juggling life's RESPONSIBILITIES

BIBLICAL HELP FOR THE MARRIED WOMAN

juggling life's RESPONSIBILITIES

BIBLICAL HELP FOR THE MARRIED WOMAN

ANNE ELLIOTT

REGULAR BAPTIST PRESS
1300 North Meacham Road
Schaumburg, Illinois 60173-4806

All Scripture quotations, unless otherwise noted, are from the New King James Version. Copyright © 1979, 1980, 1982 by Thomas Nelson, Inc. Used by permission. All rights reserved.

Quotations on pages 26 and 30 are from *Answering the Key Questions about the Family.* © 1984 by John MacArthur, Jr. All rights reserved. Used by permission.

Quotations on page 28 and 252 are from *Growing Kids God's Way: Biblical Ethics for Parenting.* © 1998 by Gary and Anne Marie Ezzo. Used by permission.

Quotation on pages 30 and 31 is from *What Every Mom Needs* by Elisa Morgan and Carol Kuykendall. © 1995 by M.O.P.S. International, Inc. Used by permission of The Zondervan Corporation.

Quotations on pages 33, 178, 211, and 222 are from *The Gentle Ways of the Beautiful Woman: A Practical Guide to Spiritual Beauty.* © 1987, 1990 by Anne Ortlund. Reprint, 1998 (3 vols. in 1). Used by permission.

Quotations on pages 79, 91, and 100–102 are from "Family News from Dr. James Dobson," February 1995. Focus on the Family, Colorado Springs, Colo. Used by permission.

Quotations on pages 152 and 153 are from *Birth by Design: The Expectant Parent's Handbook.* © 1999 by Growing Families International. Used by permission.

Quotations on pages 201–203 are from *What Every Child Should Know along the Way.* © 1998 by Parent-WiseSolutions, Inc., Mt. Pleasant, SC. Used by permission.

Quotation on page 220 is from *A Mother's Heart* by Jean Fleming. © 1982. Used by permission of NavPress, www.navpress.com. All rights reserved.

Quotation on page 225 is from *The Hidden Art of Homemaking* by Edith Schaeffer. © 1971. Used by permission of Tyndale House. All rights reserved.

Quotation on pages 271–274 is from "Missions in the Home." Used by permission of Baptist Mid-Missions.

Quotation on page 275 is from *My Utmost for His Highest* by Oswald Chambers. © 1935 by Dodd Mead & Co.; renewed 1963 by Oswald Chambers Publications Assoc. Ltd. Used by permission of Discovery House Publishers, Box 3566, Grand Rapids, MI 49501. All rights reserved.

Quotation on page 281 is from *What Is a Family?* by Edith Schaeffer. © 1975. Used by permission of Baker Book House. All rights reserved.

Regular Baptist Press is not responsible for the contents of any book, periodical, or off-site Web page referenced in this publication. Reference in this publication to any Web site, product, process, service, or company does not constitute its endorsement or recommendation by Regular Baptist Press.

JUGGLING LIFE'S RESPONSIBILITIES:
BIBLICAL HELP FOR THE MARRIED WOMAN
© 2005
Regular Baptist Press • Schaumburg, Illinois
www.regularbaptistpress.org • 1-800-727-4440
All rights reserved
Printed in U.S.A.
RBP5313 • ISBN: 1-59402-153-8

Dedication

To Kraig,
who sees past my imperfections and loves me anyway,

and to my grandmother, Ruth Root,
who, by living it before me, taught me that a
God-centered life is more fulfilling than any other.

Acknowledgments

Thank You, Lord, for so many godly examples . . .

— for my mother, Virginia Haasch, who quietly reminded me over and over again that home is the nicest place for a woman to be;

— for Judy Sargent, who invested unselfishly into my teenage life and pushed me to seek You first;

— for Terri Jenkin, who trained up her children in the way they should go;

— for Anne Ortlund, whose obedience in writing Your words changed the course of my life;

— for my father, Stephen Haasch, who taught me to do right when "only the squirrels will see";

— for Jodi Demerly, who was first to hear of the dreams for this book and believed that You wanted me to write it;

— for Anne Marie Ezzo, who stayed up late one night to help a young mom like me;

— for Eve Haynes, who wrote me notes each week and filled them with Your Word;

— for Claire Ulik, who saw the vision and helped me take off the rough edges;

— for Sherry Jo Wheeler, who laughed and cried with me and loves You with all her heart;

— for all my friends online, who let me into their hearts and gave me a reason to keep going;

— for Linda Glasford, whose encouragement kept me trying;

— for Valerie and Pat, my editors, who took a chance on this book so that women's hearts could be touched;

— for my husband, Kraig, and our four children, who cheerfully ate Taco Bell so this book could be finished;

— for Jesus, Your Son, Who laid down His life that others might live.

CONTENTS

Preface 9

Introduction: God's Design for You 11

CHAPTER 1   Setting Priorities 13

CHAPTER 2   Fulfilling Your God-given Roles 23

PART 1: YOUR GOD   39

CHAPTER 3   Thinking Biblically 41

CHAPTER 4   Tapping into God's Power 53

CHAPTER 5   Knowing God Intimately 63

PART 2: YOUR HUSBAND   79

CHAPTER 6   Submitting to Your Husband's Leadership   83

CHAPTER 7   Being Your Husband's Best Friend 97

CHAPTER 8   Making Your Marriage a Priority 115

PART 3: YOUR CHILDREN   123

CHAPTER 9   Being a Godly Mother 127

CHAPTER 10   Filtering the Parenting Advice 139

CHAPTER 11   Realizing That Children Are a Blessing 149

CHAPTER 12   Loving and Teaching Your Children 163

PART 4: YOUR HOME   175

CHAPTER 13   Being a Faithful Steward. 177

CHAPTER 14   Wisely Building Your Home 197

CHAPTER 15   Creating a Peaceful Sanctuary 219

PART 5: YOUR WORLD   231

CHAPTER 16   Contributing to the Body of Christ. 235

CHAPTER 17   Learning from Older Women 245

CHAPTER 18   Ministering to Lost People 257

CONCLUSION   God's Plan for Your Future 281

P R E F A C E

As women we have so many questions, and what do we do first? Should a busy mom place a priority on her home? her kids? a job to pay the bills? What about serving in her church? helping a sick friend? Where will she ever find the time to develop a close relationship with God among all her other responsibilities?

The answers? Look into God's Word. Perhaps you've been studying the Bible for many years. If so, *Juggling Life's Responsibilities: Biblical Help for the Married Woman* will not only be a good review for you, but hopefully it also will motivate you to share your wisdom with the women coming behind you. Or perhaps this is the first time you've ever considered what God thinks about women and their roles in society. *Juggling . . .* might radically challenge your views while showing you how to find fulfillment as a woman of God.

However, knowing what the Bible says is not enough. We need to put Biblical truth into practice. *Juggling . . .* provides Bible study and mentoring to help you do just that. Begin by asking the Lord to open your eyes and show you wonderful things from His Word. Ask Him to search your heart and challenge your mind so that you will never be the same again!

HOW TO USE THIS BOOK

Juggling Life's Responsibilities is an introduction to what the Bible teaches about five major relationships of a woman. I have been praying that this book will minister to the following groups of women:

- Single women who are seeking God's priorities for their lives
- Engaged women or new brides
- Married women who need affirmation in their marriages, are struggling with their spouses, or have marriages that have failed
- Mothers, especially those with young children

- Ministry wives seeking for ways to encourage the women they influence
- Older women looking for opportunities to minister to younger women

Group Study. I am also praying that you'll read *Juggling . . . ,* not just in the privacy of your home, but with other women in your church. Each woman in your study group could read the chapter at home, and then you all could meet weekly for encouragement, accountability, and additional study.

Personal Growth. At the end of each chapter you'll find ideas to help with personal growth. For instance, there are recommendations for verses to memorize. Perhaps each woman could write out the week's verse(s) on 3" x 5" cards and post them in prominent places at home or work. When you come together again, you can begin by saying the verses by memory, adding accountability to your group.

Study Guide. A study guide is also provided with each chapter. During your group meeting, read the Bible verses together and discuss possible answers. This is an excellent time for the older women to share their wisdom with the younger ones.

Group Project. At the conclusion of your meeting, review the group project and have a time of prayer (and maybe some light refreshments). Make goals for the following week and ask if certain women would visit the local library and read one of the books listed at the end of the chapter as a complementary resource.

A Study Partner. If a group of women from your church is unavailable, ask the Lord to give you someone! He may want you to read *Juggling . . .* with your husband or your mom. The possibilities are endless. You might have a close friend or a neighbor you hardly know who would enjoy studying with you. You might be able to start an Internet study group.

However you use *Juggling . . . ,* may it challenge your heart and mind so that you, your family, your relationships, and even your church will never be the same again!

INTRODUCTION

God's Design for You

POINT TO PONDER
"For I know the thoughts that I think toward you, says the LORD, thoughts of peace and not of evil, to give you a future and a hope"
(Jeremiah 29:11).

We had a monster thunderstorm in our town one summer. On a late afternoon, muggy and typical for June, the clouds rolled in, and we were afraid we wouldn't get our hamburgers grilled soon enough to avoid getting soaked. We ate our picnic in the living room instead of on the back porch, and after supper we watched *Wheel of Fortune* instead of playing in the backyard. Even the game show was interrupted by flashing thunderstorm warnings and messages about tornadoes.

Yet just as the winning contestant tried to guess the final puzzle, my oldest son looked out the window and exclaimed with delight. The brightest rainbows I have ever seen formed complete semicircles across the eastern sky. We all stopped worrying about the storm and ran to the front of the house to gaze at the sight (and to snap pictures with our cameras). The rainbows supplied the perfect ending to an otherwise disappointing day.

Later that night I walked outside and looked up at the sky. The moon was bright. Fingerlike clouds stretched between the stars, and lightning bugs danced in the cool breeze.

On nights like that one I think about my life, about how God can reach into the storms I've created, paint a beautiful rainbow with His love, chase away the fears, and orchestrate a breathtaking design for the rest of my days. He longs to make my life beautiful. In response, He wants me to praise Him.

No matter where you are in life right now, God has such a plan for you. His ideas as expressed in the Bible may not be popular or politically correct. However, they are perfect, and because they are, they will fulfill you, delight you, and complete you as you learn to walk in obedience to them.

I believe any woman can become an expert on the home and family. How? By paying attention to the Chief Expert, God Himself. "His divine power has given to us all things that pertain to life and godliness, through the knowledge of Him" (2 Pet. 1:3). So we're going to talk together about the priorities God wants us to have and how we can fulfill our God-given roles. You can begin to work on having a living, exciting relationship with God. If you're married, you can have a loving relationship with your happy husband. If you have been blessed with children, you can begin to become a godly mother. No matter what your home is like, you can learn to make it a haven from the world, a true pleasure to come home to! Finally, you can begin to expand your vision of what God wants to do with your life by ministering to your spiritual family (the church) and by reaching those in your circle of influence who need the Lord.

God has a design for each woman. He does not want to stifle us; He wants to perfect us. He wants our lives to burst with color. Like those rainbows. He wants us to be a splash of beauty in a sky full of storms.

Are you curious to see what God's design is? Welcome! Let's explore this topic together.

CHAPTER *1* ONE

Setting Priorities

POINT TO PONDER
*"Trust in the LORD with all your heart, and
lean not on your own understanding; in all
your ways acknowledge Him, and He shall
direct your paths" (Proverbs 3:5, 6).*

My worst kitchen failures come when I feel too busy to cook—when I'm juggling a bunch of projects. I wait until the last minute to start; then I look for a recipe that is fast, easy, and requires no defrosting. Grabbing up the first recipe with these promises, I run into the kitchen to start. The first few "easy" steps aren't so easy—or quick.

Then I see step three: "Marinate overnight in the refrigerator."

If I would just take the time to read a recipe first, we wouldn't have Taco Bell for supper so often!

Know What You're Living For

Wouldn't it be a shame if your life got so busy . . . if you had so many balls in the air . . . that you reached the end of your life only to find it had been a waste? Even worse, what if you thought your life was a success, but God considered it a waste?

The apostle Paul probably had this thought in mind when

he wrote, "For we must all appear before the judgment seat of Christ, that each one may receive the things done in the body, according to what he has done, whether good or bad" (2 Cor. 5:10). The thought of standing before Christ, the One Who died for me, inspires me to live completely for Him.

I'm reminded of the story about a man rescued by a stranger. The rescued man pledged his life to the stranger who saved him. From then on he served the stranger in any way possible to show his gratitude.

I also remember the parable Jesus told about the man who planned a trip to a faraway country. He called three of his servants to him and entrusted a sum of money to each one. The first two servants took the money and invested it wisely, presenting it to their master when he returned. But the third servant hid his money in the ground, where it could not earn interest for his master (Matt. 25:14–30).

God has given each of us a lifetime to work for Him. Yet it is so easy to forget that truth! We sit down to make new goals and plans (usually on New Year's Eve), and we dream.

We dream we have enough money to do anything we want.

I know exactly what I want my dream house to look like. It has two stories and a Victorian wraparound porch. The perfectly manicured yard has flowers tastefully arranged around the walkways and architecture. Inside I'll have a formal living room that isn't too formal to enjoy. I'd also like a music room with a grand piano, a luxurious chair to read a good book in, a few built-in bookcases to house my reading collection, and a crackling fire in the fireplace. I'd like a big, homey kitchen accessible to the family room. My husband would like a big-screen TV so he could keep better track of his favorite sports' teams. Upstairs I want a master bedroom with a private sitting area. Our private bath needs a sunken bathtub with a gurgling waterfall and a skylight. I'd like a spot to sit down when I put on my makeup and do my

Setting Priorities 15

hair. I'd like to have bedrooms for the kids, as well as a sewing room. The kids vote for a toy room (we might need a third floor!), and we all want a garage large enough for several cars and all our hobbies.

I want to be able to buy whatever I need or want—whenever I need or want it! I want the various gadgets and gizmos I see in the catalogs we receive so frequently.

I don't want to have to worry about money. I want more money at the end of our month! I want to be carefree! (Did I mention I'd also like a maid and my husband would like a gardener?)

We also dream of having fame and success . . . of having our names written in history books . . . of being sought after for our knowledge . . . of smiling at the crowds who have come to see us, confident and polished. We dream of accomplishing something no one else has ever accomplished . . . and being rewarded for it!

So we dream and dream and dream.

Then we work hard to reach our dreams, never stopping to ask ourselves if what we're working so hard for will satisfy.

God's dreams for us are much different. Does that mean He doesn't want us to have a comfortable home, quality things, or reasonable paychecks? Does that mean if we serve Him, we will lead isolated, lonely, frustrated lives?

Of course not! Jesus said, "I have come that they may have life, and that they may have it more abundantly" (John 10:10).

But Satan's first lie—and one he still uses today—is that God is somehow trying to rob us of the good life. He deceived Eve in the same way.

> And the woman said to the serpent, "We may eat the fruit of the trees of the garden; but of the fruit of the tree which is in the midst of the garden, God has said, 'You shall not eat it, nor shall you touch it, lest you die.' " Then the serpent said to the woman, "You will not surely die. For God knows that in the day you eat of it your eyes will be opened, and you will be like God, knowing good and evil" (Gen. 3:2–5).

Know What God Plans for You

So Eve ate the fruit, thinking God did not have her best interests in mind. She learned she was wrong!

God has big desires for your life too. His desires for you revolve around His great love for you and the rest of humanity.

He desires an intimate relationship with you, one where you and He can walk and talk closely with each other. He wants you to know, "Yes, I have loved you with an everlasting love; therefore with lovingkindness I have drawn you" (Jer. 31:3). He wants you to love Him too! Fifteen times the Word of God talks about loving the Lord.[1] For example, "You shall love the LORD your God with all your heart, with all your soul, and with all your might" (Deut. 6:5).

God wants to make you into a beautiful woman with a godly character. Note what He said through Paul in Ephesians 2:10, "For we are His workmanship, *created in Christ Jesus for good works,* which God prepared beforehand that we should walk in them" (emphasis added), and through John in 1 John 3:2, "Beloved, now we are children of God; and it has not yet been revealed what we shall be, but we know that when He is revealed, *we shall be like Him,* for we shall see Him as He is" (emphasis added).

And God desires to use you in a big way. He said, "For I know the thoughts that I think toward you, says the LORD, thoughts of peace and not of evil, to give you a future and a hope" (Jer. 29:11).

Remember that this One Who cares so much for you is the almighty God of the universe. Our God created all things by the words of His mouth. He is omnipresent ("free from the laws or limitations of space"), He is omniscient (has "perfect knowledge"), and He is omnipotent (possesses "absolute power").[2] There is no one like our God!

Yet even more mind-boggling is the truth that the King of

Setting Priorities 17

the universe wants a personal relationship with you! He desires your love, affection, and loyalty.

When God created light, water, flowers, and wind, He did so by speaking. But when God created the first person, He lovingly took the dust on the ground and gently formed a man with His own fingers. Then He leaned down and breathed into man the "breath of life." What a loving God we serve!

So why did God go to all the trouble of making us in the first place? Why was He not satisfied with the beauty of the flowers and the magnificence of the animal kingdom?

The purpose of our lives, as stated in God's Word, is to bring glory to God. The Old Testament states, "Everyone who is called by My name, whom I have created for My glory; I have formed him, yes, *I have made him*" (Isa. 43:7, emphasis added). And the New Testament says: "For by Him all things were created that are in heaven and that are on earth, visible and invisible, whether thrones or dominions or principalities or powers. All things were created through Him and *for Him*" (Col. 1:16, emphasis added). Revelation 4:11 reiterates: "You are worthy, O Lord, to receive glory and honor and power; for You created all things, and by Your will they exist and were created."

Know that your life has purpose, dear woman! No matter how unimportant you feel sometimes, remember God has great plans for you. He has so much invested in you! If you still doubt His love for you, take a few minutes to read Psalm 139. He cares about your deepest thoughts, your loneliest cares. He knew you and formed you in your mother's womb. He thinks about you all day long. He loves you!

And God wants you to love Him. Scripture says: "Now by this we know that we know Him, if we keep His commandments. He who says, 'I know Him,' and does not keep His commandments, is a liar, and the truth is not in him" (1 John 2:3, 4).

God wants to cultivate His character in your life—traits like love, joy, peace, long-suffering, kindness, goodness, faithfulness, gentleness, and self-control (Gal. 5:22, 23).

He wants you to know Him through His Word. The psalmist said, "I will delight myself in Your statutes; I will not forget Your word" (Ps. 119:16).

God wants to have fellowship with you. That's why you have the Bible: "That which we have seen and heard we declare to you, that you also may have fellowship with us; and truly our fellowship is with the Father and with His Son Jesus Christ" (1 John 1:3).

Know What Is Important

Why have I spent so much time showing you from God's Word what a mighty, wonderful God we serve? Because I want you to realize that your entire life must revolve around Him. Before we talk about loving our husbands, reading to our kids, or baking cookies for our neighbors, we must share common ground concerning our priorities.

Realize that your husband is not your first priority; God is! Your life does not revolve around your kids; it revolves around God! Your aim in life must not be to influence the world; God must influence you! Again the Bible says it best: "But seek first the kingdom of God and His righteousness, and all these things shall be added to you" (Matt. 6:33).

Seek God by spending time alone with Him each day and by consciously walking with Him throughout each day. In part 1 we will discuss some practical ways to do this.

As your thoughts and your life begin to center on God, you will find the other priorities of your life appropriately lining up.

The New Testament, for instance, is clear that our spiritual family—especially our local church—should have a high priority in our lives. However, each time the Bible gives instructions to the church on matters of behavior, we find many applications of how

Setting Priorities   **19**

a Christian family should conduct itself. Realize God wants you to serve Him in your physical family. That means your husband, your children, and your extended family should have a high priority in your life. Home is where you begin to learn to walk in obedience to God by practicing such commands as "love one another," "submit to one another," and "serve one another."[3] Therefore, we're going to spend a lot of time in this book talking about some practical ways to serve God by serving those closest to you.

Your spiritual family will benefit from the strength of your physical family. Never meaning to put down the importance of your physical family, I want to stress that we must not neglect our eternal spiritual family. Learning to function in healthy church relationships is a priority that is sadly missing in the lives of many Christians today. After we talk about practically loving your physical family, we're going to concentrate on what roles you should play in your spiritual family, both your local church and the Body of Christ around the world.

In fact, we need to lift our eyes to this world next. How can you meet the needs of those who don't know God? How can you reach them—by telling them what God's Word says and by showing them His love through you—when you have babies underfoot and a mountain of laundry to do, as well as soup to make for your pastor's wife who is sick? We'll be sure to talk about that challenge!

IN SUMMARY

God has great plans for you! He wants to bless you and make you a blessing to others. Trust Him. Then when the world's priorities (Mark 4:19) entice you, turn your eyes to Christ instead.

> When [Jesus] had called the people to Himself, with His disciples also, He said to them, "Whoever desires to come after Me, let him deny himself, and take up his cross, and follow Me. For whoever desires to save his life will lose it, but whoever loses his life for My sake and the

gospel's will save it. For what will it profit a man if he gains the whole world, and loses his own soul? Or what will a man give in exchange for his soul?" (Mark 8:34–37).

EXTRA CREDIT ASSIGNMENT

Memorize Ephesians 2:10 and recite it to a minimum of five women.

> "For we are His workmanship, created in Christ Jesus for good works, which God prepared beforehand that we should walk in them" (Ephesians 2:10).

STUDY GUIDE

1. According to John 10:10, why did Jesus come to earth? Can you name some Christian women who seem to have abundant life? What do you think their secret is?
2. According to Colossians 1:16, why did God create all things? List some things created by God mentioned in this verse. According to Revelation 4:11, does God allow any accidents? How do you think evil people and terrible circumstances can be part of God's will?
3. According to Matthew 6:33, what should our top priority be? After reading verses 25–34, list some things God will handle for us when our priorities are straight.
4. According to Mark 4:19, what are the world's priorities? List some logical consequences of making these things your priorities.
5. After reading Mark 8:34–37, list some things you would have to give up in your own life if you were to make God your top priority. Ask God to help you realize the eternal value of a relationship with Him.

Setting Priorities   21

GROUP PROJECT

Each woman in your group should spend some quiet moments by herself to write a purpose statement for her life. Encourage each woman to list one goal for improvement in each priority area (God, physical family, spiritual family, world). These goals should be measurable and easily attainable in the next month. For instance, a goal for the priority of God might be "I will read my Bible every morning at breakfast."

After each woman has written a purpose statement and some goals, let the ladies share their work with each other. If possible, have each woman choose an accountability partner who will check the progress on her goals one month from today. Be sure to mark this date on your calendars!

EXTRA READING

✔ Kramer, Rita W. *Peanut Butter on My Pillow.* Nashville: Thomas Nelson Publishers, 1980. This funny yet practical book describes how to get control over your priorities as a wife and mother. Currently out of print.

✔ Ortlund, Anne. *The Gentle Ways of the Beautiful Woman: A Practical Guide to Spiritual Beauty.* Reprint (3 vols. in 1), New York: Inspirational Press, 1998. Volume 1 of this book is titled *Disciplines of the Beautiful Woman* (© 1984 by Word, Inc., Waco, Texas). In this classic Ortlund discusses setting priorities, making goals, scheduling your daily life, organizing your life behind the scenes, and God's view of a beautiful woman.

NOTES

1. Deuteronomy 6:5; 11:1, 13, 22; 13:3; 19:9; 30:6, 16, 20; Joshua 22:5; 23:11; Psalm 31:23; Matthew 22:37; Mark 12:30; Luke 10:27.

2. Merrill F. Unger, *The New Unger's Bible Dictionary*, rev. & updated (Chicago: Moody Press, 1988), 942.

3. 1 John 3:11; Ephesians 5:21; Galatians 5:13.

CHAPTER **2** TWO

Fulfilling Your God-given Roles

POINT TO PONDER
"A wife is a hedge against the alienation that comes from being human"
(Karen Burton Mains).[1]

W hy did God create women? What role does He expect you to fill? Genesis 2 gives the account of how God created the first man, Adam. As soon as God formed Adam, He planted a garden where Adam could live. Then God made the plants—lovely to look at and their fruit luscious to eat—grow up around Adam. The Tree of Life stood in the center of the garden, and rivers flowed out from the garden. What a place! It sounds like the place I want to escape to when I've had a hard day.

But it wasn't enough, not in God's opinion. God determined to find a helper for Adam, one suited to Adam's needs. God paraded the animals in front of Adam, allowing him to name each creature. (So if you ever wondered why a giraffe is called a giraffe . . .) None of these animal helpers were suitable, however.

So Adam got sleepy, and God got busy—busy making a perfect companion for the new man. And man's best friend was—no! not a dog! It was a woman!

From that moment on, the wise Creator of all the universe decreed that the best companion for a man is a woman. Men were to leave their parents' homes and be joined in a permanent way to their wives.

I have discovered four roles that God, through His Word, instructs women to play: helper to man, mother of children, manager of a home, and minister to the world.

These roles continue to be controversial in our society, but I can find nowhere in Scripture where it appears God has changed His mind. God created these roles, and He continues to sanction them. It is only when we as women determine to abide within the boundaries set by Him that we find true peace, joy, and fulfillment.

Helper to Man

It should come as no surprise that modern psychology shows how much our husbands need us. In Genesis 2 God carefully made a helper for Adam, someone comparable to him who would complete him (Gen. 2:18–25).

You see, women are perfect complements to men. Men tend to be logical and analytical, to have goals, and to see the "big picture." Women often excel in communication, emotions, fine details, relationships, and attention to "today" (as opposed to the big picture). What a creative God we serve to have made us in this way!

When a man and woman love each other, they start to work for the other person's good instead of their own. And while society often teaches us to compete with men, I know from personal experience that when I strive to be a helper to my husband, I feel a wonderful "job satisfaction."

But how can we be competent helpers to our husbands? We'll discuss this topic in part 2. (No fair peeking ahead. God has some other roles for us to fill too!)

Mother of Children

As soon as God made Adam and Eve, He blessed them and said to them, "Be fruitful and multiply; fill the earth and subdue it; have dominion over the fish of the sea, over the birds of the air, and over every living thing that moves on the earth" (Gen. 1:28). Two more times in Genesis, God gave a similar command to "be fruitful and multiply"—to Noah (Gen. 9:1, 7) and to Jacob (Gen. 35:11)—and He has never revoked this command.

Environmentalists predict the collapse of mother earth because of overpopulation. But God predicts blessing to those who have children: "Who is like the LORD our God, Who dwells on high. . . . He grants the barren woman a home, like a joyful mother of children. Praise the LORD!" (Ps. 113:5, 9). "Behold, children are a heritage from the LORD, the fruit of the womb is a reward. Like arrows in the hand of a warrior, so are the children of one's youth. Happy is the man who has his quiver full of them; they shall not be ashamed, but shall speak with their enemies in the gate" (Ps. 127:3–5).

So how can we begin to view our children as blessings and gifts from Almighty God? You guessed it . . . we'll discuss that subject in part 3.

Manager of a Home

I first became excited about the possibilities of managing a home when I was four or five years old. I followed my mother around the kitchen and the house, intent on learning how to be a good mommy. My first attempt at homemaking took place with the help of my older brother. We excitedly took my toy broom, mop, and vacuum, filled the bathroom sink with sudsy water, and "cleaned" my bedroom walls and floor. My mother has since then taught me a little moderation.

But now I have a little daughter of my own, and guess what!? She follows me around! At the tender age of eighteen months, she emptied the container of baby wipes and "cleaned" all the furniture with them.

My family's women aren't the only ones who are bent toward keeping a home. A quick glance at the home section of any bookstore or magazine rack will show you the popularity of making a home cozy and inviting. This bent is God's design—don't fight it!

Paul told Titus to admonish the older women to teach the younger women to be "homemakers" (Titus 2:5). The original Greek word indicates that women are to be guardians of their homes, "a stayer at home, i.e. domestically inclined."[2]

John MacArthur, a renowned pastor and Bible teacher, wrote, "Nothing in Scripture . . . specifically forbids women from working, as long as they are fulfilling the priority in the home (Proverbs 31). The exalted place for a wife, however, is the home. The world calls her out, not the Lord. The ultimate decision is a personal one that each woman must make in submission to her husband's authority."[3]

So we're going to devote a good portion, part 4, of this book to developing the skills of an effective homemaker.

Minister to the World

The final role God designed for women is also intended for men, that is, the role of witnessing of His salvation throughout the world. The Lord commanded the apostles in Matthew 28:18 and 19 to make disciples of all nations and again in Acts 1:8 to be witnesses in the entire world. He distinctively made these commands to men, but I see many instances in the Bible of women who helped carry them out.

For example, the Lord opened the heart of Lydia, a seller of purple, as she listened to the apostle Paul. In Acts 16:14 and 15 we read that Lydia's "household" came to Christ and that she offered her home to God's servants: "And when she and her household were baptized, she begged us, saying, 'If you have judged

Fulfilling Your God-given Roles　　　　27

me to be faithful to the Lord, come to my house and stay.' "

In Acts 9:36 we read of Tabitha, who was "full of good works and charitable deeds."

Eleven more times the New Testament encouraged early believers to live lives full of "good works"—twice specifically speaking to women (1 Tim. 2:10; 5:10).[4] The apostle Peter explained that when unbelievers observe our good works, they will glorify God (1 Pet. 2:12). Of course, Jesus Himself said the same thing to His disciples when He told them, "Let your light so shine before men, that they may see your good works and glorify your Father in heaven" (Matt. 5:16).

Indeed, the famous Proverbs 31 woman is known for her good works. "She extends her hand to the poor, yes, she reaches out her hands to the needy" (Prov. 31:20).

So we will spend time in part 5 talking about how we can learn to "stir up love and good works" (Heb. 10:24) and thereby reach the world with the love of Christ.

Hurdles to Overcome

We've discussed our priorities and the roles God wants us women to play. Now we need to discuss some common hurdles we might face. Consider these concepts starting points for the chapters to come.

Independence

Author Jani Ortlund wrote:

> Almost anything done in the name of a woman's independence is celebrated as raw courage. Women are seen to be more intelligent if they value a life of autonomy as richer and fuller than that of a homemaker. . . . Over and over again, we are encouraged to set our own rules, to define our own terms. Through TV commercials and sitcoms and talk shows, through books and movies, through speeches and political movements, we've been

told that true happiness comes when we learn to enhance our self-respect apart from any connection with others, even those we should naturally love the most.[5]

We women are taught to be independent of all others. We don't need help from anyone. Yet how Biblical is this attitude?

I decided to see if the word "independent" is even in the Bible. I couldn't recall any place, so imagine my surprise when I found it is used twice, both in the same verse of Scripture: "Nevertheless, neither is man independent of woman, nor woman independent of man, in the Lord" (1 Cor. 11:11).

Wow! What a mind-opener! The context of this verse (we'll discuss how important context is later) is summed up a few verses earlier: "But I want you to know that the head of every man is Christ, the head of woman is man, and the head of Christ is God" (1 Cor. 11:3).

Wow again! You see, God created you to be a helper to that man you're married to—yes, the same man who snores and forgets to pick up his dirty clothes. A better word to describe all family relationships might be "interdependency," defined as "mutually dependent." Gary and Anne Marie Ezzo observed,

> The best way to describe this [interdependent] family is to imagine a group of people holding hands in a circle, each looking in toward one another. This family structure allows for the sending and receiving of signals by each member of the family: from Mom and Dad to the children, from the children to each other, and from the children back to Mom and Dad.[6]

Resist the urge to be independent! Accept help from your mother-in-law when she wants to tell you how her son loves his cinnamon rolls baked just so. Graciously thank those who offer to bring you supper when you're pregnant and not feeling well. Teach your children to learn from one another, not alienate themselves from the siblings who may be there for them the rest of their lives.

Careers

"Careerism" is the "practice of seeking one's professional advancement by all possible means." By all possible means? Oh, that worries me! What about the woman who sacrifices her husband for the pursuit of her career? Or, more frequently, her children? Will the sacrifice be worth it in the end?

Many American mothers began working outside the home for two primary reasons: they needed the additional money or they wanted to get out of the house. Homemaking had come to signify slavery in a way. Women envied their husbands, who were able to leave in the morning, make their ways in the world, and come home to nicely prepared dinners. The wife, on the other hand, was left with whining children and the dull repetition of dishes, laundry, baking, gardening, diapering, and cleaning.

I really do understand feeling like this; I've felt this way many times myself! In fact, this book was born out of the frustration I felt at being "home alone." I struggled with my feelings, knowing I should be a good wife and that my work was in my home, but the feelings didn't always cooperate with my brain.

As always, however, the Word of God has the power to change our thinking. I typed several passages of Scripture about what God expects of women, and I taped them to the cabinet near where I do dishes (a most detestable job, in my opinion). As I scrubbed day-old dishes and pouted and sulked, the words of those Scriptures started to wash away the selfishness in my heart and change my mind.

Did I say "selfishness"? Yes! I know it was definitely selfishness in my case. I wanted to get out of the house so I could do something important in the world—like make a fortune for myself. But God's standards are selfless, and His Word requires a higher standard.

Many women work to bring in money that is sorely needed in the family. If this is your situation, I urge you to prayerfully bring the matter before the Lord. Read chapter 13; then study your family finances carefully to determine if the benefits of working are actually worth it! It might take some time, but many families have found that with careful planning, Mom is able to stay home.

John MacArthur was asked his opinion of mothers working outside the home, and he replied,

> A woman who is a mother obviously has primary responsibility in the home and would therefore not be free to pursue outside employment to the detriment of the home. In fact, from my perspective as a parent, it is difficult to see how a mother could possibly do all that needs to be done in the home with the upbringing of children, hospitality, care of the needy, and work for the Lord (cf. 1 Timothy 5:3–14) and still work in an outside job.[7]

I share this opinion as well, and I hope as we move through the pages of this book I can convince you that being a wife and mother is an exciting and fulfilling career, as well as one that can be financially sound.

Homemaking

Unfortunately, ignorance of the most basic skills in keeping a home is incredibly widespread in American society. A home that is clean, pleasant, and comforting is a luxury. Elisa Morgan and Carol Kuykendall printed a "classified ad" for mothers in their book *What Every Mom Needs*. How well do your skills match the role you have been called to fill?

SITUATIONS VACANT: HOUSEWIFE/MOTHER

> Applications are invited for the position of manager to a lively team of four demanding individuals.

> The successful applicant will be required to perform the following functions: companion, counselor, financial manager, buying officer, teacher, nurse, chef, nutritionist, decorator, cleaner, driver, child care supervisor, social

Fulfilling Your God-given Roles

secretary, and recreation officer. Applicants must have unlimited energy and a strong sense of responsibility. They must be independent, self-motivated and able to work in isolation without supervision, able to work under stress, and adaptable enough to handle new developments in the life of the team, including emergencies and crises. They must be able to communicate with people of all ages, including teachers, doctors, business people, dentists, teenagers and children. A good imagination, sensitivity, warmth, and an understanding of people [are] necessary as the successful applicant will also be responsible for the mental and emotional well-being of the team.

Hours: All waking moments and a 24-hour shift when necessary.

Benefits: No guaranteed holidays, no sick leave or maternity leave. No workers' compensation.

Pay: None. Allowances by arrangement from time to time with the income-earning member of the team. Successful applicant may be allowed/required to hold second job in addition to the one advertised here.[8]

Wow! The skills required of a stay-at-home mom require a strong commitment to the task and a great desire to improve. Yet think of the memories that simple chocolate-chip cookies bring and of the serenity your family will have when they can find clean pairs of socks to wear. Homemaking skills are important to the well-being of your family.

Instead of elaborating on the reasons why so many women are lacking in these essential skills, remember instead that God's Word has the solution to all our dilemmas. We will discuss the solutions He proposes in part 4, but it's important to note that He commands us to pass our knowledge on to the next generation.

Children

One of the things God has commanded that we pass on to the next generation is the decision to love our children (Titus 2:4). Yet I have some married friends who have chosen to never have children of their own. Why? Because they have met so few children they like! Too many homes, they say, are controlled by children, little ones who have learned that temper tantrums and tears will get them their own way.

I can understand their feelings. Many children in our society can be out of control, mean, defiant, and disobedient. They can be an "unlovely" bunch!

But is it their fault? Where have they learned to be like this? From their parents? From their peers? Does it have to be this way?

No, God wants families to be happy. Having children should be a joyful experience (Ps. 127:5). Parenting can truly be a joy if moms and dads walk in holiness, teach their children to obey at an early age, and follow up with consistent love, discipline, and teaching from God's Word. We'll discuss this subject in part 3.

Hard Work

What is your attitude toward work? Over the last few years a call has gone out to work less and play more. Why? Because Americans are tired, stressed, and emotionally spent.

So the common advice has been to get more rest. Relax. Enjoy yourself. Have fun.

I'm afraid, however, that with this added fun has come added stress. Why? Because now the laundry isn't getting done, and not having clean underwear certainly adds stress to your life! Because we don't take the time to balance the checkbook, eating out can cause bounced checks. Because we aren't inclined to cook a healthy meal, reducing our nutrition to convenience foods can reduce our health and energy.

God endorses rest. Repeatedly throughout the Old Testa-

Fulfilling Your God-given Roles   33

ment, God commanded the Israelites to take a rest from their labor. He even required them to rest their livestock and their land. Slaves were to be set free after a certain number of years. Women were to rest after giving birth. God Himself rested after the six days of creation!

But notice each of these rest periods followed a period of labor. For instance, "Six days you shall labor and do all your work, but the seventh day is the Sabbath of the LORD your God. In it you shall do no work" (Exod. 20:9, 10). "Six years you shall sow your land and gather in its produce, but the seventh year you shall let it rest and lie fallow" (Exod. 23:10, 11).

I think the emphasis in America has shifted so far toward rest that we have forgotten we should work six times as much as we rest.

Anne Ortlund wisely wrote,

> Hard work never hurt anybody. It's only a bad attitude toward work that causes the gears to grind, the tensions to mount. That's why our work done in God's will should only bring physical fatigue—from which rest will bounce us back—but not emotional or spiritual fatigue.[9]

Being a homemaker, a wife, and a mother is hard work! But accepting your responsibilities will bring relief and freedom, not anxiety and bondage.

Contentment

One of the biggest challenges to fulfilling the role into which God has placed you is learning contentment. What is contentment? According to my Bible dictionary, "the word means 'sufficiency.' . . . It is that disposition of mind, through grace, in which one is independent of outward circumstances . . . , so as not to be moved by envy . . . , anxiety . . . , and repining."[10]

Through God's grace we accept the positions into which God has placed us. We are not swayed by our circumstances (your best friend has a part-time job now and can afford such great clothes), nor by envy (you resent that your husband doesn't have to stay home with the "little monsters"), nor by anxiety (you fear you'll never be able to afford to stay at home), nor by discontent (you dream of the days when you were "free and single"). Instead we are filled with peace, love, trust, and joy. With excitement we accept God's assignment to us as wives and mothers!

IN SUMMARY

Think of God as your employer and your home as your career center. The day you accepted your new job as "wife," you accepted a difficult assignment. But it is worth it! The pay with God is exceptional! He rewards you with many "perks" and benefits.

First of all, God wants to give you a lifelong companion, friend, confidant, and helper in your husband. Proverbs 5:18 and 19 suggest that a man and woman committed to each other for life can always be captivated by each other's love. This commitment takes work, of course, and we will talk about some practical ideas to help you remain committed. But marriage for life is God's command, and He will bless you for your commitment by giving you a relationship that is a true picture of His love for you (Eph. 5:22–33). As you become the kind of wife God wants you to be, your husband will be grateful (Prov. 18:22; 31:10, 11, 28).

Second, training your children in godliness positions them to follow in your footsteps. Let's read what Scripture has to say to wise parents:

> The curse of the LORD is on the house of the wicked, but He blesses the home of the just (Prov. 3:33).
>
> Train up a child in the way he should go, and when he is old he will not depart from it (Prov. 22:6).
>
> Correct your son, and he will give you rest; yes, he will give delight to your soul (Prov. 29:17).

Fulfilling Your God-given Roles

The Bible also says that "a wise son makes a glad father, but a foolish son is the grief of his mother" (Prov. 10:1). While I may attempt to train my children by taking them to church once or twice a week, reading Christian books to them, and teaching them Bible verses, I realize that when they get older they may *choose* to turn from God and live in disobedience. Such a scenario would break my heart! Therefore, I'm endeavoring to train them in godliness from the earliest age, consistently following through day by day, year after year.

I have purposed in my heart to follow the advice of Moses, teaching the principles of God's Word when we sit in our house, when we walk by the way, when we lie down, and when we rise up (Deut. 6:4–9). I am learning that my responsibility is to lead a life of integrity. I pray that when my children are grown, my life will have blessed theirs.

> The righteous man walks in his integrity; His children are blessed after him (Prov. 20:7).

> And you, fathers, do not provoke your children to wrath, but bring them up in the training and admonition of the Lord (Eph. 6:4).

God has more perks for those who follow Him.

• He gives you joy and happiness (Ps.113:5–9; 127:3–5).

• Your home environment, no matter how rich or poor, can be filled with peace (Prov. 17:1; 24:3, 4; Phil. 4:7–9).

• You can have a feeling of accomplishment and fulfillment (Prov. 31:28–31).

• You have friends and mentors who love you and want the best for you (Titus 2:3–5).

• You have the opportunity to influence the world for Christ (Prov. 22:29; Phil. 2:15, 16).

I know there are many, many more reasons to follow God's design for you, His woman. I pray they will become evident to you as you read this book and apply some of the principles to your life. In the meantime, you have an assignment. Look at the faces of the women you know and those you meet. Observe which women are truly joyful, which women have radiant faces (Ps. 34:5), which women exhibit the peace of God even in stressful circumstances, and which women have children who are a joy to be around. Ask yourself if these women are following God's advice or the world's. Ask them if obedience to God has been worth it all!

EXTRA CREDIT ASSIGNMENT

Memorize 1 Peter 2:9 and recite it to a minimum of five women.

> "But you are a chosen generation, a royal priesthood, a holy nation, His own special people, that you may proclaim the praises of Him who called you out of darkness into His marvelous light" (1 Peter 2:9).

STUDY GUIDE

1. According to Genesis 2:18, why did God create women? How can a woman fulfill this purpose for her husband?
2. Read Genesis 1:28, 9:1, 7, and 35:11. Who was God speaking to in each passage? What was the specific command? Were any promises attached to these commands?
3. What source of happiness does Psalm 113:9 mention? Who is the source of joy in Psalm 127:3–5. What blessings are listed in these verses?
4. After reading Titus 2:3–5, list the qualities that should be taught to young women. Why do young women need to learn these qualities?

5. According to 1 Peter 2:12, why should we live good lives? When will God get the glory?
6. Draw a simple chain of command for a family, using 1 Corinthians 11:3 and 11 as a guide.
7. What promise does Galatians 6:9 contain?

GROUP PROJECT

Each woman in your group should make a list of the activities she is involved in. To see her priorities, have her mark a 1 by everything that relates to God, a 2 by everything that relates to her husband, a 3 by everything that relates to her children, a 4 by everything that relates to her home, a 5 by everything that relates to her church, and a 6 by everything that helps her share Christ with the unsaved. What things are not marked? As a group, brainstorm ways to better match your activities with God's roles for you as a wife or mother. If possible, pair older women with younger women and have them work together on this project.

EXTRA READING

✔ Ortlund, Jani. *Fearlessly Feminine: Boldly Living God's Plan for Womanhood.* Sisters, OR: Multnomah Publishers, 2000. Ortlund courageously covers common sources of fear, such as the fear of the restraints of Biblical femininity and the fear of vulnerability in a godly marriage.

✔ Pride, Mary. *All the Way Home.* Wheaton, IL: Crossway Books, 1989. This thought-provoking book goes into greater detail on the roles of family members.

NOTES

1. Karen Burton Mains, "For Better, for Worse," *Moody Monthly* (February 1983): 35.

2. James Strong, *Strong's Exhaustive Concordance* (Nashville: Abington Press, 1890).

3. John MacArthur, Jr., *Answering the Key Questions about the Family* (Panorama City, CA: Grace to You, 1984), 10.

4. Matthew 5:16; Ephesians 2:10; 1 Timothy 2:10; 5:10; 6:18; Titus 2:7, 14; 3:8, 14; Hebrews 10:24; 1 Peter 2:12.

5. Jani Ortlund, *Fearlessly Feminine: Boldly Living God's Plan for Womanhood* (Sisters, OR: Multnomah Publishers, 2000), 37, 38.

6. Gary and Anne Marie Ezzo, *Growing Kids God's Way, 5th ed.* (Simi Valley, CA: Growing Families International, 1998), 270.

7. MacArthur, 10.

8. Elisa Morgan and Carol Kuykendall, *What Every Mom Needs* (Grand Rapids: Zondervan Publishing House, 1995), 31.

9. Anne Ortlund, *The Gentle Ways of the Beautiful Woman: A Practical Guide to Spiritual Beauty* (reprint, 3 vols. in 1, New York: Inspirational Press, 1998), 31.

10. Merrill F. Unger, *The New Unger's Bible Dictionary*, rev. and updated (Chicago: Moody Press, 1988), 254. See also 2 Corinthians 9:8; Philippians 4:11; 1 Timothy 6:6–8; James 3:16; Matthew 6:24, 34; 1 Corinthians 10:10.

PART *1* ONE

Your God

POINT TO PONDER

"That He would grant you, according to the riches of His glory, to be strengthened with might through His Spirit in the inner man, that Christ may dwell in your hearts through faith; that you, being rooted and grounded in love, may be able to comprehend with all the saints what is the width and length and depth and height—to know the love of Christ which passes knowledge; that you may be filled with all the fullness of God" (Ephesians 3:16–19).

How much do you love God? Do you find it hard, as I sometimes do, to love a God you've never seen, never met, never touched? Do you sometimes wonder if God loves you as much as Christians claim He does?

As we already discussed, the Bible says we will find ultimate peace and fulfillment when we line up our lives according to God's priorities, the roles He has designed for us. I want to take some time to discuss with you your relationship to God.

The amazing thing about God is that we can know Him at all! Many religions and cultures have worshiped gods of all sorts, but as King David prayed, "Among the gods there is none like

You, O Lord; nor are there any works like Your works" (Ps. 86:8). Despite His greatness (or perhaps, because of it), He wants to reach us so we can have a loving relationship.

The Bible pictures this loving relationship by calling God our Father. For example, Psalm 103:13 likens God to a father who pities his children. Some other Scripture verses that paint God as a father are as follows: "For your Father knows the things you have need of before you ask Him" (Matt. 6:8); "For you did not receive the spirit of bondage again to fear, but you received the Spirit of adoption by whom we cry out, 'Abba [or, papa], Father.' The Spirit Himself bears witness with our spirit that we are children of God . . ." (Rom. 8:15–17).

Remember that the same God Who created all things in six days walked in the Garden in the cool of the day to talk with Adam and Eve, His creatures (Gen. 3:8). Remember, too, that this powerful God had dinner in Abraham's tent (Gen. 18) and that He spent so much time with David that He identified David as "a man after My own heart" (Acts 13:22).

God desires to know you and for you to know Him. But He also desires for you to love Him. Jesus said that this commandment is the greatest: "You shall love the Lord your God with all your heart, with all your soul, with all your mind, and with all your strength" (Mark 12:30).

How can we love God? By keeping His commandments. Jesus said, "If you love Me, keep My commandments" (John 14:15).

How can we keep His commandments? The answer is found in Psalm 119:9–11: "How can a young man cleanse his way? By taking heed according to Your word. With my whole heart I have sought You; oh, let me not wander from Your commandments! Your word I have hidden in my heart, that I might not sin against You!"

So join me as we discover how to know and love God, making Him top priority in our lives and in our homes.

CHAPTER **3** THREE

Thinking Biblically

POINT TO PONDER
"Now, O Israel, listen to the statutes and the judgments which I teach you to observe, that you may live" (Deuteronomy 4:1).

Moses stood before the Children of Israel, who had been wandering in the wilderness for forty years because of rebellion against God. They were eager to enter the Promised Land. He reminded them that obedience to God brings blessing. But Moses knew that when blessings come, humankind tends to forget God. So he stood before them, reviewing with them God's commands.

You shall not add to the word which I command you, nor take anything from it, that you may keep the commandments of the LORD your God which I command you. . . . Be careful to observe them; *for this is your wisdom and your understanding* in the sight of the peoples who will hear all these statutes. . . . Only take heed to yourself, and diligently keep yourself, *lest you forget the things your eyes have seen,* and *lest they depart from your heart* all the days of your life. . . . The LORD said to me, "Gather the people to Me, and I will let them hear My words, that they may learn to *fear Me* all the days they live on the earth, and that they may *teach their children"* (Deut. 4:2–10, emphasis added).

41

We Need Wisdom

God's primary concern for His chosen people, Israel, was that they remember what they had learned, fear God, and teach their children and grandchildren.

Such an undertaking demands great wisdom. What is wisdom? The dictionary defines wisdom as "common sense or good judgment."

God's definition goes a little further: "The fear of the LORD is the beginning of wisdom; *a good understanding have all those who do His commandments.* His praise endures forever" (Ps. 111:10, emphasis added).

Women especially need wisdom. Each of us needs wisdom to be a loving wife, a godly mother, a devoted friend, and a capable leader in many different roles. But am I alone in the feeling that many women do not know how to think through issues and make decisions based on the "fear of the LORD"?

American culture wants to do all the thinking for us. For example, many of us have learned to trust information that is fed to us by "experts"; after all, they have our best interests at heart, right? Or we do things the way they've been done for generations in our families, because the traditional way is the best way, right? What we learned in school is especially trustworthy because knowledge is power and textbooks are full of knowledge, right? Our friends give us the best advice because they've already been through whatever we're going through and they care so much about us, right?

Obviously the answer is sometimes no. It would be a wonderful world if we could trust everyone else to give us consistently excellent advice. However, we can't even trust ourselves: "The heart is deceitful above all things, and desperately wicked; who can know it?" (Jer. 17:9).

Nevertheless, we try many sources for wisdom. Television is an easy place to get answers to our questions. A typical half-hour

Thinking Biblically

news broadcast has all the top stories, as well as the weather, tips on household maintenance, health advice, and how to take care of our pets. Magazines entice us when we're in the checkout aisle. They make huge promises:

"Lose twenty pounds in five days!"

"Find out the truth about . . . " (insert latest disaster)

"Rid your body of cancer overnight"

"How to help your child make straight *As*"

These days we also have to sort through the immense amount of information available on the Internet. And then we have libraries and local bookstores. Sorting through it all can be confusing.

A proverb clarifies the struggle: "The first one to plead his cause seems right, until his neighbor comes and examines him" (Prov. 18:17).

When I was pregnant with my first child, I was determined to be the best mother in the world. So I spent those nine months immersing myself in all the knowledge I could find. I think I read every book on parenting that our local library offered. I love to read anyway, so that investigation was fun! I took all the magazines my doctor gave me and read all the articles. But when my son was born, I felt overwhelmed! Why hadn't my baby read the same books I had?! Why didn't the advice I had received work?

Maybe you've done the same thing. You see, we are vulnerable to misinformation at certain times in our lives. Major life changes (such as pregnancy) cause us to question our values. We graduate from high school or college and wonder what we're supposed to do with our lives. We fall in love and have to make decisions such as how to get along with this man we're committed to. Fatigue, a shortage of money in the bank, stressful holidays, and crying babies—all these leave our minds in a mush and open to dangerous trends.

We're also vulnerable just because we're women. Now I don't like to admit that any more than you do! But the Bible records illustration after illustration of women who tended to make bad decisions. The most famous is Eve. That sneaky serpent had no trouble at all convincing her that God didn't love her and was hiding things from her. The Bible doesn't mince any words; it says she was "deceived" (1 Tim. 2:14).

We all hate deception! But Eve wasn't the only one. Sarai deceived herself into thinking God couldn't keep His promise of a son, so she suggested to Abram that maybe her handmaiden could bear him a child instead (Gen. 16:1, 2). Imagine how sorry she must have felt when she actually did conceive years later!

Lot's wife was told not to look back at the city of Sodom when her family fled early that fateful morning. But she thought a little glance at her home wouldn't hurt; she missed her friends and her lovely things already! She chose to disobey, she looked back, and God turned her into a pillar of salt (Gen. 19:1–26).

I think our culture as a whole has been deceived. Remember how Moses warned the Israelites of the danger of forgetting God when prosperous times come? America has become a prosperous nation. Many of us, as a result, have stopped thinking Biblically. During the last century, many parents certainly had God's morals on their hearts. However, as time passed, even many Christian parents stopped teaching God's morals to their children and grandchildren. When teen pregnancy rates began to climb and other indications of social decline became evident, the parents were bewildered. A generation gap had occurred because the values on the parents' hearts were not transferred to the hearts of the children.

I don't know what your situation is, but I know I want to pass on godly wisdom to my children. I want to be an example to other women in my church. I want to impact my world! To do these things I need to know why I believe what I believe. I need to know how to think. I need wisdom!

Thinking Biblically   45

The Source of Wisdom

How can we gain wisdom? How can we go from naïve to knowledgeable and wise? How can we learn to think? The Bible, the book of all comfort, gives the answer: "If any of you lacks wisdom, let him ask of God, who gives to all liberally and without reproach, and it will be given to him" (James 1:5).

God is the source of all wisdom, just as He is the source of everything. We need to learn to walk in step with Him each day so that we can draw from the wisdom He offers us. We need to think His thoughts, not our own. We need to evaluate all beliefs from His perspective, not our own limited vision.

After my first son's birth, a godly woman brought a passage of Scripture to my attention. I would like you to memorize these verses—to hide Psalm 1 in your heart—so you can meditate and chew on them all day long.

> Blessed is the man who walks not in the counsel of the ungodly [ungodly magazines, new age philosophies, etc.], nor stands in the path of sinners, nor sits in the seat of the scornful [who are your friends?]; but his delight is in the law of the LORD, and in His law he meditates day and night. [Does God's Word fill your mind?] He shall be like a tree planted by the rivers of water, that brings forth its fruit in its season, whose leaf also shall not wither; and whatever he does shall prosper. [Isn't that what you want for your home?] The ungodly are not so, but are like the chaff which the wind drives away. [Ever noticed how the "latest" advice never lasts?] Therefore the ungodly shall not stand in the judgment, nor sinners in the congregation of the righteous. For the LORD knows the way of the righteous, but the way of the ungodly shall perish.

While it's easy to *say* we should get all of our wisdom and advice from God's Word, what do we *do* in reality? Christian Overman wrote a book called *Assumptions That Affect Our Lives.* In it he lists twenty-four major distinctions between the way the world thinks and the way the Bible wants us to think.

For instance, the world wants us to believe we have no mandate from any source above ourselves. Secular society says that truth is measured by humankind's intellect and reasoned judgment; in other words, no divine standard or measure of truth exists. The ancient Greek Protagoras said it well: "Man is the measure of all things." However, we know that truth is determined by God independently of mankind. God's Word is the measure of all things. Humankind's opinion does not affect it in any way.

Overman made many more comparisons, but obviously he was saying that God and His Word are our ultimate authorities.[1]

But can you see where even Christians fall into some of the traps of worldly thinking?

Do you remember the account of Lot's wife? She and her family had to flee the city of Sodom before God destroyed it because of its wickedness. Then she looked back at the city and all she had left behind, directly disobeying God's command not to look, and God turned her into a pillar of salt.

How did Lot and his wife get into that awful situation in the first place? Did they start out trying to think in "unbiblical" ways?

No, I don't think so. The first time we read about Lot in the Bible, he was in the company of his uncle Abram, who was leaving the home of his father and journeying to a land to which he had never been. Abram walked in faith and in obedience to God (Gen. 12:1–5).

The next time we read of Lot, his servants were bickering with Abram's servants. They all had so many flocks and herds that the land could not support them. So Abram suggested they separate. He offered to let Lot have the first choice of where to live (Gen. 13:1–13).

Lot looked out over the Jordan River valley and saw that it was green and well-watered, like one big garden! Two cities stood in the valley, Sodom and Gomorrah, so living there would be

Thinking Biblically

easy. He chose the valley, and eventually he moved his family's tents all the way to Sodom and took up residence.

However, Lot failed to consider the reputation of the two cities, that the men of Sodom were "exceedingly wicked and sinful against the LORD" (Gen. 13:13). Lot put himself into a position where it would be easy to walk "in the counsel of the ungodly" and to stand "in the path of sinners" and to sit "in the seat of the scornful."

Sometime later God had to destroy the wicked cities, but on Abraham's insistence, He sent two angels to Sodom to fetch Lot and his family (Gen. 19:1–26). They found Lot sitting at the gate of Sodom. His sitting at the gate probably meant he had considerable importance in the town. The city gates were a place of honor, since all who entered the town had to pass through them. Lot had made the citizens of Sodom his closest companions. "Do not be deceived: 'Evil company corrupts good habits' " (1 Cor. 15:33). "He who walks with wise men will be wise, but the companion of fools will be destroyed" (Prov. 13:20).

The result of this infamous account is that Lot's family and home were destroyed, as well as his good name. But the destruction came because of a gradual movement toward the ungodly— their counsel and companionship.

It takes work to resist this gradual assault on our senses. The apostle Paul said we are at war:

> For though we walk in the flesh, we do not war according to the flesh. For the weapons of our warfare are not carnal but mighty in God for pulling down strongholds, casting down arguments and every high thing that exalts itself against the knowledge of God, bringing every thought into captivity to the obedience of Christ (2 Cor. 10:3–5).

So let's get to work and bring our thinking, our philosophy, and our choices into alignment with God's Word. What will God do for you if you choose to think His thoughts?

48 JUGGLING LIFE'S RESPONSIBILITIES

• *God will increase your knowledge.* "Call to Me, and I will answer you, and show you great and mighty things, which you do not know" (Jer. 33:3). "The fear of the LORD is the beginning of knowledge, but fools despise wisdom and instruction" (Prov. 1:7).

• *God will instruct you and guide you.* "I will instruct you and teach you in the way you should go; I will guide you with My eye" (Ps. 32:8).

• *God will grant mercy to you in your decisions.* "Many sorrows shall be to the wicked; but he who trusts in the LORD, mercy shall surround him" (Ps. 32:10).

• *God will give you not only wisdom and knowledge but joy.* "For God gives wisdom and knowledge and joy to a man who is good in His sight" (Eccles. 2:26).

• *God will let you know Him more personally.* "Then you will understand the fear of the LORD, and find the knowledge of God. For the LORD gives wisdom; from His mouth come knowledge and understanding" (Prov. 2:5, 6).

• *God will shield you.* "He stores up sound wisdom for the upright; He is a shield to those who walk uprightly" (Prov. 2:7).

• *God will help you make decisions.* "Your word is a lamp to my feet and a light to my path. . . . The entrance of Your words gives light; it gives understanding to the simple" (Ps. 119:105, 130).

• *God will make you prosperous and successful.* "This Book of the Law shall not depart from your mouth, but you shall meditate in it day and night, that you may observe to do according to all that is written in it. For then you will make your way prosperous, and then you will have good success" (Josh. 1:8).

More could be said about each of these points, so we'll spend the rest of the book discussing the wonderful things God can do in your life if you are willing to do things God's way. Before we go on, however, let's discuss for a moment what applying God's Word to your life really means.

Thinking Biblically 49

Remember that your mind is the gateway to all your actions, and you need to guard carefully against wrong thoughts entering. "Keep [or guard] your heart with all diligence, for out of it spring the issues of life" (Prov. 4:23). Let the Word of God guard your heart. In one of his most famous psalms, Psalm 119 (which would be a good one to memorize), David prayed, "Your word I have hidden in my heart, that I might not sin against You" (Ps. 119:11).

You are probably familiar with these Scripture verses, but how easy it is to memorize a verse and not let its meaning sink into your life! Paul commended the church in Berea because the believers "received the word with all readiness, and searched the Scriptures daily to find out whether these things were so" (Acts 17:11). I know that only rarely in my life have I taken a sermon I've heard and compared it carefully to the Scriptures to be sure it was accurate. Yet the Bible urges us to let it be our comparison for *all* things, not just sermons. For instance, can you spot inaccuracies in a movie you watch or in a book you read, quoting the exact Scripture that tells you why there is an error? The only way to excel at this practice is to "search the Scriptures daily" and hide God's Word in your heart.

How will you know what kind of woman, wife, or mother God wants you to be? How will you know how to train your children or love your husband? How will you know what impact you should have on the world? The apostle Paul wisely told us how we can know God's mind on any subject.

> I beseech you therefore, brethren, by the mercies of God, that you present your bodies a living sacrifice, holy, acceptable to God, which is your reasonable service. *And do not be conformed to this world, but be transformed by the renewing of your mind,* that you may prove what is that good and acceptable and perfect will of God (Rom. 12:1, 2, emphasis added).

We are to renew our minds, never conforming to the world's wisdom, so that we can discern God's will. Renewing our minds and evaluating things in the light of Scripture take a lot of effort. Sometimes what God expects from us is radically different from what the world expects. However, don't be persuaded by *my* words (or you'll be falling into that same old trap of "not thinking"). Go ahead—"search the Scriptures daily."

The Opponents of Wisdom

Before we get into specifics, I want to warn you about some opposition you may face as you implement God's ways. You *will* face opposition (2 Tim. 3:12). Remember, the way God thinks and the way the world thinks are complete opposites. So what can you do when you're tempted to think the world's thoughts?

• *Don't be afraid to be different.* "For God has not given us a spirit of fear, but of power and of love and of a sound mind" (2 Tim. 1:7). Notice that a spirit of fear (of other's opinions) does not come from God. He gives us a sound mind capable of thinking clearly and rationally. Don't forget that "the LORD is my light and my salvation; whom shall I fear? The LORD is the strength of my life; of whom shall I be afraid?" (Ps. 27:1).

• *Don't jump on every bandwagon.* An idea may be new and popular, but is it Biblical? Does it tend to go to extremes?

• *Don't compare yourself to others.* God's opinion of you is all that counts. Paul warned that "we dare not class ourselves or compare ourselves with those who commend themselves. But they, measuring themselves by themselves, and comparing themselves among themselves, are not wise" (2 Cor. 10:12). How do your beliefs compare with God's Word?

• *Beware of counterfeits.* Just because someone quotes a Scripture verse doesn't mean he or she is quoting it accurately or within the correct context! Many people base their opinions on a phrase of a Bible verse, ripped out of context, devoid of its

Thinking Biblically

original intent. Study the Scriptures! Also consider if the person giving advice is qualified.[2]

• *Don't close your mind.* God is working in your heart to make you into His image. Don't resist Him because something He is teaching you is different or strange. Allow His Word to work in your life, leaving in His hands the consequences of any changes you make.

IN SUMMARY

God wants to see you become wise and develop a heart like His. This process takes time and commitment to the truth. When I was in high school, I taped the following lines on my wall to remind me that the little things count and that over time God would develop His wisdom in me.

Sow a thought, reap an action.
Sow an action, reap a habit.
Sow a habit, reap a character.

EXTRA CREDIT ASSIGNMENT

Memorize 2 Timothy 1:7 and recite it to a minimum of five women.

> "For God has not given us a spirit of fear, but of power and of love and of a sound mind" (2 Timothy 1:7).

STUDY GUIDE

1. After reading Deuteronomy 4:1 and 2, list some practical ways we can learn to think Biblically.
2. According to Psalm 111:10, where does wisdom begin? What does it mean to "fear the LORD"?
3. According to Jeremiah 17:9, we should not trust our own

judgment. Why not? Summarize an example from your own life when you followed your heart and the circumstance turned out badly. Can you quote a Scripture verse that shows why your heart deceived you?

4. Do you think it's fair to say women are more vulnerable than men to being deceived? Read 1 Timothy 2:11–15 and think of how it differs from our culture's opinion.

5. According to James 1:5, how can you find wisdom? When God gives you wisdom, is it easy to follow?

6. In Proverbs 3:5 and 6, what is God's recipe for success?

7. Read 2 Corinthians 10:5 and list the things we need to have constantly under our control. Write down some practical ways to do this. (See also Proverbs 4:23.)

GROUP PROJECT

Choose a current event and write down responses you have observed in people because of this event. Using Scripture as a resource, brainstorm ways these responses agree or disagree with God's wisdom.

EXTRA READING

✔ Overman, Christian. *Assumptions That Affect Our Lives*. Simi Valley, CA: Micah 6:8, 1996. I highly recommend this book as a resource for analyzing your worldview. This book was much more readable than I thought it would be! You can order it at 1-800-474-6264 or www.gfi.org.

NOTES

1. Christian Overman, *Assumptions That Affect Our Lives* (Simi Valley, CA: Micah 6:8, 1996), 253–259.

2. First Timothy 3:1–7 and Titus 1:5–9 give the qualifications for bishops. These lists of character qualities would be a good place to start when checking the Biblical qualifications of a person.

CHAPTER *4* FOUR

Tapping into God's Power

POINT TO PONDER
"But thanks be to God, who gives us the victory through our Lord Jesus Christ"
(1 Corinthians 15:57).

I come from a rich tradition of gardeners. My grandmother grew beautiful flowers. Often we found her in the garden, a giant hat protecting her face from the sun, meticulously pruning her roses or trimming the edges of the walkways. My mother has a talent for turning out vast amounts of vegetables from her garden. She enjoys the bounty throughout her long New York winters and shares with many friends. My mother-in-law has a heart for flowers. She can turn a barren lot into a bevy of flowers, and I've secretly thought of calling *Better Homes and Gardens* to recommend that they visit her!

But my thumb is black. I've never had a houseplant last longer than a few months. The former occupant of our home left me a treasure of rosebushes and landscapers' delights, but I've managed to neglect them and turn them into stalks without leaves. The one time I attempted a vegetable garden, I gave up mid-season because of my great fear of bugs!

53

I did manage to get two tomato plants to grow one time. I bought the plants, along with a bag of potting soil, from an Amish farmer, and I plopped them into the ground behind my home. I sent my husband to the store for some stakes and twine, and as the weeks went by, I carefully watered and pruned and tied and loved those tomato plants.

One summer day I proudly picked some luscious tomatoes from their vines and paraded them into the house for supper. Never had a tomato tasted so juicy! I envisioned myself continuing to pick them for the rest of the summer and turning into a domestic kitchen goddess who could can sauces and turn out Italian dishes with a flourish.

You can imagine my great disappointment one morning when I saw that several vines were starting to wither. What had I done wrong? I had faithfully watered them! I had tied them to stakes, protecting them from wind and storms! Only yesterday they had been so healthy.

A careful look through the leaves revealed my problem. I had visitors! On one stalk, and also on the ground, were fat tomato worms. Oooh! Gross! I have memories of my father squashing them under his shoe when I was a little girl. I knew I didn't have the guts (pardon the pun) to do that!

While my gardening skills haven't improved much, those tomato plants taught me a lot about how to be spiritually fruitful. We've made it our goal to be godly women, with our priorities in order, and we've established that a strong relationship with God is our first priority. Now we're going to learn how to be fruitful for God.

The Source of Power

The night before Jesus' death, He sat down for a final meal with His disciples. John 13—18 records His words of instruction and love for them. The disciples didn't realize what was about to

Tapping into God's Power

happen at Calvary, but Jesus did. He knew that He would be leaving them for awhile. He knew that they would be confused and feel abandoned. He knew also that the Holy Spirit would come and guide them. Jesus knew what great things these humble men would do for God.

Jesus wanted them to know the source of their power. If they thought that Jesus had to be physically present in order for them to do great things for God, then how would they function when He was crucified, buried, arose, and ascended into Heaven? On the other hand, they needed to understand that without Him, they had no power at all.

Jesus used a simple illustration to teach them. He said, "I am the true vine, and My Father is the vinedresser" (John 15:1). Then He explained the source of their power—and ours.

God wants us to bear much fruit. He has been planning for it from the beginning of time. Ephesians 2:10 states, "For we are His workmanship, created in Christ Jesus for good works, which God prepared beforehand that we should walk in them." Other places in Scripture describe these fruits of good works, and we'll discuss them more in chapter 9.

As a successful gardener, God works in our lives so that the maximum amount of fruit is produced. He carefully prunes us, getting rid of the sin in our lives and stripping us of the things that will keep fruit from growing.

How does He do this pruning? Jesus said that the only way we can truly be cleansed of the sin and selfishness in our hearts is through His cleansing Word.

Difficult circumstances should drive us to His Word. The discovery of sin in our lives should push us to His Word. The environment of our past should help us realize how much we need God's Word. As we live in the world, watch television, and otherwise pick up the world's thinking patterns, we need to regularly return to the Word for pruning. Otherwise these worldly "growths" can sap our energy and prevent us from bearing much fruit.

As branches, we must remain connected to the vine, Jesus Christ. A tomato branch can't grow tomatoes when its connection to the vine is pinched, restricting the nutrients from the main vine. We need to learn to fellowship with Christ, to enjoy quality time with Him, or to "abide," as John 15:4 puts it.

We don't have any power to do good in ourselves. When we trusted in Christ, God gave us a new life in Christ. Ephesians explains that "even when we were dead in trespasses, [God] made us alive together with Christ. . . . For by grace you have been saved through faith, and that not of yourselves; it is the gift of God, not of works, lest anyone should boast" (Eph. 2:5, 8, 9).

Now we want to have the power to bear the fruit of good works, but we need to remember to abide in Christ. We just can't bear fruit by ourselves. However, when we do abide, the result is *much* fruit!

How was the apostle Paul able to have joy in difficult circumstances, even to be content as he rotted in a Roman jail? His secret was to abide in Christ: "I can do all things through Christ who strengthens me" (Phil. 4:13).

So what is the key? Abiding in Christ. Don't lose your close relationship with Him Who is your life-giving vine, for without Him you can accomplish nothing of worth.

The Results of God's Power

I'm always more motivated when I know the end result. Since I love to eat fresh tomatoes, I am certainly more motivated to grow tomatoes than, say, turnips.

In the same way, God wants to work in an awesome way in our lives. Why, then, should we abide in Christ?

First, we will know the will of God. "If you abide in Me, and My words abide in you, you will ask what you desire, and it

Tapping into God's Power   57

shall be done for you" (John 15:7). God promises to answer our prayers, knowing, of course, that when we abide in Him and His Word, we'll know God's will and pray accordingly.

> Behold, the LORD's hand is not shortened, that it cannot save; nor His ear heavy, that it cannot hear. But your iniquities have separated you from your God; and your sins have hidden His face from you, so that He will not hear (Isa. 59:1, 2).

When sin destroys our fellowship with God, we suddenly can't see what God's will is. We pray, but our prayers are filled with sinful, selfish desires. Then we complain that God doesn't answer our prayers. In reality, we accuse God of not being strong enough, kind enough, or caring enough to hear us. But has the almighty God's hand suddenly grown so short that it can't reach us? Is He asleep? Is He deaf?

No! The problem lies in us. Our fellowship with the Vine has been broken. We need to return immediately to the Word for cleansing.

2. *Second, when we abide in Christ, we will give the glory to God.* "By this My Father is glorified, that you bear much fruit" (John 15:8). Pride can make us think that we can be spiritual giants all by ourselves. If we just dress a certain way, put a spiritual look on our faces, and use all the right words, then everyone will see how holy we are.

In reality, when we abide in Christ, all the glory goes to God. Two of my favorite verses read, "My soul shall make its boast in the LORD; the humble shall hear of it and be glad. . . . They looked to Him and were radiant, and their faces were not ashamed" (Ps. 34:2, 5). When we're plugged into God, drawing our power from Him, the peaceable fruits of righteousness shine out of our faces.

3. *Third, when we abide in Christ, we will know the love of God.* Jesus said, "As the Father loved Me, I also have loved you; abide in My love" (John 15:9). Consider how much God loved His Son. Then

realize how much Christ loved you to give His life for you.

We should love others in the same way. We tend, however, to love them based upon their merits—how nice they look, how well they treat us. "But God demonstrates His own love toward us, in that while we were still sinners, Christ died for us" (Rom. 5:8). We don't love others because they are precious to us; we love them because they are precious to God.

Fourth, when we abide in Christ, we feel *loved by God.* When my child is obedient, she certainly feels my loving favor more than when she is disobedient. When she does wrong, we both feel rather yucky. Our fellowship can't be restored until I confront her and she asks for forgiveness.

This point flows into *the fifth point: When we abide in Christ, our joy is full.* One morning as I was working, my son was playing with cars next to my desk. He had fun sifting through his car container and telling me why each car was special to him. Even though I was busy, we had a good time talking and laughing and enjoying each other's company.

Only moments later, he became angry with his little sister without cause. He yelled at her and snatched her toy from her hands. Suddenly he felt my displeasure! Instead of fun, he shed tears. Instead of joy, he felt misery.

Jesus said, "If you keep My commandments, you will abide in My love, just as I have kept My Father's commandments and abide in His love. These things I have spoken to you, that My joy may remain in you, and that your joy may be full" (John 15:10, 11).

Abiding in Christ, our Vine, is the most wonderful place we can be!

The Requirements for Power

Jesus' plan for a power-filled spiritual life can be summarized with three phrases. We must be obedient to God, friends with God, and chosen by God.

Tapping into God's Power   59

We can sum up obedience to God with one word: love. Jesus said, "This is My commandment, that you love one another as I have loved you. Greater love has no one than this, than to lay down one's life for his friends" (John 15:12, 13).

How can we abide in Christ? By abiding in His Word. What fruit will be produced? Love for others. Love is the thermometer that tells you how well you're doing in the number one priority of life, your relationship with God. You can learn to think Biblically, taking Scripture in context and applying it with wisdom. But if you are unloving to your husband, something is wrong. You can keep a clean house and have hospitality to the world, but if you're unloving to your children, your relationship with God is not right. Obedience to God is directly measured by the amount of love you show.

Jesus said, "You are My friends if you do whatever I command you" (John 15:14). When your heart is cleansed from sin, you have confidence to approach God's presence. You can be sure that you're walking in His will. The rest of your priorities will fall into place.

God must be our number one priority. Unless He is first in our lives, we will not abide in Him. Without a firm attachment to Christ and His Word, our spiritual lives will wither. We won't bear much fruit. What little fruit we have won't remain. We won't be sure that the rest of our lives are in line with the will of God.

But marvel, dear woman, that from the beginning of time God saw you and chose *you* to bear much fruit (John 15:16). He has great plans for your life, as we've seen, and He wants your fruit to remain.

IN SUMMARY

Abide in Christ—He is the source of your power. Abide in His Word—the Bible is the source of your cleansing. Abide in His command to love others—it is the source of your joy. Abiding is *your* choice. Throughout the rest of this book you'll learn many practical tips on *how* to abide. I'll show you how to arrange your day so that God's Word takes priority and can have the opportunity to cleanse you. I'll show you how to love your husband and children, and how to share your love with the rest of the world.

But your responsibility is to stop trying to take control of your own life. God wants all the glory for the fruit you bear, and you must humbly relinquish control to Him. Learn to make a *daily* choice to abide with Christ.

EXTRA CREDIT ASSIGNMENT

Memorize this passage of Scripture by learning one verse at a time; then recite it to a minimum of five women.

> "But God, who is rich in mercy, because of His great love with which He loved us, even when we were dead in trespasses, made us alive together with Christ (by grace you have been saved), and raised us up together, and made us sit together in the heavenly places in Christ Jesus, that in the ages to come He might show the exceeding riches of His grace in His kindness toward us in Christ Jesus. For by grace you have been saved through faith, and that not of yourselves; it is the gift of God, not of works, lest anyone should boast. For we are His workmanship, created in Christ Jesus for good works, which God prepared beforehand that we should walk in them" (Ephesians 2:4–10).

Tapping into God's Power

～ STUDY GUIDE ～

1. Read Isaiah 64:6 and 7. Thinking back on your life before you trusted Christ, list specific instances of the truth of these verses.
2. According to Romans 3:19, why do laws exist?
3. According to Ephesians 2:8–10, what has God done for you? How long has He had you in His plans?
4. After reading 2 Corinthians 6:16, name some ways that being the temple of God affects you as a wife, mother, homemaker, church member, and witness to the unsaved.
5. What is the command given in John 15:4? List the three things mentioned in John 15 that will help you obey Jesus' command.

GROUP PROJECT

Plan a time to go out under the stars at night. Have someone read aloud or recite Isaiah 55:8 and 9. Lie on your backs on the grass, and after a few minutes of quietly meditating on these verses, sing some praise songs to God under the night sky.

EXTRA READING

✔ Ketcham, Robert T. *God's Provision for Normal Christian Living.* Schaumburg, IL, Regular Baptist Press, 1990. You can order this classic from Regular Baptist Press at www.regular baptistpress.org or 1-800-727-4440.

✔ Ortlund, Anne. *The Gentle Ways of the Beautiful Woman: A Practical Guide to Spiritual Beauty.* Reprint (3 vols. in 1), New York: Inspirational Press, 1998. The second volume is *Disciplines of the Heart: Tuning Your Inner Life to God* (© 1987 by Anne Ortlund). Ortlund clearly explains how to die to ourselves and be victorious in our spiritual lives.

CHAPTER **5** FIVE

Knowing God Intimately

POINT TO PONDER
"The law of Your mouth is better to me than thousands of coins of gold and silver. . . . I have not departed from Your judgments, for You Yourself have taught me"
(Psalm 119:72, 102).

So you want to make God the top priority in your life? You want to walk in His ways and follow His will? Then you must know Him intimately. We have already seen that knowing God intimately means knowing His Word. The Bible has been described as God's love letter to us. Knowing what God's Word says means we know what God Himself thinks.

I beseech you therefore, brethren, by the mercies of God, that you present your bodies a living sacrifice, holy, acceptable to God, which is your reasonable service. And do not be conformed to this world, but *be transformed by the renewing of your mind*, that you may prove what is that good and acceptable and perfect will of God (Rom. 12:1, 2, emphasis added).

63

How to Read the Bible

Many people struggle with the thought of reading God's Word from cover to cover. (We can stay up until midnight reading romance novels, but we dread reading a page of our Bibles.) The Bible can be difficult to understand and oh, so convicting! Some passages are dull, and we wonder how they could ever apply to us.

Then there is the matter of interpretation. It's like the man who wasn't sure what to do with his life, so his pastor recommended he read his Bible. He wasn't sure where to start, so he decided to randomly open it and see what he found. The first verse he read was how Judas "threw down the pieces of silver in the temple and departed, and went and hanged himself" (Matt. 27:5). Unsure what God might be trying to tell him, he decided to try a different verse. The next verse he randomly opened to said, "Go and do likewise" (Luke 10:37).

This story is silly, but it is important to understand the context of the verses we read. Obviously the best way to see the context of the verses is to start at the beginning and read through. Starting at the beginning helps us see the "plot."

If you have never read the Bible before, starting on the first page of Genesis and beginning to read may be difficult. It may be wise for you to start with the life of Christ as told in the New Testament book of John. Sometime during your Christian life, however, you need to start at the beginning of the Bible and get the big picture of what God has done for humankind. Jot down questions you have. Look up the answers in a reliable Bible commentary. (See resources at the end of this chapter.) Ask your husband for help (1 Cor. 14:35). Don't forget to ask the Holy Spirit, Who lives in you, to help you understand what you are reading.

Whether you are somewhat familiar or quite familiar with the Bible, you can never go wrong by reading the Bible verse by verse, chapter by chapter. That way you will have the most protection against error.

Knowing God Intimately

Do you remember how Satan tempted Jesus in the wilderness? The Devil himself quoted Scripture to Jesus: "If You are the Son of God, throw Yourself down. For it is written: 'He shall give His angels charge over you,' and, 'In their hands they shall bear you up, lest you dash your foot against a stone' " (Matt. 4:6).

I know if Satan had quoted Scripture to me, my defenses would have immediately lowered. But not Jesus. Why? Because Jesus recognized that Satan had not quoted the verses correctly. Satan quoted from Psalm 91:11 and 12, but he left out the phrase shown here in italics: "For He shall give His angels charge over you, *to keep you in all your ways.*"

Eve committed a similar offense in the Garden by adding to what God had said. God commanded, "But of the tree of the knowledge of good and evil you shall not eat, for in the day that you eat of it you shall surely die" (Gen. 2:17). Eve added to this command when she told Satan, "God has said, 'You shall not eat it, *nor shall you touch it*, lest you die' " (Gen. 3:3, emphasis added).

And the deceptions continue even in our time. How will you know whether the things you hear and read are true? By comparing them to God's Word—including the context!

It may help you to use a translation of the Bible that divides the passages of Scripture into paragraphs instead of verses. It is much easier to see the flow of thought when the text is written in paragraph form. It's also easier to tell which verses are Hebrew poetry, which verses are quotations, and which verses are narratives. Even if you use a traditional verse format (such as the King James Version or the New American Standard Bible), pay attention to the flow of thought so you don't take anything out of context.

You should also learn about the writer and the intended audience. For instance, knowing that a learned physician wrote the book of Luke to a non-Jewish friend may help you decide to recommend it to an educated skeptic friend of yours. Also, knowing that Paul wrote the book of Philippians when he was in prison may help you realize just what he meant when he wrote, "Rejoice in the Lord always. Again I will say, rejoice!" (Phil. 4:4). Since the *epistle* to the Philippians is a *letter* to the Christians who lived in the ancient city of Philippi, you may even decide to look up the account of how Paul first visited the city of Philippi. You would find this background by using the cross-references in your Bible, by looking up the word "Philippi" in a concordance, or by reading about the history of the book of Philippians in a good commentary. (Acts 16 records the account of the Philippian church.)

You also need to remember the cultural surroundings of what you are reading. What was the geography like? What was the political climate? How did the people dress and eat? A great example would be the story Jesus told in Matthew 20:1–16. If you read in the King James Version that each worker received a penny for a day's work, you would be surprised indeed. But knowing that this penny, also called a denarius, was equal to a full day's wage will greatly help you understand what Jesus was saying.

Gordon D. Fee and Douglas Stuart wrote a book titled *How to Read the Bible for All Its Worth.* In this book they pointed out that "the most important contextual question you will ever ask, and it must be asked over and over of every sentence and every paragraph, is, 'What's the point?' "[1]

God has given us the ability to reason and use common sense. While you shouldn't forget to first pray and ask God for wisdom as you read, be sure to apply your thinking skills to the Bible as you read it (James 1:5). As you form opinions and beliefs, ask yourself if they adhere to the message of the Bible as a whole or if you have pulled them out of context to suit a point you wish to make. Remember that the Holy Spirit guided men to write the Bible and that He now resides in your heart to guide you in your understanding. Frequently ask, "What's the point?" or, rather, "What's God's point?"

Knowing God Intimately 67

Many books can guide you in your reading and study of the Word of God. I have listed some of my personal favorites in the resources at the end of this chapter.

Consistent Study

If you are a woman who is juggling family and home responsibilities, you will probably struggle to find time to read the Bible. However, it is important to become consistent. Why? Because God's Word is your spiritual food. How long can you go without food? "As newborn babes, desire the pure milk of the word, that you may grow thereby" (1 Pet. 2:2). A newborn baby needs to eat every few hours, around the clock. Although sweet, he or she can be insistent when it's time to eat again! Likewise you should insist that feeding on God's Word has top priority in your day!

But speaking of newborn babies . . .

Some seasons of your life are busier than others! A close friend and mentor of mine showed me her journal so I could see my name written there. She prays for me faithfully every day, as well as for her entire church family and other friends and loved ones. With her prayer time, she also reads four or five chapters in the Bible, studies another chapter in depth, memorizes Scripture in large chunks, and takes copious notes to file away for future study. And this was just her morning routine! She had an entirely different routine after lunch and yet another for bedtime. No wonder she seems to be a godly woman!

But I was discouraged. When I saw her last, I had a preschooler and a year-old baby; plus I was pregnant with my third child. I was busily involved in a home business and preparing to be a missionary overseas. My family traveled extensively, and my husband worked sixty or more hours each week. I wasted precious energy for over a day as I plotted how I could manage a devotional routine similar to hers. Thankfully the Lord was faithful to remind me of Psalm 1:2 (remember, Psalm 1 is one of my favorite Scripture passages!): "But his delight is in the law of the LORD, and in His law he *meditates* day and night" (emphasis added).

I was always taught that to meditate does *not* mean I sit in a yoga position in my living room, burning incense candles and attempting to empty my mind. Actually, it means to *fill* my mind—in this case, with God's Word. A picture I like is a cow that chews some grass, swallows it, then brings it up later to chew on again and again. That's meditation I can do!

So when you're a new wife with the responsibility of making a home for yourself and your husband, take some time to paint or cross-stitch (or whatever else) some "meditation verses" for your walls. You may want to place the words of 1 Corinthians 13, the "love chapter," over your bed so you're prepared for your first quarrel. You might consider handwriting the words of Proverbs 31 and taping them to your kitchen cabinet so you can meditate on the excellent wife described there as you learn to do your dishes faithfully.

When babies begin to arrive, keep your Bible right by your chair so you can feed yourself on Proverbs as you feed your little one. As more babies fill your home and your older ones want your attention when you're feeding the baby, keep an index card next to your chair. You may want to copy verses on it about love or patience.

Post this verse beside your bed: "A little sleep, a little slumber, a little folding of the hands to sleep—so shall your poverty come on you like a prowler, and your need like an armed man" (Prov. 6:10, 11).

The point is that God wants us to meditate on His Word. You can do that no matter how busy you are, no matter what stage of life you are in. Don't be bound to the tradition of a "quiet time." The important thing is that you feed on God's Word as often as you can.

Having said that, though, it is important that you "eat" a

well-balanced diet. As I said earlier, it is always wiser to read verse-by-verse through the Bible rather than a solitary verse here and there. You may want to consider plopping your little one into a playpen and hiding in the bedroom so you can read a few verses from where you left off yesterday. Then choose a verse to meditate on, and write it in a spiral 3" x 5" notebook. Prop this notebook on your kitchen counter, and you will have your own perpetual calendar. Now it will be easy to meditate on this verse each day.

Choosing a place to study God's Word will help you be consistent. Even if the bathroom is the only quiet room in your house, be prepared with a pen and your Bible, as well as a notebook to write down thoughts and questions. Think about your daily routines and choose a spot where you can have a little bit of privacy for a few minutes.

If your family is large or your time is short, you may need to set your alarm a few minutes earlier or go to bed a little later. When your children are older, you might be able to have leisurely devotions each morning with chilled orange juice and a bran muffin, but for now be creative in making time with God a priority.

If spending time with God is a new habit for you, it will take time to do it consistently. Ask God to help you! Studies have shown that forging a new habit can take up to two months. So patiently start to make your Bible study a permanent fixture in your day, and don't quit if you mess up sometimes.

Memorization

I want to take just a moment to share with you some secrets of memorization. Memorization is just a step beyond meditation. If you "chew the cud" with a Bible verse each day, in no time at all you will have committed it to memory. Don't let the word "memorize" scare you away!

David prayed, "How can a young man cleanse his way? By taking heed according to Your word. With my whole heart I have sought You; oh, let me not wander from Your commandments! Your word I have hidden in my heart, that I might not sin against You" (Ps. 119:9–11).

The following passages of Scripture are "must haves" in your memory bank. I'm sure I've missed some, but this list will get you started.

Exodus 20:1–17	Psalm 119	Romans 13
Psalm 1	Psalm 139	1 Corinthians 13
Psalm 8	Psalm 150	Galatians 5:16–26
Psalm 15	Proverbs 31:10–31	Philippians 1—4
Psalm 19	Isaiah 53	Titus 2
Psalm 23	Matthew 5—7	Hebrews 4:9–16
Psalm 34	John 3:1–21	James 1—5
Psalm 86	John 14—17	1 Peter 3:1–6
Psalm 90	Romans 8	1 John 2
Psalm 100	Romans 12	

As you memorize, remember that the more of your five senses you involve in each verse, the easier it will be to remember. Be creative as you memorize. You may also learn more quickly by *teaching* the verses. If you have children, you are surrounded by students who need God's Word in their hearts, so recite those verses *with* them at every opportunity.

My best advice for memorization is probably to find someone to hold you accountable. You may want to consider an older woman in your church, someone who is patient and understanding and wise. Ask her to suggest verses as well. Tell her you need someone to pray for you as you memorize, and ask her if you can quote your verses to her.

Prayer

A dear friend of mine belongs to a church that tells her she may pray only to her priest or recite only prayers the church has

Knowing God Intimately

given her. When she and her husband came to our home for a meal, she was astonished that my husband thanked the Lord so freely for the food. How dare we talk to God in such an intimate manner!

Another friend of mine is going to the Middle East as a missionary. Five times each day the people in that culture drop to their knees, face the East, and pray a prayer. Not to pray would be to add years of suffering to their time in Hell, so these dear people are faithful to call upon their god.

The Bible tells us that we may "come boldly to the throne of grace, that we may obtain mercy and find grace to help in time of need" (Heb. 4:16). I'm afraid we don't realize what a great privilege prayer is! Again, consider our God. Isaiah saw God in a vision, and these are the words he wrote:

> In the year that King Uzziah died, I saw the Lord sitting on a throne, high and lifted up, and the train of His robe filled the temple. Above it stood seraphim; each one had six wings: with two he covered his face, with two he covered his feet, and with two he flew. And one cried to another and said: "Holy, holy, holy is the LORD of hosts; the whole earth is full of His glory!" And the posts of the door were shaken by the voice of him who cried out, and the house was filled with smoke. So I said: "Woe is me, for I am undone! Because I am a man of unclean lips, and I dwell in the midst of a people of unclean lips; for my eyes have seen the King, the LORD of hosts" (Isa. 6:1–5).

Yet this God, Whose appearance and holiness struck terror into the heart of Isaiah, invites us to come boldly into His presence.

> And whatever things you ask in prayer, believing, you will receive (Matt. 21:22).

> Ask, and it will be given to you; seek, and you will find; knock, and it will be opened to you. For everyone who asks receives, and he who seeks finds, and to him who knocks it will be opened. Or what man is there among you who, if his son asks for bread, will give him a stone?

> Or if he asks for a fish, will he give him a serpent? If you then, being evil, know how to give good gifts to your children, how much more will your Father who is in heaven give good things to those who ask Him! (Matt. 7:7–11).

Other Scripture verses are like these—verses that beckon us to draw near to our Father's throne in confidence. We don't need to pray to a priest. Jesus is the high priest Who intercedes for us. We don't need to worry about getting all the words just right. The Holy Spirit makes our prayers clear to our righteous God.

When Jesus' disciples came to Him and asked Him to teach them to pray, Jesus answered with these words:

> Our Father in heaven, hallowed be Your name. Your kingdom come. Your will be done on earth as it is in heaven. Give us day by day our daily bread. And forgive us our sins, for we also forgive everyone who is indebted to us. And do not lead us into temptation, but deliver us from the evil one (Luke 11:2–4).

The first thing I see we should do when we pray is address God as our Father. Remember, God is the *perfect* Father. He doesn't lose His temper. He always keeps His promises. He loves us unconditionally.

Next we should praise Him. To praise is to compliment. Tell God how wonderful He is. In any love relationship, praising someone not only makes him or her feel wonderful, but it also increases your feelings of love as well.

Tell God you are satisfied with His will for you. Take your worries to Him, of course, but be content with your circumstances, knowing He wants to use your life—including your sufferings—to bring about His ultimate purposes.

Ask Him to supply your needs. Be specific. "Be anxious for nothing, but in everything by prayer and supplication, with thanksgiving, let your requests be made known to God" (Phil. 4:6).

Restore your fellowship with Him by confessing your sins to Him. Don't build a wall of unrepentance between you and

Knowing God Intimately

God. Quickly, immediately—as soon as you realize you've done wrong—go to God and confess.

Talk to God about your other relationships. Ask His help in forgiving others. Your willingness to forgive those who have wronged you is a picture of God's willingness to forgive you. You do not forgive because the other person is lovely—because he or she might not be! You forgive because God, as a result of what Jesus did on the cross, forgives you.

Finally, secure God's help in fighting evil in your life. Remember, you are totally unable to fight sin without God's help.

Will God answer your prayers? Of course! Search through your Bible for the promises God gives you. Meditate on them. Memorize them. Trust Him to work in your life according to His timetable and plan. Let God be God. But believe He will answer you in His loving, perfect way.

Many godly men and women have advised that we keep a journal of our fellowship with God. You, too, may want to keep a notebook of some kind next to your Bible (and take it to church with you as well). Some women are more artistically inclined than I am, and they write long, loving prayers to God. I do well to scratch out a quick list of the requests I make and the verses I want to learn. But, quick list or flowery paragraph, it is a blessing to see God answer! Many times I have looked over my journal from years past and cried new tears over the ways God has worked in my life. A backward glance can help you trust God more. You see *why* He brought that circumstance into your life. You see *how* He will work good through each event.

Don't forget to list your blessings as well as your requests. Just as Johnson Oatman's gospel song says, "When upon life's billows you are tempest-tossed, / When you are discouraged, thinking all is lost, / Count your many blessings—name them one by one, / And it will surprise you what the Lord hath done."[2]

I want to share one other "ritual" I do during my personal

prayer time. I keep my church hymnal close by. Each day I sing a hymn (I started with hymn 1), or I read the words if I don't know the tune. If you or your children play a musical instrument, this practice can become a daily praise and worship time for your family. The words of hymns are not inspired Scripture, but as you sing and pray them to God, the melodies will fill your heart and lift your spirit. God's Word tells us that "speaking to one another in psalms and hymns and spiritual songs, singing and making melody in your heart to the Lord" (Eph. 5:19) evidences being filled with the Spirit.

Planning Ahead

Finally, I want to encourage you to save your journals, your sermon notes, your memory verse cards, and all your church papers. Even if you are one of those enviable people who can discipline themselves to throw away all unimportant pieces of paper, don't throw away your Biblical knowledge!

Why? You never know how God will use you. You are like a sponge. When God's Word is poured into your heart, you fill up with knowledge. But if that knowledge sits in you without being squeezed into the lives of others, you will start to "mold." You may not see any use for your knowledge now, but be prepared. We will discuss some possible ideas for service in a later chapter.

For the moment, let me tell you what I did. (I learned this trick both from my mother and from author Anne Ortlund, in her book *Disciplines of the Beautiful Woman*.) Arm yourself with a pile of file folders and a box (you can get fancier if you want to). I made a file folder for each book of the Bible (yes, all sixty-six of them!). I also made an alphabetical file for general topics. Then when you study the word "prayer" as it is used in the Bible, you can drop your notes under the letter *P*. When your pastor preaches on Psalm 23, drop your notes into the "Psalms" folder.

IN SUMMARY

Knowing God is an adventure. You can know God first and foremost through His Word. No matter what stage of life you're in, learn to walk with God each day. Talk to God as you would talk to a loving father, asking for wisdom and instruction, bringing your concerns to Him freely. Prepare to serve God by saving the insights He gives you. Let your knowledge and growing love for God spill out into the lives of others.

EXTRA CREDIT ASSIGNMENT

Memorize this passage of Scripture by learning one verse at a time; then recite it to a minimum of five women.

> "How can a young man cleanse his way? By taking heed according to Your word. With my whole heart I have sought You; oh, let me not wander from Your commandments! Your word I have hidden in my heart, that I might not sin against You" (Psalm 119:9–11).

STUDY GUIDE

1. According to 1 Corinthians 14:35, women should ask questions of their husbands at home. Why do you think the Bible recommends this action? Could this apply to women whose husbands don't know Christ? What other benefits could a wife gain from doing this?
2. Read 1 Peter 2:2. List the similarities between a newborn baby and a newborn Christian.
3. What is the law of God? According to Psalm 1:2, how are we to feel about it? How will this happen?

JUGGLING LIFE'S RESPONSIBILITIES

4. After reading Hebrews 4:14–16, describe Christ's role in Heaven now.
5. According to Isaiah 30:19, how will God respond to the prayers of His people? If you have children, how is your daily response to their legitimate requests the same or different?
6. Read Philippians 4:6. Do you have a specific list of the needs you should regularly take to God?
7. Read Ephesians 5:18–21. What are some ways we can tell that God's Spirit is filling our lives?

GROUP PROJECT

One of the greatest things your group can do to encourage one another is to choose accountability partners. If possible, pair older women with younger women. You may choose Scripture memorization as your first project, or you may decide just to meet for coffee and discuss what you've been reading in your Bible time. Be sure to include prayer times together. Get out your calendars and plan your first meeting now!

EXTRA READING

✔ Christenson, Evelyn, with Viola Blake. *What Happens When Women Pray.* Wheaton, IL: Scripture Press Publications, Victor Books, 1991. This book will give you plenty of ideas for your own prayer life, as well as the dynamics that occur when women in the church pray.

✔ Fee, Gordon D., and Douglas Stuart, *How to Read the Bible for All Its Worth: A Guide to Understanding the Bible.* Grand Rapids: Harper Collins Publishers, Zondervan Publishing House, 1982. This book explains in simple terms how to read your Bible thoughtfully. It will also point you to more resources than I could ever describe here.

✔ LaHaye, Tim. *How to Study the Bible for Yourself.* Eugene, OR: Harvest House Publishers, 1998. I was amazed at how

Knowing God Intimately   **77**

much "meat" is packed into this easy-to-read manual for Bible reading and Bible study. LaHaye simply explains how to read and how to study, using practical, time-proven methods.

✔ Strong, James. *Strong's Exhaustive Concordance.* Nashville: Abingdon Press, 1890. This concordance lists every word in the King James Version of the Bible. It also features a unique numbering system that allows you to see the original Greek or Hebrew meaning of the word you're looking up. This feature allows people like you and me, those who can't read these languages, to have more insight into a passage of Scripture.

✔ Walvoord, John F., and Roy B. Zuck, eds. *The Bible Knowledge Commentary: An Exposition of the Scriptures by Dallas Seminary Faculty.* Wheaton, IL: Scripture Press, Victor Books, 1983, 1985. This two-volume set, one for the Old Testament and one for the New Testament, is based on the New International Version of the Bible. You will find the commentaries helpful no matter what version you are reading. I like these books because not only do the editors give a verse-by-verse commentary of the Bible in an easy-to-read format, but the introductions to the books of the Bible are priceless. These are usually the first books I pick up when I have a Bible question.

NOTES

1. Gordon D. Fee and Douglas Stuart, *How to Read the Bible for All Its Worth: A Guide to Understanding the Bible* (Grand Rapids: Harper Collins Publishers, Zondervan Publishing House, 1982), 24.

2. Excerpt from "Count Your Blessings" by Johnson Oatman, Jr.

PART 2 TWO

Your Husband

POINT TO PONDER

*"George Gilder, the brilliant social commentator
and author of* Men and Marriage, *believes wom-
en are actually more important to the stability
and productivity of men than men are to the
well-being of women. I'm inclined to agree.
When a wife believes in her husband and deeply
respects him, he gains the confidence necessary
to compete successfully and live responsibly.
She gives him a reason to harness his mascu-
line energy—to build a home, obtain and keep
a job, remain sober, live within the law, spend
money wisely, etc. Without positive feminine
influence, he may redirect the power of testos-
terone in a way that is destructive to himself
and to society at large" (James C. Dobson).*[1]

What a wonderful privilege God has given you—to be the wife of a man! The creation of Eve by God was a unique event. She was made for the purpose of being a companion and a helper for Adam. You see, God has special plans for the family, plans that are different from those He made for any other "institution," such as the government or the church.

God gave several jobs to the "first family," Adam and Eve. They were to fill the earth with children, and they were to have dominion over the animals on the earth (Gen. 1:28). They were a beautiful picture of the relationship between Christ and His church (Eph. 5:22–33).

The role the woman has in a marriage relationship is unique. Adam needed a helper suitable to him (not one of the animals). He needed a companion. He needed someone on whom he could pour all his love. He needed someone to give him children. No other creature fit this description. So God lovingly made Eve from Adam's flesh.

Likewise, when God in eternity past looked ahead and saw you, He already had a plan for your life. He intended for you to be a wife. While you may plot and plan what you want to do with your life, keep in mind that your greatest fulfillment will come when you do what *God* wants.

Consider the worth God gives to you. When your husband married you, God granted him the favor of heaven: "He who finds a wife finds a good thing, and obtains favor from the LORD" (Prov. 18:22). God gave your husband a great treasure, worth more than earthly wealth. "Who can find a virtuous wife? For her worth is far above rubies" (Prov. 31:10). Your husband received an inheritance from the King of Kings and the Lord of Lords when he married you: "Houses and riches are an inheritance from fathers, but a prudent wife is from the LORD" (Prov. 19:14). Never underestimate the worth you have in God's eyes!

Therefore, it makes sense that if you want to have a wonderful, fulfilling marriage, you need to learn what God expects of you as a wife. You see, God gave you a free will. That means you have a choice. Do you want to follow your plans or God's? His best for us depends upon our doing things His way, but God will never force us. He will never tie us down. He wants us to *want to*.

Don't grow discouraged if some days are harder than others.

Your Husband   81

God knows that marriage takes practice and patience. Did you know He commanded the men in the nation of Israel to stay home with their wives for one year? "When a man has taken a new wife, he shall not go out to war or be charged with any business; he shall be free at home one year, and *bring happiness to his wife* whom he has taken" (Deut. 24:5, emphasis added).

Wouldn't that be great? Well, some days . . . Can you imagine being in the same house with that man, day in and day out, for a whole year!? We would learn to love each other, no doubt, but not with the love the world typically thinks of. Oh, the first few days would be very romantic. But as the irritants grow and the frustrations mount, true love would emerge. Love that loves in spite of the other person. Love that forgives. Love that continues.

So, since your first married paycheck probably didn't last a whole year, you may still be in that "practice" period. Let's talk about what God requires in a wife and how to perfect those characteristics in a practical way.

NOTES

1. James C. Dobson, "Family News from Dr. James Dobson" (Colorado Springs: Focus on the Family, February 1995), 2.

CHAPTER **6** SIX

Submitting to Your Husband's Leadership

POINT TO PONDER

*"Therefore submit to God. . . . Humble yourselves
in the sight of the Lord, and He will lift you up"
(James 4:7, 10).*

What does a godly wife look like? No, I don't mean on the outside, although that *is* important. I'm talking about her character and how that character shapes her behavior. How specific does God get in His Word? The most famous command He has given wives is probably found in Ephesians 5:22: "Wives, submit to your own husbands, as to the Lord."

But under the umbrella of submission we have a whole list of other characteristics. Compare yourself to the following Scripture verses:

> The heart of her husband safely trusts her; so he will have no lack of gain. She does him good and not evil all the days of her life (Prov. 31:11, 12).

> Confess your trespasses to one another, and pray for one another, that you may be healed. The effective, fervent prayer of a righteous man [woman] avails much (James 5:16).

> Let nothing be done through selfish ambition or con-

> ceit, but in lowliness of mind let each esteem others better than himself. Let each of you look out not only for his own interests, but also for the interests of others (Phil. 2:3, 4).
>
> Finally, all of you be of one mind, having compassion for one another; love as brothers, be tenderhearted, be courteous; not returning evil for evil or reviling for reviling, but on the contrary blessing, knowing that you were called to this, that you may inherit a blessing (1 Pet. 3:8, 9).

Of course, all of us have to hang our heads and admit that we've fallen down on the job at one time or another. (Hey, what a great opportunity to practice what we learned about meditation in part 1! The Scripture references here make great "chew-the-cud" material.)

It is not easy to be a godly wife. But the Spirit of God lives in you. You are a new creature in Christ. Not an old, patched-up creature. You are reborn. Even more, Christ abides with you, and in His power you *do* have the ability to fulfill the duties He has called you to do.

And one vital duty is submission. Someone has said that the most important thing a man can do for his kids is to love their mother. If that is true, then the most important thing a mother can do for her kids is to respect their father.

The Importance of Submission

Why is submission so important? The number one reason is explained in Ephesians 5, right after the command, "Wives, submit to your own husbands, as to the Lord."

> For the husband is head of the wife, as also Christ is head of the church; and He is the Savior of the body. Therefore, just as the church is subject to Christ, so let the wives be to their own husbands in everything (Eph. 5:23, 24).

A proper relationship to your husband pictures for the world the relationship believers have with Christ. The church submits to Christ. You submit to your husband. But the church isn't always

Submitting to Your Husband's Leadership 85

obedient to Christ. Uh oh. Wives aren't always obedient either.

The apostle Paul continued in Ephesians to talk about how much Christ loves the church, and he instructed husbands to love their wives in the same way. But that is your husband's responsibility. We must resist the tendency to condition our obedience on the amount of love we receive. We must submit—period, and Paul says we are to submit "in everything."

In return you are blessed with a right relationship to God, children who learn to obey by example, and a next-door neighbor who wants to know, "Why are you so different?" You're likely to have a husband who adores you as well, but that should not be your motive. Submit to your husband "as to the Lord."

How Submission Works

"What exactly does it mean to submit?" you ask. Well, it does not mean inferiority or that the woman never gets to express her opinion. The Amplified Bible puts it this way:

> And let the wife see that she respects and reverences her husband—that she notices him, regards him, honors him, prefers him, venerates and esteems him, and that she defers to him, praises him, and loves and admires him exceedingly.

That verse is just packed!

Do you notice him? Do you notice his accomplishments? Did you notice that he put his dirty clothes in the laundry hamper?

Do you regard him? Do you look into his eyes when he talks to you? Do you memorize the curves of his face so that someday, should the Lord take him Home, you'll have them stashed away in your mind's scrapbook?

Do you honor him? In front of the kids? In front of your friends? In front of your mom? In front of the pastor?

Do you prefer him? If you had to choose between spending time with him or shopping with your best friend, which would it be?

Do you venerate him? Don't worry—I had to look that one

up too! Do you regard him with reverence? Do you refer to him with names of endearment or with jokes and ridicule?

Do you esteem him? Do you prize him? Do you find your thoughts returning to him over and over again throughout the day?

Do you defer to him? Do you ask him his opinion before buying an expensive sweater? Do you say, "Let's see what Dad thinks," before you give a child permission to go camping with his friend's family?

Do you praise him? How long has it been since you've given him a compliment? How long since you gave him one in front of others?

Do you admire him exceedingly? Do you wish you could be as godly as he is? or as patient? or as loving? Do you dwell on his good qualities?

All these things come easily when we're dating, but they start becoming difficult after the wedding ring has been slipped on (maybe even the engagement ring). But love—and these things are expressions of love—is a choice. We must consciously choose to submit to our husbands. Maybe we should add some of these activities to our "to do" list, right up there with "brush my teeth."

Of course, submission also brings with it an attitude of teachableness and a willingness to yield. Those are difficult, I admit.

Kraig and I had our first big argument as husband and wife about how to set up the kitchen cupboards. As a little girl, I had pictured myself setting up my own kitchen. I would put everything just so. But, alas, my husband lived in our little apartment for a few weeks before the wedding, and he had all the spoons and cups arranged the way *he* liked them.

We arrived home from our honeymoon late at night. He carried me over the threshold, just as I'd pictured. We fell into bed, weary from driving all day, and he left for work early the next morning. I remember waking up and thinking, "Today is the day I become a *real* housewife."

Submitting to Your Husband's Leadership   87

So I hit the kitchen as soon as I could. I pulled everything out of the cupboards and set the dishes all over the floor and table. Then I took a sheet of paper and carefully planned the placement of each piece. It took me all day (I was new at this, after all), but when it was done, I was so proud!

Then he came home.

"Didn't you like the glasses on the left side of the sink, Anne?"

"Oh, well, they were fine, but my mom always put them on the right side. It's easier to grab them with your right hand that way," I said.

"Anne, I'm left-handed!"

And so it went, cupboard by cupboard. He would ask why I did something, and I would try to come up with a good answer. He would answer back, and I would cry. And in the end, he put all the dishes back the way they were while I sulked in front of the TV.

We're not proud of that night, but it was just the beginning of the lessons God had to teach me (and still is teaching me). You see, I wasn't willing for Kraig to teach me anything. What could a man possibly know about cooking? (Quite a bit, I soon found out!) I wasn't willing to yield either.

But what happens if we yield? I recently observed a man and his wife pull into a gravel parking lot in their minivan. They were the first to arrive, so the man—who was driving—got to choose how to park. There were no lines to indicate how to park. He parked at a funny angle. Even I thought so! The wife gently asked him if he thought it might make it difficult for other cars to park if he remained in that position. He looked around, shrugged, and said, "Looks fine to me!"

If I had been that wife, I probably would have opened my big mouth and waxed eloquent about the virtues of parking neatly and about considering others above yourself. But this wife calmly kept quiet as her husband walked around the vehicle, opened her door for her, and assisted her to the ground. They then held hands and strolled toward the building. (And you know what? All the other cars parked like that too!)

Submission is a gift and a blessing. God has decreed it, and God Himself will reward those who obey.

So let's flesh out this command just a bit more. What does a typical *unsubmissive* wife look like?

She loves to relive her husband's failures. She will never forgive him or let him forget the mistakes he has made. She can pull out a list and tell you exactly what he did to anger her on October 29, 2002. Of course, the larger the crowd she can tell about it, the better she feels about herself.

She is a fearful woman. She has a questioning attitude. She rides in the passenger seat with white knuckles, gasping with obvious worry at every turn he makes. When he is in front of a crowd, she has her hand by her ear, signaling him to be louder, softer, more emphatic, less domineering, or whatever else comes to her mind.

She undermines his authority. She smiles at the children while their dad instructs them but then whispers to them to do it another way. It'll be okay. She'll make sure Daddy doesn't mind.

She calls her best friend at the first sign of a disagreement. Or worse—she runs home to Mom!

On the other hand, *the submissive wife is willing to allow God to teach her husband.* Peter instructed wives to "be submissive to your own husbands, that even if some do not obey the word, they, without a word, may be won by the conduct of their wives, when they observe your chaste conduct accompanied by fear" (1 Pet. 3:1, 2).[1]

It may be difficult for us to accept that our husbands will not want to change just to please us or because of a romantic feeling. But again, the power is with God, not us. God's power to change *your* life is also effective in changing your husband's life.

Submitting to Your Husband's Leadership 89

Your husband may love the Lord already. But no man is perfect. Instead of trying to change her husband, a submissive wife steps back and allows God to change him on His almighty timetable. She allows her sweet spirit to create a climate where her husband can hear God's voice, not her nagging.

In contrast, let this word picture from Proverbs grip you: "The contentions of a wife are a continual dripping" (Prov. 19:13).

The submissive wife is also a trusting woman. It may not be that she truly trusts her husband in all that he does, but she is willing to trust God. She knows that God has placed her under her husband's leadership. Therefore, she realizes that God is in control of each situation they face. She knows that God has commanded that she obey and honor her husband. So she calmly trusts God to lead her husband, and she acts out her beliefs by calmly following him.

This trust reminds me of Job, not because he was "ultra-spiritual" or because he never feared storms or sicknesses or death. But maybe in spite of his fear, Job was willing to trust God. It is in this context that Job stated, "Though He slay me, yet will I trust Him" (Job 13:15).

When your husband feels your confidence in God, he will gain the confidence to be the leader he needs to be.

The submissive wife is also careful to build up her husband's confidence in other ways. Do you know your husband's dreams? Do not ridicule those dreams! Build him up! Your husband will not hear encouraging words from the world around him. His coworkers will tear him down. Images he sees on television will make him feel inadequate. But you are his helper, his "flesh of his flesh." Encourage his dreams, praise him, cast your vote for him.

You will become a refuge for him. Make his home a castle that shuts out the world's negative messages. Fill his sanctuary with laughter, hugs, smiles, and compliments. Encourage him to share his secrets, with you being a good listener. Put your book down. Turn off the TV. Look in his eyes and nod. Don't interrupt. Don't try to teach him. Don't be his mother. Be his best friend.

Also build him up in public. Encourage him with an e-mail at work or a loving note on his napkin. Tuck words of affirmation into his pants pocket. Send him a big bunch of helium balloons that say, "You're the best _____ [you fill in the blank] in the world!"

Compliment him in front of others. Tell his friends about some of his accomplishments. Show his picture to others, like a grandmother brags about her grandkids.

And that one flaw that bothers you the most? Vow never to mention it to him or bring it up in public. Is he overly conscious of his large ears? Never, never ridicule him! Instead, lovingly compliment him on his handsome eyebrows. Tell his boss what a wise financial manager your husband is with the family budget. Brag to his mother about how he always hangs up his shirts. Peter put it this way: "And above all things have fervent love for one another, for 'love will cover a multitude of sins' " (1 Pet. 4:8).

Are you seeing the many facets involved in submission to your husband? It really comes down to submitting your plans and dreams to those of your husband. I know that in American society, those are fighting words. As youngsters, girls are taught to think "career" right along with the boys. But is this emphasis Biblical? I think not. The Creator of the human race had a specific purpose for creating women—we've already seen this purpose. God created Eve to be a helper to Adam.

This is not to say that women are incapable of having excellent careers. They are. This is not to say that women should not be well-educated. They should be. But the moment you said, "I do," you accepted a new role, a new "career." This new career is to be a helper to your husband.

Ask your husband what he needs from you as his helper. You may be surprised how specific he is. If he says that the biggest

Submitting to Your Husband's Leadership

help you can be to him right now would be to continue in your career, then you have his blessing (and I believe God's as well).

But I challenge you to broaden your horizons. Ask your husband if a clean, organized home would help him. Maybe he is afraid to tell you what he really thinks because he cares about you and knows how much you dislike housekeeping. But accept his honesty and strive to meet his needs.

Maybe he needs a nutritious breakfast each morning.

Maybe he needs you to begin handling the finances or to allow him to handle them.

Maybe he needs a few minutes of quiet time from the kids each evening.

Maybe he needs to move across the country, away from your family, so that he can follow the leading of God in his life.

Are you willing to be his helper? Are you brave enough to ask him what he needs? Do you trust God?

James Dobson made this observation:

> Unfortunately, millions of marriages are in trouble today because of an inability of the sexes to get along. Perhaps the fundamental problem is one of selfishness. We're so intent on satisfying our own desires that we fail to recognize the longings of our partners. The institution of marriage works best when we think less about ourselves and more about the ones we love. Again, the basic needs of each gender are straightforward. Women need to be loved, not just on Valentine's Day, but all year around, and men need to be respected, especially when the going gets tough.[2]

Maybe you need to sit down and, in humility, make a list of the areas where you have been serving yourself instead of serving your husband:

- Not making his dinner; making him eat too much take-out food
- Not cleaning out his coffeepot
- Not hanging up his clothes for him

92 JUGGLING LIFE'S RESPONSIBILITIES

- Not replacing pencils that you borrow from his desk
- Not kissing him as soon as he gets home
- Not complimenting him daily
- Not holding his hand in public
- Not calling about that overcharge on a credit card bill so he doesn't have to do it
- Not holding the children to the same standard because you don't feel like disciplining them
- Not fixing his lunch for him

In the small ways, begin to demonstrate to your husband that you will follow his leadership in your life. You do not need to make a speech or a big production. Take simple steps instead toward being a consistent and godly wife. Be humble. Be teachable.

And be permanent. I cannot leave this discussion without observing that the most crucial way you must be submissive is by staying with your husband. Vow to stand by him "so long as you both shall live," with no exceptions.

Not feeling those loving feelings? Fold his underwear, type his memos, kiss him even if he has bad breath, whether the feelings are there or not. Feelings often follow action.

Has he been unfaithful to you? Remain faithful to him. Pray for a forgiving spirit, remembering that Jesus told Peter to forgive—not seven times but seventy times seven! Also remember Joseph, whose brothers sold him into slavery. Adopt his philosophy as your own: "But as for you, you meant evil against me; but God meant it for good, in order to bring it about as it is this day, to save many people alive" (Gen. 50:20). You will not be able to forgive and withhold bitterness on your own; you must rest in God's power, in His strength to make you what He wants you to be.

And if your husband is unsaved or even unkind? In her book *Me? Obey Him?* Elizabeth Rice Handford maintained that wives can change their husbands' hearts simply by being obedient to God's Word. "How blessed is the woman who will take God at

Submitting to Your Husband's Leadership 93

His Word, believe Him, obey Him, and leave the consequences to Him!"[3]

Remember, God loves your husband more than you do.

IN SUMMARY

As you begin to trust in God, walking in simple obedience to His Word, you will begin to become a lovely picture of an excellent wife.

EXTRA CREDIT ASSIGNMENT

Memorize this passage of Scripture by learning one verse at a time; then recite it to a minimum of five women.

"Who can find a virtuous wife? For her worth is far above rubies. The heart of her husband safely trusts her; so he will have no lack of gain. She does him good and not evil all the days of her life" (Proverbs 31:10–12).

STUDY GUIDE

1. According to 1 Peter 3:1 and 2, if a husband does not obey God's Word, what is God's remedy? What things should a wife do, and what things should she *not* do?
2. What does Proverbs 21:9 say is worse than living on a corner of a roof? Why?
3. Read Job 13:15. In your opinion, what is the worst thing that could happen to your marriage? How could you show trust in God and a submissive spirit in that situation?
4. Read 1 Peter 4:8. Make a list of some of your husband's sins that are hard to cover. Now make a list of *your* worst sins.

Draw a red cross over the paper to remind you of Christ's love for both of you as sinners. Now throw the paper away!

5. Read about a forgiving spirit in Genesis 50:20. Why is it difficult to forgive? What attitude toward God does an unforgiving spirit show?

GROUP PROJECT

Proverbs 19:13 says that "the contentions of a wife are a continual dripping." As a group, find some way to act out the "continual dripping" talked about in this verse. Maybe someone's shed has a drippy roof, or maybe you could take turns standing under a drip from a gutter. After experiencing the verse, pray together, asking God for His divine help in your lives as you work to overcome being contentious.

EXTRA READING

✔ Cooper, Darien B. *You Can Be the Wife of a Happy Husband*. Wheaton, IL: Scripture Press Publications, Victor Books, 1974. A woman who has lived the principles in this book recommended it to me. I just had to buy it!

✔ Handford, Elizabeth Rice. *Me? Obey Him?* Rev. ed. Murfreesboro, TN: Sword of the Lord Publishers, 1994. One of the best books ever written on marriage. Even if you can't imagine submitting in "everything" to that husband of yours, read this book so you can see another side of the issue.

✔ Swindoll, Charles R. *Strike the Original Match*. Carol Stream, IL: Tyndale House, 1990. Whether our marriages are brand-new or have been in existence for years, we all need the author's practical ideas for adding more love to our relationships.

NOTES

1. First Peter 3:1–6 is an excellent passage to study if you struggle with submitting to an unsaved husband or one who is disobedient to the Word. Note the example of Sarah, whose account you can read beginning in Genesis 12.

2. James C. Dobson, "Family News from Dr. James Dobson" (Colorado Springs: Focus on the Family, February 1995), 4.

3. Elizabeth Rice Handford, *Me? Obey Him?* rev. ed. (Murfreesboro, TN: Sword of the Lord Publishers, 1994), 48.

CHAPTER 7 SEVEN

Being Your Husband's Best Friend

POINT TO PONDER
"First time he kissed me, he but only kissed
The fingers of this hand wherewith I write;
And ever since, it grew more clean and white"
(Elizabeth Barrett Browning).[1]

It struck me as odd when I first read Titus 2 and discovered that older women are supposed to teach younger women to love their husbands. "Can love be taught?" I asked myself. A love that is taught doesn't seem to have too much in common with romance-novel love. To love my husband means that pink hearts float above us when he walks into the room . . . that I cannot bear to be apart from him . . . that he brings me roses and candy and I read impassioned sonnets to him.

Yet reality hits me when I realize that all around me are couples who feel no love for each other. I think of the children I know, many of whom have parents who continually yell or throw things at each other.

I have been taught that love is a choice. Love is self-sacrificing, and love will continue, despite the odds. Love is what Christ did for us on the cross, dying for our sins even though we were His mortal enemies.

So imagine my surprise when I discovered that the Greek word for "love" in Titus 2:4 is *philandros*. This word implies fondness, affection, and friendship. While loving my husband unconditionally is certainly Scriptural, for that is how I am to love all people (1 Corinthians 13 is just one example of this command in Scripture), that is not the type of love described here.

No, older women are to instruct the younger women to be their husbands' best friends! So I began to brainstorm about ways women could show friendship and affection to their husbands. My list is by no means complete . . . nor is my list full of original ideas. In fact, some points are further discussions of what we talked about in chapter 6. Remember, God is a God of creativity, and we are created in His image. So have fun and be creative in coming up with even more ideas on your own! On to the list . . .

Be Your Husband's Spiritual Support

I don't put this idea of being your husband's spiritual support first to sound pious. Actually it's easy for me to pray for the folks on the church prayer list but difficult to remember to pray for my husband.

My best friend and her husband started a habit on their wedding night of always praying together before falling off to sleep. I think that will always be a special time for them! But it is a habit my husband and I never developed.

Since we are both talkers, we tend to drift off to sleep talking a mile a minute. Sometimes we'll both be reading separate books, and we'll stop every few minutes to give each other a running commentary. I used to be slightly jealous of my friend, wondering if my marriage would ever be as good as hers. After all, my husband and I didn't pray together before bed at night. So as a good, nagging wife, I finally pestered my husband into praying aloud before we went to sleep. Instead of talking to me,

Being Your Husband's Best Friend 99

he would dutifully remember all the foreign missionaries and so on; then he would turn over and go to sleep.

That was when I began to realize that his talking to me at night was his personal way of sharing his heart with me. What a privilege to hear my husband's dreams and desires and goals! And what a privilege to be able to pray over his dreams—not before bed but the next morning in the shower.

So we're back to our old ways. Now I take it as my personal mission to pray over the test he's giving in science class at 10:12 A.M. I talk to God about the girls who are disrespectful in seventh period. I even bring such matters as football games and paychecks before the throne of God. My praying for my husband pleases God and draws my husband and me closer to each other.

> Confess your trespasses to one another, and pray for one another, that you may be healed. The effective, fervent prayer of a righteous [woman] avails much (James 5:16).

I can support my husband spiritually in other ways as well. These do not include nagging him into religious fervor. Remember the words of Peter to women married to unbelievers:

> Wives, likewise, be submissive to your own husbands, that even if some do not obey the word, they, without a word, may be won by the conduct of their wives (1 Pet. 3:1).

God has not called us to the pulpit of marriage. God has called us to a meek and quiet spirit, serving our husbands and edifying them in the little things we do.

Maybe you should make a list right now of the ways you can encourage your husband spiritually—quietly, unobtrusively, humbly.

Encourage Your Husband

In my opinion, a true friend is someone who believes in me. Every woman has days when life seems impossible, when she feels like giving up. Most women I know have someone special to whom they turn when they are at their lowest—a special buddy, a sister, or mother. A listening ear, a hug, or encouraging words are enough to send them on their way rejuvenated.

On the contrary, most men I know never open up like that to other men. I could "psychoanalyze" men and try to list some reasons why this may be, but I would like to remind you again that God made Eve to be a companion and a helper to Adam. A wife should be the person closest to her husband. This is God's plan.

So what can a man do if his wife is not an encouragement to him? What damage takes place if a man opens his heart to his wife and shares his deepest hurts, yet she ridicules him or belittles him? That man will be wounded deeply!

But if, when no one else believes in him, she looks him in the eyes and says, "I trust you," that man can be instilled with the courage of Daniel. I dare you to try it with your husband!

At times, of course, we may not believe in our husbands. Sometimes guys make mistakes. Sometimes they act irresponsibly, or they lose their temper, or they speak too quickly.

In moments like these, it is vital that you *choose* to see only the best in your husband (bathing him in prayer, of course). Choose to list his good qualities. Remind him of his successes. Tell him you are praying for him. Touch his face and say, "Look at me, Honey. Do you remember the time you _____ [fill in the blank with something good he did once]? You can do it again, Hon! I know you can!"

James Dobson told this story of a confidence-building wife:

> My friend E.V. Hill . . . is a dynamic black minister and the senior pastor at Mount Zion Missionary Baptist Church in Los Angeles. He lost his precious wife, Jane, to cancer a few years ago. In one of the most moving messages I've ever heard, Dr. Hill spoke about Jane at her funeral and described the ways this "classy lady" made him a better man.
>
> As a struggling young preacher, E.V. had trouble earning a living. That led him to invest the family's scarce resources,

Being Your Husband's Best Friend

over Jane's objections, in the purchase of a service station. She felt her husband lacked the time and expertise to oversee his investment, which proved to be accurate. Eventually, the station went broke and E.V. lost his shirt in the deal.

It was a critical time in the life of this young man. He had failed at something important, and his wife would have been justified in saying, "I told you so." But Jane had an intuitive understanding of her husband's vulnerability. Thus, when E.V. called to tell her that he had lost the station, she said simply, "All right."

E.V. came home that night expecting his wife to be pouting over his foolish investment. Instead, she sat down with him and said, "I've been doing some figuring. I figure that you don't smoke and you don't drink. If you smoked and drank, you would have lost as much as you lost in the service station. So, it's six in one hand and a half-dozen in the other. Let's forget it."

Jane could have shattered her husband's confidence at that delicate juncture. The male ego is surprisingly fragile, especially during times of failure and embarrassment. That's why E.V. needed to hear her say, "I still believe in you," and that is precisely the message she conveyed to him.

Shortly after the fiasco with the service station, E.V. came home one night and found the house dark. When he opened the door, he saw that Jane had prepared a candlelight dinner for two.

"What meaneth thou this?" he said with characteristic humor.

"Well," said Jane, "we're going to eat by candlelight tonight."

E.V. thought that was a great idea and went into the bathroom to wash his hands. He tried unsuccessfully to turn on the light. Then he felt his way into the bedroom and flipped another switch. Darkness prevailed. The young pastor went back to the dining room and asked Jane why the electricity was off. She began to cry.

"You work so hard, and we're trying," said Jane, "but it's pretty rough. I didn't have quite enough money to pay the light bill. I didn't want you to know about it, so I thought we would just eat by candlelight."

Dr. Hill described his wife's words with intense emotion: "She could have said, 'I've never been in this situation before. I was reared in the home of Dr. Caruthers, and we never had our lights cut off.' She could have broken my spirit; she could have ruined me; she could have demoralized me. But instead she said, 'Somehow or another we'll get these lights on. But let's eat tonight by candlelight.' "

E.V. continued, "She was my protector. [Some years ago] I received quite a few death threats, and one night I received notice that I would be killed the next day. I woke up thankful to be alive. But I noticed that she was gone. I looked out the window and my car was gone. I went outside, and finally, saw her driving up in her robe. I said, 'Where have you been?' She said, 'I . . . I . . . it just occurred to me that they [could have] put a bomb in that car last night, and if you had gotten in there you would have been blown away. So I got up and drove it. It's all right.' "[2]

Dobson concluded,

Jane Hill must have been an incredible lady. Of her many gifts and attributes, I am most impressed by her awareness of the role she played in strengthening and supporting her husband. E.V. Hill is a powerful Christian leader today. Who would have believed that he needed his wife to build and preserve his confidence? But that is the way men are made. Most of us are a little shaky inside, especially during early adulthood.[3]

The Word of God describes this kind of love so eloquently as love that "thinks no evil; does not rejoice in iniquity, but rejoices in the truth; bears all things, believes all things, hopes all things, endures all things" (1 Cor. 13:5–7).

I believe that encouraging your husband is the number one thing you can do for him. Is he a plumber? Encourage him to be a *great* plumber! Is he a businessman? Encourage him to be a *great* businessman! Believe in him no matter what, regardless of who is trying to convince him he is a failure. He will repay you with his undying love.

Be a Good Listener

One summer during high school I had the biggest crush on a boy I knew. I was determined to use all my feminine wiles to attract his attention, but I didn't know exactly how to do that. So in typical Anne-fashion, I decided to look it up at the library.

Thankfully the library book I consulted didn't advise me to dress seductively or to apply my mascara just so. It simply said to be a good listener!

The great experiment was on: The next time I saw this boy, I looked him right in the eyes and asked him a question. As he began to answer, I dutifully nodded, donned an interested expression, and said "mmm" and "hmmm" in all the right places. To my surprise, he kept talking! And the more he talked, the more I found myself really listening. Instead of trying to formulate a response or butt in to his narrative, I bit my tongue and continued to nod. It was tough, but I kept looking him in the eyes. We sat there talking for over an hour, an unheard-of feat for me.

A week or so later, he called me and asked me on a date!

Don't hold your breath—I have no more exciting news to share concerning this romance. But I have living proof that this practice works well with husbands too.

Think about it. Who has time to listen to your husband at work? His job is to take orders, not to philosophize. Who cares about his strategy to increase profits by 500 percent? Do his friends listen to him? No, no. They are probably all too busy trying to prove they know more than he does.

But you have plenty of time! When you were dating, didn't you gaze into his eyes for hours at a time, approving of all his ideals and ambitions? But if your husband is typical, the talkative man you married probably became a lot quieter a few days after the wedding ceremony.

Why? Maybe because *you* started talking! And if you're anything like me (and most women I know), you haven't stopped talking yet. After all, you haven't seen him all day, and you have so much to share!

But so does he. How are your listening skills? Do you periodically mumble an "uh huh," while in your head you are planning your grocery list? Or do you really involve yourself in the conversation?

So many times we treat perfect strangers with more respect than we give our husbands. Recently while at the Laundromat, I sat at a table and listened to a lady whom I had never met before. Before my clothes were dry, she had told me about all her forty-some nieces and nephews and had listed every gift she had received for Christmas. But when I got home, I didn't have enough time to hear my husband tell me the score of the football game.

Do you want to keep your love alive? Learn to be a good listener!

Spend Time Together

Just as spending time reading your Bible and praying will cause you to fall in love with the Lord, spending time with your husband will renew your feelings of love for your husband.

I met my future husband five weeks into my freshman year of Bible college. I had lofty goals for my first semester. I had set aside certain times each day for study and practice, since I was a music major. I remember my feeling of pride as I sat by the lake one September afternoon, studying the first headache-giving chapter of my Psychology 101 textbook. Other freshmen were

Being Your Husband's Best Friend

playing basketball or shopping at the mall or strolling beside the lake near me. *Not me!* I would memorize the theories of the great philosophers so I could graduate in four years at the top of my class!

Then I met Kraig. I remember how easy it was to rationalize that I *needed* to spend time with him rather than study, that I *needed* to talk to him on the phone until midnight rather than sleep, that I *needed* to meet him at 6:00 A.M. for a healthy breakfast. Being with him every possible moment was my one consuming passion.

Of course, it is practical for those first romantic flames to have cooled some during marriage. Now your husband has a job and must support his family. You have responsibilities in the home and with your children. But you also need to guard against you and your husband becoming "ships that pass in the night." Life has a way of creeping away, continually becoming more hectic, harried, and helter-skelter. Your other commitments may begin to crowd out the one to whom you have committed your life.

I made a list one year, during an especially busy season of my life, of all the time commitments I had. My list contained more than twenty items. I felt so overwhelmed! So I showed it to my husband, hoping he would help me sort out the things that were necessary from those that weren't. He looked it over for a few minutes and said, "You didn't put my name on this list!"

I could have cried! I felt he should be understanding and willing to step back and wait for my life to slow down. However, I learned an important lesson that day. After my time with God, time spent with my husband should be top priority.

A wise couple I know has developed some rituals into their life as a system of checks and balances to keep their priorities in order. One ritual is that each Thursday night belongs to their marriage. They will not allow any other commitment, except emergencies, to crowd out that time together.

Some Thursdays they go out to a nice restaurant or to a hockey game, hiring a trusted babysitter to play with their children at home. They can't afford to do that every week, though, so they spend some Thursdays watching Sherlock Holmes videos brought home from the public library. Some Thursdays he cooks Chinese food for her; sometimes she makes Italian for him. They might read books to each other or give each other back rubs. They might play board games or look through magazines to pick out items they would like someday in their dream home. Of course, they plan ahead to make the evening romantic as well.

Other couples reserve Saturday mornings for each other, using their time at breakfast to pray over their goals. The point isn't what method you use, but rather that you maintain the priority of your relationship by allowing plenty of time for the relationship to blossom. And sometimes penciling in time for your husband tells him that he is important to you . . . that you enjoy his company . . . that he is more fun than a sitcom or a good book.

Ask, "How Can I Help You?"

We discussed this subject in chapter 6, but I want to remind you that a good friend is always willing to lend a helping hand. The first step toward assisting your husband is to ask, "How can I help you?" Be ready to act on his suggestions! Even if you have few appointments on your calendar, bring your schedule to him and let him see you adding his wishes to your "to do" list. Then before you tackle the other projects you had planned, do his first.

The second step toward assisting your husband is to think, *How can I serve him?* The difference is your attitude. The outward, helpful things you do are good. The inward, servant spirit you have is better. What is your motive? "And whatever you do in word or deed, do all in the name of the Lord Jesus, giving thanks to God the Father through Him" (Col. 3:17). By the way, do you

Being Your Husband's Best Friend   **107**

know what verse follows this one? "Wives, submit to your own husbands, as is fitting in the Lord" (Col. 3:18). Interesting, huh?

Enrapture Your Husband with Your Love

One of the best ways you can show friendship to your husband is through the intimate love you give him. Remember, no other relationship he has can satisfy his physical needs as you can. The Bible states that a husband is to "rejoice with the wife of [his] youth" and to be "enraptured with her love" (Prov. 5:18, 19). Yet some women are not willing to allow their husbands to come into this innermost sanctuary of their lives.

Modern researchers are just now discovering what God's Word has maintained all along: that men and women need each other! Your husband needs your love, and many times that love is best expressed physically. Maybe he desires to share his innermost thoughts with you, but because you shy away from his physical advances, he thinks you do not love him. On the contrary, you might think that he only desires your body and that he doesn't really love you for who you are.

Instead of getting caught up in self-help books, turn to the Lord. What does His Word say?

> Marriage is honorable among all, and the bed undefiled (Heb. 13:4).

> Let the husband render to his wife the affection due her, and likewise also the wife to her husband. The wife does not have authority over her own body, but the husband does. And likewise the husband does not have authority over his own body, but the wife does. Do not deprive one another except with consent for a time, that you may give yourselves to fasting and prayer; and come together again so that Satan does not tempt you because of your lack of self-control (1 Cor. 7:3–5).

If you have trouble in this area, may I suggest you memorize Colossians 3:12–17 and recite these verses whenever you are tempted to withhold your physical affection from your husband? Using these verses, the Holy Spirit will remind you to be kind, humble, long-suffering, and thankful; to bear with your husband; to forgive him (as Christ forgave you); to put on love, the bond of perfection; to let God's peace rule in your heart and His Word dwell in you richly; and to sing to the Lord in your heart (try to have a headache while doing that one!).

While these verses are not typically used in this context, I challenge you to apply them to your marriage. God's Word is powerful to change you, and His power will help you "render to your [husband] the affection due [him]."

Your reward? Your husband will be enraptured with your love! Wow, doesn't that sound like it's straight out of a steamy romance novel? Whoo-weee!

Give Your Husband Little Gifts

It is true that to some people gifts are extremely important. You can spot these people easily; they are always giving gifts to you! According to Gary Chapman, the author of *The Five Love Languages,* some people think a well-timed box wrapped with ribbons and bows means you love them and were thinking of them. To other people, a box covered with silly wrapping paper means that now they have to return something to the store because they didn't really want it. Why won't you sit down and just talk to them?

It is a matter of speaking someone's language—his or her *love* language.[4] You know your husband best. If he is a gift-giver, then you can be sure that he shows people he cares by using that method. If you never give gifts to him, he probably thinks you don't love him very much.

Even if your husband doesn't speak the love language of gifts—if he has never noticed that birthdays and Valentine's Day are for candy and cards—you should still bless him with the

Being Your Husband's Best Friend 109

occasional gift. Why? Because it will show *others* that you love him.

My husband is a high school teacher. So every year I have fun embarrassing him. My children and I all head to the store, where we find the biggest, gushiest helium balloon we can find. Then we attach candy, flowers, teddy bears, and other lovey-dovey items. Next we drive to his school. We obtain permission from the office to visit his classroom, and we walk in unannounced. My kids rush in with the goodies, and all the ninth grade girls ooh and ahh. Then I make a point of kissing him soundly in front of the class.

Now who knows that I love him? My children. The store clerks. The school office and all his fellow teachers. Everyone we passed in the hall. All those impressionable high schoolers, many of whom come from broken homes. And of course, my husband knows!

If my husband spoke the love language of gift-giving, he would be eternally grateful for this display of affection. And I would have had fun planning it all. But since he doesn't particularly care one way or the other about gifts, I get to eat some of the candy!

My advice to you? Go to your local library and check out some idea books. Always have in your home a supply of wrapping paper, gift bags, bows, cards, and cellophane tape. Brainstorm with your friends to get some new ideas. Then, if gift-giving isn't your strength, schedule some giving events on your calendar. Have fun!

Be Only His

Titus 2 commands the older women in a church to teach the younger women specific things. Two lessons, and possibly the most important two, are "to be discreet" and "chaste." Different Bible versions, as well as the original Greek, use several descriptive words—such as "self-control," "innocence," "a clean heart," and "purity"—to enhance the meanings of these words.

An unfaithful wife first becomes unfaithful in her mind, and your mind is what you must guard most. King Solomon, a man who wasn't known for his pure ways, wrote, "Keep your heart with all diligence, for out of it spring the issues of life" (Prov. 4:23). He had learned from experience that our thought-life controls our actions, and our actions have consequences.

Being a wife, especially if you have a career besides your duties to your husband, children, and home, has several "occupational hazards." In their book *The Curious Waltz of the Working Woman,* Karen S. Linamen and Linda Holland listed several reasons why working women may be more vulnerable to extramarital affairs. "Exposure is one reason. For eight hours each day, five days a week, we're exposed to countless numbers of relationships with male co-workers, bosses, clients, vendors, patients, subordinates, laborers, consultants, etc."[5]

Another reason is "professional intimacy."[6] You are required to invest energy, brainpower, and time with others in your work setting. The common goals of your workplace often bind you together as you share challenges and triumphs.

Then there is "emotional need." Linamen and Holland conclude, "The stress and pressures of holding down two full-time jobs (one that pays and one that doesn't) can create areas of need that leave women vulnerable to the lure of romantic entanglements."[7]

Paul gave wise advice when he instructed young women to be "keepers at home" (Titus 2:5, KJV). For, then, the woman is exposed more to her husband than to any other man; she can share common goals and challenges with her best friend, her life's mate; and in a loving, caring relationship, she and her husband will meet each other's deepest emotional needs.

However, even a stay-at-home wife must guard her heart. No

husband is perfect, and no marriage is flawless. Your husband may be away from you for long hours, leaving you hungry for adult company. You may not feel as though you can share common goals with him other than "please change Baby's diaper, dear" and "don't forget to take out the trash." You may have legitimate emotional needs that are not being met.

If you are home most of the time, I warn you to guard your heart. Guard what you allow into your heart by way of television and reading materials. Do not fantasize about what *could* be (the Bible calls us to be *content;* Phil. 4:11; Heb. 13:5). Find someone to whom you can be accountable for your actions (more on this subject in part 5). Frequently verbalize your commitment to your husband, "For out of the abundance of the heart the mouth speaks" (Matt. 12:34). Be sure that you remain in God's Word and in prayer, for only God is able to keep us from sin. Finally, maintain a thankful heart for the man, the marriage, and the circumstances into which God has placed you.

IN SUMMARY

Take it as a personal challenge to become your husband's best friend. While you may think a love relationship like that is out of reach for you and your husband, don't despair. The God Who commanded us women to love our husbands is also the God Who will empower us to obey Him. The blessings to be gained are worth all the effort. So determine in your heart to love your husband, no matter what, for the rest of your life.

EXTRA CREDIT ASSIGNMENT

Memorize this passage of Scripture by learning one verse at a time; then recite it to a minimum of five women.

> "Love suffers long and is kind; love does not envy; love does not parade itself, is not puffed up; does not behave rudely, does not seek its own, is not provoked, thinks no evil; does not rejoice in iniquity, but rejoices in the truth; bears all things, believes all things, hopes all things, endures all things. Love never fails" (1 Corinthians 13:4–8).

STUDY GUIDE

1. According to James 5:16, what is the quickest way to healing in your marriage? Do you think your husband should be the first to come to you or should you go to *him* first?
2. According to Colossians 3:17 and 18, who are you pleasing when you submit to your husband? What other things do these verses tell believers to do?
3. Read Proverbs 5:18 and 19 and describe some emotions that should be part of a Biblical marriage.
4. According to 1 Corinthians 7:3–5, who has control over your body? What are the *only* reasons listed for denying your husband the sexual fulfillment he needs?
5. Read Hebrews 13:4 and 5 and Philippians 4:11. What character quality should lie at the heart of your marriage? What is covetousness?

GROUP PROJECT

As a group, plan a "date night" for each couple represented. For those couples who have children, volunteer to babysit for free. Help one another plan creative activities that will fit into each family's budget. As needed, lend pretty candles, soft music, and beautiful china to one another. See the following resources for more ideas.

EXTRA READING

✔ Arp, Dave, and Claudia Arp. *52 Dates for You and Your Mate*. Nashville: Thomas Nelson Publishers, 1993. Here are some ideas to get you started, for all budgets and interests.

✔ Chapman, Gary D. *The Five Love Languages: How to Express Heartfelt Commitment to Your Mate*. Chicago: Northfield Publishing, 1992. We've already discussed gift-giving, but read this book for advice on all the love languages and how they can strengthen your marriage.

✔ Smalley, Gary. *For Better or For Best*. Rev. ed. Grand Rapids: Zondervan Publishing House, Pyranee Books, 1988. My husband and I received this book as a wedding present, and oh, did we need it! The book was so helpful that we loaned it to several other couples. Eventually it became lost, but we pray that other couples were helped by reading it.

NOTES

1. Elizabeth Barrett Browning, "Sonnets from the Portuguese."

2. James C. Dobson, "Family News from Dr. James Dobson" (Colorado Springs: Focus on the Family, February 1995), 3.

3. Dobson, 3.

4. Gary Chapman, *The Five Languages of Love: How to Express Heartfelt Commitment to Your Mate* (Chicago: Northfield Publishing, 1992).

5. Karen S. Linamen and Linda Holland, *The Curious Waltz of the Working Woman* (Ventura, CA: Gospel Light Publications, Regal Books), 166.

6. Ibid., 167.

7. Ibid.

CHAPTER **8** EIGHT

Making Your Marriage a Priority

POINT TO PONDER

"The sentiments expressed by the man of this house do not necessarily comply with those of the management."[1]

Have you ever noticed how easily a small child can be sidetracked? "Son, please go upstairs and grab a pair of socks from your dresser drawer so we can go to the store." "Yes, Mommy." And off the five-year-old runs—willingly, happily, obediently. Quickly he gets to the bottom of the stairs. He sees his robot-spaceman, built proudly of Legos earlier that day. Suddenly he isn't climbing the stairs to his bedroom; he is climbing a foaming volcano on Mars, bravely seeking to defend the world.

At the top of the stairs he sees his gold-colored race car. Mars is forgotten as he careens the car wildly across the hall to his bedroom. He zooms to the finish line at the open door to his bedroom, barely beating an army tank.

Ah! The army tank! He shakes all the green soldiers from their compartment inside. Whoa! He grabs the tank and rolls daringly across the floor, crashing into the container that holds his puzzles, and the one-hundred-piece "Daniel and the Lions'

115

116 JUGGLING LIFE'S RESPONSIBILITIES

Den" puzzle flops to the floor. "Son, did you find your socks?"

One of the challenges of parenting is teaching our children how to be responsible and timely without quenching their incredible imagination. One of the challenges our Heavenly Father has is keeping us, His adult children, on task with the assignments He has given us. We, like our children, are so easily sidetracked!

Before the birth of my Lego-loving, race-car driving, Army-commanding, puzzle-building son, my husband and I learned a big lesson about being sidetracked. We had been married about nineteen months when we learned we were expecting a baby. Of course we were excited to be new parents. Now we would be a "family"—not just a "couple" anymore!

But were we correct? Did having a baby complete our family? Weren't we a family already? We were not clear on what Scripture says about the priority of the marriage relationship, so we were easily led by the world's opinion during that vulnerable time. I'll share some of the results of our misunderstanding in part 3, but for now let's talk about what happened to get us sidetracked in the first place.

The Importance of Marriage

Throughout the pregnancy, we forgot our marriage should be a priority over our soon-coming child. We forgot that if our baby's parents didn't have a strong marriage, our baby would not be raised in a Christ-honoring home. Instead, we focused our attention and energy on making our baby the center of our home. We were sidetracked from our original mission!

You see, your relationship to your husband reveals your relationship to God. How can you be a good mother, a godly mother, if your relationship to God is not right? You can have a consistent daily devotional and prayer time, yet if you are crabby with your husband, your relationship to God is not right. You

Making Your Marriage a Priority

can serve in various ministries in your church, yet if you do not lovingly submit to your husband's leadership, your relationship to God is not right. Your marriage is primary!

Your relationship to your husband also reveals who you really are. Someone can compliment me on my sweet personality, but my sarcasm to my husband at breakfast reveals my heart.

As 1 Corinthians 13:1–3 explains,

> Though I speak with the tongues of men and of angels, but have not love, I have become sounding brass or a clanging cymbal. And though I have the gift of prophecy, and understand all mysteries and all knowledge, and though I have all faith, so that I could remove mountains, but have not love, I am nothing. And though I bestow all my goods to feed the poor, and though I give my body to be burned, but have not love, it profits me nothing.

How can you serve God as a mother if you will not obey Him regarding your husband? And if you dream of great deeds, missionary endeavors, and crusades for the cause of Christ—stop! Your marriage is your priority! Obey God in the small yet oh-so-difficult things, and He will bless you in the big things. Don't get sidetracked.

Why Marriage Is Important

Why is marriage such a high priority to God? First of all, He is the One Who created marriage, blessed it, and called it good (Gen. 2:18–24). Notice that the first family He created was a family of *two*. He added children later, for the express purpose of filling the earth. If your family consists of just you and your husband, rejoice! You are a complete family in God's eyes. If God has given you extra credit assignments in the form of kids, rejoice—but don't complete the extra credit and forget the regular homework He gave you. Your primary assignment is to your husband. If you have faithfully trained your children and now they are grown and leaving home, rejoice! Now you can commit more time than ever to your husband. What fun you can have, just the two of you!

As you and your husband faithfully obey God by working at this thing called marriage, your children will be blessed with a working, everyday model. You see, your husband's faithful obedience to God pictures Christ's obedience to His Heavenly Father. Your cheerful submission to your husband pictures the church's joyful service to Christ (Eph. 5:22–33).

When I took driver's education in high school, we used a textbook with instructions on how to change a tire, check the oil, and perform basic maintenance checks on our car. In all honesty, I didn't learn a thing! My mind is not mechanically oriented, and all the reading and studying of charts in the world could never prepare me for a flat tire! But my dad took me out to the driveway with a rag and some tools, lifted the hood of the car, and *showed* me some necessary skills. I must confess that I'm still mechanically challenged, but I learned far more by working beside my dad than I ever did from reading a textbook.

Your children learn by observing. How will you teach them to obey God if you do not submit to your husband? Your home is the best place to ingrain into their little hearts the character qualities of kindness, forgiveness, responsibility, and servant-hood. "Do what I say and not what I do" just doesn't work with your kids. No, your marriage—a model—is priority!

How to Make Marriage a Priority

There are several action steps you can take to begin making your marriage a priority. Basically the steps lead to one goal: unity. You and your husband must be united in every way. And as uncomfortable as the concept may be, if you two disagree, you should budge first! Of course, if your husband is asking you to directly disobey God, you have an obligation to follow the Lord first, but examine your heart carefully to be sure your motive is pure.

Making Your Marriage a Priority 119

You and your husband need to be a united authority. Settle disagreements privately. Don't challenge Daddy's authority in front of the kids. How can your son or daughter learn to obey without question if Mom is always questioning? Encourage your kids to obey right away, with a happy spirit; then pray about the matter. Talk to your husband later, when you've both cooled down. Have a submissive heart and tell him your concerns. Agree to abide with his decision. You will be amazed at the peace that will reign in your home as you set an example of submission in front of your children.

You and your husband need to have a united attitude. Have you discussed your parenting philosophies? Do you know how your husband wants you to discipline the kids? Do you agree? If not, settle the matter right away! More importantly, support your husband's opinions, both in public and in private. This does not mean you can never question your husband or that you can never bring to his attention something he has possibly not thought of before. But your attitude must be one with his.

You and your husband also need to have united actions. What child hasn't tried to work his parents against each other? Thomas wants Caleb to spend the afternoon with him. Thomas knows that Daddy might say no, so he goes to Mommy first. She says it's fine with her. When Daddy balks at the idea, Thomas says that Mommy said it was okay.

Mommy would have done better to defer to her husband. "Thomas, ask Daddy first" or "Daddy has a headache today, honey, so why don't we wait and invite Caleb another day?"

Another easy way to be sure your actions are united is to know what your husband's goals are for your family and consistently work to carry them out. Has your husband noticed that your daughter whines frequently? Join forces with your husband to help your daughter overcome her bad habit. Trust the Lord's wisdom in making your husband the head of your home, and learn to unite on his goals for your family.

Don't forget to share with your husband the things that happen in his absence. If your husband is the CEO of your home, you are the daily operations manager. It is critical that you give your husband a full report of the daily happenings so he can make wise decisions. You know your husband best, and you'll know if a "full report" to him means a half-hour conversation or a two-minute overview. However, help him be involved in the decisions, especially the ones that involve your children.

Finally, be united in action with your husband by communicating your affection for him in a public way. Beth,[2] a friend of mine, grew up in a home where her parents were never affectionate with each other, at least not in front of her and her brothers. At the age of twenty-four, she married Keith. Keith was from a home where physical affection came much easier. From the beginning of their relationship, Keith felt it was important to hold Beth's hand in public, open her car door for her, and welcome her with a kiss when she dropped by his office. At first Beth was embarrassed. Keith was puzzled about why she pulled away from his advances. But they were patient with each other, and, over time, they came to understand each other's backgrounds and to accept each other's ways.

Eventually they had children of their own. Even though it was against her nature, Beth made an effort to return her husband's affections and even to initiate some of her own, especially in front of the kids. She and Keith had determined in their hearts to show their kids by example that they loved each other, that they were committed to each other, that they enjoyed each other's company, and that this marriage would last!

IN SUMMARY

Your children need to see your love in action. Your credibility is at stake in your marriage relationship. Your actions

Making Your Marriage a Priority 121

toward your husband—your willingness to submit to him, to love him, to make him a priority in your life—will say more to your kids about your relationship to God than any sermon you could preach to them. Their future marriages may depend on your example as well! Give your children the heritage of a happy and secure home, a home filled with true love and obedience to God's plan for the family.

EXTRA CREDIT ASSIGNMENT

Memorize this passage of Scripture by learning one verse at a time; then recite it to a minimum of five women.

> "Wives, submit to your own husbands, as to the Lord. For the husband is head of the wife, as also Christ is head of the church; and He is the Savior of the body. Therefore, just as the church is subject to Christ, so let the wives be to their own husbands in everything" (Ephesians 5:22–24).

STUDY GUIDE

1. Read Genesis 2:18–25. According to verse 24, marriage should take priority over what other relationship? What are some practical ways to do this?
2. According to Deuteronomy 24:5, how did God establish the priority of marriage in the nation of Israel? List some things that would have to happen if a couple tried to do this in our culture today.
3. After reading 1 Corinthians 13:1–3, list some worthy activities that are meaningless without love. Now rewrite these verses using activities you are involved in that will be meaningless if you don't have love.

GROUP PROJECT

Sometimes it is difficult to be open in a group about your marriage difficulties. But as James 5:16 implies, being accountable to others is a positive way to bring about change. If the group is willing, have a time of confession together. Bring a box of tissues and allow plenty of time for everyone to share her needs. Close by kneeling together, with your arms around one another, asking God for His forgiveness and thanking Him for His healing. Sing a song of praise to Him!

EXTRA READING

✔ Ezzo, Gary, and Anne Marie Ezzo. Rev. ed. *Reflections of Moral Innocence*. Simi Valley, CA: Growing Families International, 1995. This book and a set of audiotapes deals with how to teach your children about sex. However, our family was blessed as we also learned about the Biblical principles of marriage in a fun way.

✔ Dillow, Linda. *Creative Counterpart: Becoming the Woman, Wife, and Mother You've Longed to Be.* Nashville: Nelson Books, 2003.

✔ Dillow, Linda, and Lorraine Pintus. *Intimate Issues: 21 Questions Christian Women Ask about Sex*. Colorado Springs: Waterbrook Press, 1999.

NOTES

1. Source unknown.
2. Names have been changed to protect privacy.

PART *3* THREE

Your Children

POINT TO PONDER

"The father of the righteous will greatly rejoice, and he who begets a wise child will delight in him. Let your father and your mother be glad, and let her who bore you rejoice"
(Proverbs 23:24, 25).

I laid down my cross-stitch project with a sigh. My four-year-old son had been exceedingly disobedient all morning, and I had a headache. My toddler had the stomach flu, so I had been up most of the night with her. I knew the queasy feeling in my own swollen stomach was just morning sickness, but I was miserable anyway. I was sitting in my children's playroom so I could keep my eyes on them while I finished sewing a friend's wedding present. The wedding was on Saturday, yet I had so much still to do! How would I ever finish on time? To top it off, my pink embroidery floss had a knot in it.

(On days like this I sometimes wish I could escape the heavy demands of motherhood, don't you? Maybe I could sneak out of the house after midnight, drive across the border into Canada, change my name, and start a new life!)

Using my needle, I began to work at the knot in my floss. As I stared at the stubborn knot, a verse from the pastor's sermon the day before suddenly came into my head: "For a thousand years in Your sight are like yesterday when it is past, and like a watch in the night" (Ps. 90:4). I began to picture the piece of thread as my life. So short! Used so quickly! The knot reminded me of my season in life at the moment, the season of motherhood. Such a short time in which to be the best mother possible!

So a thousand years were "like a watch in the night" in God's sight? I thought of the hours I had spent beside my sick daughter's bed the previous night. At the time I had been exhausted, the care had been tedious, and the hours had dragged by. Yet the night was over. It had passed as quickly as the stomach flu!

That was the day I realized how precious the time is that I have with my children. This realization was not a miracle potion in my life. I did not instantly become more patient with my kids. The queasy stomach didn't go away, nor did my headache. But it was the beginning of an attitude change for me.

Do you feel overwhelmed with the duties of mothering as well? Do you sometimes feel as though the job is too much for you? Do you wish you could quit?

God knows how you feel. He wants to comfort you, to strengthen you, and to give you the wisdom you need for your task.

When the Israelites had been exiled in Babylon for years because of their sin, God looked down on the people in their misery and asked the prophet Isaiah to give them a message of comfort. He promised the people not only that He would deliver them from their bondage and take them back to their homeland, but also that He would send the Messiah as He had promised. Then He reminded them of some principles that apply to mothers as well.

> The grass withers, the flower fades, but the word of our God stands forever (Isa. 40:8).

No matter what our circumstances, God's Word will never fail! We can take comfort in His wisdom.

> Who has measured the waters in the hollow of His hand, measured heaven with a span and calculated the dust of

> the earth in a measure? Weighed the mountains in scales and the hills in a balance? Who has directed the Spirit of the LORD, or as His counselor has taught Him? With whom did He take counsel, and who instructed Him, and taught Him in the path of justice? Who taught Him knowledge, and showed Him the way of understanding? (Isa. 40:12–14).

God's wisdom and power far exceed our own. We can take comfort in His power.

> Lift up your eyes on high, and see who has created these things, who brings out their host [the stars] by number; He calls them all by name, by the greatness of His might and the strength of His power; not one is missing (Isa. 40:26).

If God cares about the stars in their infinity, think of how much He cares about you and your family, people for whom He has given His only Son (John 3:16). We can take comfort in His love.

> Have you not known? Have you not heard? The everlasting God, the LORD, the Creator of the ends of the earth, neither faints nor is weary. His understanding is unsearchable. He gives power to the weak, and to those who have no might He increases strength. Even the youths shall faint and be weary, and the young men shall utterly fall, but those who wait on the LORD shall renew their strength; they shall mount up with wings like eagles, they shall run and not be weary, they shall walk and not faint (Isa. 40:28–31).

Young mothers (and older ones too) are often tired and without strength. Yet God is never without strength. We can take comfort in His strength.

As we begin to talk about the monumental task we have of mothering our children to the glory of God, take comfort in God. He is not too small for the job. Indeed, His power is limitless and His resources are inexhaustible.

> He will feed His flock like a shepherd; He will gather the lambs with His arm, and carry them in His bosom, and gently lead those who are with young (Isa. 40:11).

Now to Him who is able to do exceedingly abundantly above all that we ask or think, according to the power that works in us, to Him be glory in the church by Christ Jesus to all generations, forever and ever. Amen (Eph. 3:20, 21).

CHAPTER *9* NINE

Being a Godly Mother

POINT TO PONDER

"It is usually best to have a nap right after lunch. After lunch, simply say, in a breezy, cheerful, self-confident, firm but not harsh, assured but not domineering, soft but audible tone, 'It is time to have our NAPPIE now.' If you have done this properly, most children, not all children, will usually, not always, sometimes, go to bed without protesting" *(Marvin J. Gersh).[1]*

How much advice have *you* received to help you be a better mother? How does anyone know what it takes to be a great mom? The world is ready to dole out its share of advice; but as we have learned, it is our responsibility to take the advice we hear and compare it to God's Word. But where do we start? What is God's design for a mother? I have found several "motherly" responsibilities in God's Word. They are quite basic.

The Duties of a Mother

First, I can see that God's Word commands mothers to love their children, and I can see evidence in Scripture that moms

127

are to teach their children. We'll explore these commands more in the next few chapters. But one special job God gives to mothers is to spiritually nurture their children.

One day as I read the account of Deborah, the judge, I noticed this motherly quality (Judges 4 and 5). Deborah, a godly woman, had watched as the Israelites rebelled against God and then lived for twenty years under the hateful captivity of the wicked king Jabin, a Canaanite. A leader in Israel, Deborah met with the people under a palm tree to settle their disputes and to speak to them about God. Finally God revealed to her His plan for delivering the Israelites from their enemies, and she even accompanied Israel's armies into battle. Deborah was responsible for bringing the people back to God. In the song of Deborah and Barak, she is described as "a mother in Israel" (Judg. 5:7).

Deborah is an example of mothers who are brave and willing to stand up for what is right and courageous as they settle disputes in the ranks. They also turn the hearts of their children to the Lord.

So how do we become this kind of mom? The answer, as always, is that God changes *our hearts*, molding us into the mothers He wants us to be. It is the same way He has helped all people fulfill His plans for their lives. Remember, "We are his workmanship [His handicraft, His work of art] created in Christ Jesus for good works" (Eph. 2:10).

Before Moses led the people of Israel from Egypt to the Promised Land, he was a shepherd who claimed he could not speak and certainly was not the man for the job (Exod. 3:11; 4:10). Zacchaeus corruptly collected taxes before Jesus touched his life and changed his character (Luke 19:2). Rahab was a prostitute, yet God allowed her to be the great, great grandmother of David and one of the women in the line of the Messiah (Heb. 11:31; Matt. 1:5). God changes lives, and He wants to make you into a mother who pleases Him.

Being a Godly Mother 129

Many women of history stand out to me as godly mothers—mothers like I want to be! One of my favorites is Susanna Wesley, the mother of John and Charles Wesley. She had so many children she had to hide under her apron to find time alone to pray. Another godly woman from more recent times is the mother of Elisabeth Elliot, author and widow of missionary-martyr Jim Elliot. Elisabeth's mother taught more by example than by word.

I'm sure you have your own list of mothers you admire. Maybe your own mother is near the top of your list. What qualities draw you to these women? What characteristics do you wish to emulate?

The Qualities of a Mother

I encourage you to start a list of godly character qualities that you desire to nurture in your own life. If possible, add Bible verses that will help you so that you can study and memorize them. Place this list in a special place (maybe inside the cover of your Bible or in your devotional notebook or journal) so you can add to it and check your progress from time to time.

Scripture already has several "lists" for us. For instance,

> Giving all diligence, add to your faith virtue, to virtue knowledge, to knowledge self-control, to self-control perseverance, to perseverance godliness, to godliness brotherly kindness, and to brotherly kindness love. For if these things are yours and abound, you will be neither barren nor unfruitful in the knowledge of our Lord Jesus Christ (2 Pet. 1:5–8).

Another good list is in 1 Timothy 6:11.

> But you, O man [or woman] of God . . . pursue righteousness, godliness, faith, love, patience, gentleness.

A list that has always been special and challenging to me is the one on the fruit of the Spirit. But before listing the fruit of the Spirit, the apostle Paul listed some fleshly works.

> Now the works of the flesh are evident, which are: adultery, fornication, uncleanness, lewdness, idolatry,

> sorcery, hatred, contentions, jealousies, outbursts of wrath, selfish ambitions, dissensions, heresies, envy, murders, drunkenness, revelries, and the like (Gal. 5:19–21).

Don't these descriptions sound just like an afternoon TV talk show? Yet how many of these have you or I been guilty of at one time or another? Don't be too quick to point your finger at others! Paul continued,

> But the fruit of the Spirit is love, joy, peace, longsuffering, kindness, goodness, faithfulness, gentleness, self-control (Gal. 5:22, 23).

Notice that the Spirit of God produces "indoor fruit"; that is, He produces the fruit inside us—in our hearts, where no one can see. Wouldn't it be so much easier if God had said that the right kind of mother is the one who perfectly juggles all the responsibilities in her life? She always wakes up at 6:00 A.M., prepares a healthy breakfast for her children, reads them exactly six Golden Books per day, makes sure all of them brush their teeth and mind their manners, and never misses a soccer game!

I know it's difficult to measure the amount of love or joy I have in my life. Yet God never gets much more specific. Instead, He allows room for creativity in the office of mothering. He gives us guidelines, or general principles, by which we can live. And He gives us His Spirit, Who will live out these beautiful qualities in our lives.

Eve, a godly woman in my former church, used to send me one card per week, each dealing with a different fruit of the Spirit, and we prayed together that God would develop these virtues in our lives. One week she wrote: "When I pray for God to work in my life, I can be assured that He will answer my prayer. But how? And when? I used to think that life would be so much easier if God would just send me a telegram. I'd picture this delivery man ringing my doorbell, handing me an envelope and inside . . . a message from God, of course. 'My child, I heard you praying, and

Being a Godly Mother

. . .' I came to an understanding some time ago that my simple daydream of telegrams was fully realized in God's Word."

Let's look more closely at what God wants us to learn from the list of the fruit of the Spirit.

1. "The fruit of the Spirit is love." The love God wants us to have toward our children is not only the sweet love that kisses them goodnight and hugs them when they're cute. No, God's love is *loving the unlovely*. Kids can be unlovely many times. They may say we're mean if we won't give them their way, yet we must respond with love. Love does what is *best* for our kids—not just what will make them happy. It takes love to see the good in our children even on days when there isn't much good to see. Remember, God's love to us in our sin is our example (see Philippians 2:1–16).

2. "The fruit of the Spirit is . . . joy." Joy is contentment in God, no matter the circumstances. Kids and moms both have trouble with joy sometimes, yet we are their character models. They will learn contentment with their circumstances when they see us practice contentment. Learn to "rejoice always" (1 Thess. 5:16; cf. Phil. 4:4), to "be content" (Phil. 4:11), to give thanks "in everything" (1 Thess. 5:18). If the God you serve decides that the best thing for you is a tough circumstance, then you can be joyful knowing that He has your ultimate good in mind. What a powerful example you can be to your children!

Regarding joy, my friend Eve wrote, "All of us get 'down' from time to time. Life is just hard. Things don't go the way we expect; we get bumped by unpleasant people. When life gets the best of me, I start thinking about what I'm going through. Next thing you know, I'm miserable. Not only am I troubled by my circumstances but disappointed in myself because God's Word tells me to be joyful, and here I am in the middle of a pity party. How do I turn this thing around?"

I copied an acrostic of the word "joy" and wrote some related thoughts in my journal some time ago. They have served me well. "How do you spell joy? J stands for Jesus, O stands for others, and Y stands for yourself. Focus on the source of my joy, Jesus Christ. Become involved in the lives of others. Put myself last."

Moms have many opportunities for pity parties, but we also have many opportunities to serve others—our kids and husbands especially! Next time you feel a pity party coming on, start to sing, force yourself to thank the Lord for whatever is wrong, and serve someone else immediately.

3. *"The fruit of the Spirit is . . . peace."* Jesus told His disciples, "Peace I leave with you, My peace I give to you; not as the world gives do I give to you. Let not your heart be troubled, neither let it be afraid" (John 14:27). This peace in the midst of scary times is the peace promised to us by the Spirit of God.

Every child has nightmares. At 2:30 A.M. you hear a howl coming from her bedroom. Groggily, you shove your feet into your slippers, grab your flashlight, and shuffle to her bedside. Only half awake yourself, you smooth your small daughter's hair and reassure her that no ghosts are hiding behind the toy box.

But what reassurance can you truly give her if you do not know God's peace firsthand? Do you take your fears to God? In the midst of a scary storm, when you can't see the road in front of you as you drive, do you talk to your Heavenly Father and ask Him to remove your fear? Do you trust Him when you hear your sister has cancer? When your husband is two hours late coming home from work, do you place your confidence in God before you call the highway patrol?

Remember, the peace God gives is based on His proven record. He cares for you! During frightening times, I have repeated the words of Job when he proclaimed, "Though He slay me, yet will I trust Him" (Job 13:15). I always get the jitters during thunderstorms, so I have learned to recite, "Whenever I am afraid, I will trust in You" (Ps. 56:3).

Being a Godly Mother   133

By your daily example (I pray out loud!), your children will hide those same memory verses in their hearts. Nighttime goblins and ghosts eventually will be replaced by an abiding trust in a God Who sees and hears—and "the peace of God, which surpasses all understanding, will guard your hearts and minds through Christ Jesus" (Phil. 4:7).

4. "The fruit of the Spirit is . . . longsuffering." How short is your temper these days? Whoo-weee, do mothers ever get lots of opportunities to find out! So many events during a day can try your patience and cause you to lose your temper. I was struck by the irony of this one morning when my son yelled at his sister for taking one of his toys. I was so tired of hearing him yell and listening to her holler back at him that I screamed from the kitchen, "You two stop fighting!" In the quietness of the house, I could almost hear an echo from my scream. I believe that children are born with a sin nature, but the Lord certainly convicted me about reinforcing their sin by raising my voice in anger at them. The verse He brought to my mind was, "A soft answer turns away wrath, but a harsh word stirs up anger" (Prov. 15:1).

5. "The fruit of the Spirit is . . . kindness." The woman of excellence described in Proverbs 31 "opens her mouth with wisdom, and on her tongue is the law of kindness" (v. 26). The kindness and graciousness of God is best evidenced in your life when it's the most difficult to be kind. I think home is the hardest place to obey God, don't you? Home is where you're tired . . . where supper gets burned . . . where a good night's sleep is interrupted . . . where people have bad breath and bad moods. You may be kind on Sunday morning, all dressed up in your church clothes, but are you kind on Monday morning when you have a headache and you wish you could sleep in? You may be kind when your child has straight *A*s, but are you kind when he struggles with math? You may be kind when company is coming, but are you kind when your best china is broken? Maybe we should pray David's prayer, "Set a guard, O LORD, over my mouth; keep watch over the door of my lips" (Ps. 141:3).

6. *"The fruit of the Spirit is . . . goodness."* Almost all of the forty-five references to "goodness" in the Bible mention the goodness of God. Even the inclusion of "goodness" on the list of the fruit of the Spirit refers to the goodness of God's Spirit evidenced in our lives. Humankind is not good (see Romans 3). Any act of goodness you do is simply evidence that God's grace is at work in your life. Yet the fact remains that your children will best understand the goodness of God by observing your goodness to them. How this thought reminds us to stay in the Word, soaking up the attributes of God and applying them to our lives! "Be transformed by the renewing of your mind, that you may prove what is that *good* and acceptable and perfect will of God" (Rom. 12:2, emphasis added).

7. *"The fruit of the Spirit is . . . faithfulness."* Faithfulness is trustworthiness, keeping your promises, reliability. We can learn to be faithful to our children by observing God's faithfulness. Hebrews 11:1 tells us, "Now faith is the substance of things hoped for, the evidence of things not seen." We have to learn to rely on God with a trust not based upon our feelings or our experiences but based upon the promises in His Word.

Your children learn to rely on you based upon your words. Are you faithful? When you promise to play with them, do you keep your word? "When you make a vow to God, do not delay to pay it; for He has no pleasure in fools. Pay what you have vowed—better not to vow than to vow and not pay" (Eccles. 5:4, 5). Do your children keep their promises to you? You are their first teacher! Mold their character well by consistently keeping your word.

8. *"The fruit of the Spirit is . . . gentleness."* The word for gentleness is translated "meekness" in the King James Version. Meekness is humility and having a servant's heart. When you

Being a Godly Mother 135

comb the hair of a little girl, you can do it one of two ways. You can carefully, gently, slowly detangle her hair, never pulling too sharply or making her say, "Ouch!" Or you could say, "Get your head over here! We're in a hurry!" You could rip and tear through the knots as her eyes well up with tears.

The method you choose will depend on your memories of when *you* were little. How did it feel for *your* hair to be combed? Your humble spirit will cause you to be a gentle mother, carefully teaching your children as you would want to be taught.

9. "The fruit of the Spirit is . . . self-control." One of the most obvious character flaws in kids today, according to my husband who works with high school students, is the lack of self-control. Who is to blame? If a ninth grader doesn't have enough self-control to sit still and read his homework assignment, the teacher blames the middle school. The middle school claims that the child couldn't sit still when he started sixth grade, so it must be the fault of the elementary school. Those poor teachers blame the preschool, where kids run around crazy all day. The preschool blames the parents, who never made their child behave. The parents contend, "He has always been like that! He was a colicky baby!"

Self-control is difficult to learn, harder to teach, and even more difficult to instill the older the child gets. Yet Scripture warns that "whoever has no rule over his own spirit is like a city broken down, without walls" (Prov. 25:28). Teaching your child to "rule his own spirit" must be a consistent, daily lesson, begun when he is very young—but first examine your own heart. Do you control your tongue . . . your thoughts . . . your attitudes . . . your lusts . . . your temper . . . your time . . . your money?

IN SUMMARY

The process of growing the fruit of God's Spirit in your life is not easy, nor is it always fun. Yet it is rewarding! Allow God to mold you into His image, no matter what it takes. Take your faults to Him and confess them. Ask Him to make you into the right kind of mom, one who will bring glory to Him. Mothering begins in your heart, where God makes you like Him—and then makes your children like you!

EXTRA CREDIT ASSIGNMENT

Memorize this passage of Scripture by learning one verse at a time; then recite the passage to a minimum of five women.

> "Giving all diligence, add to your faith virtue, to virtue knowledge, to knowledge self-control, to self-control perseverance, to perseverance godliness, to godliness brotherly kindness, and to brotherly kindness love. For if these things are yours and abound, you will be neither barren nor unfruitful in the knowledge of our Lord Jesus Christ" (2 Peter 1:5–8).

STUDY GUIDE

1. Compare 2 Peter 1:5–8, 1 Timothy 6:11, and Galatians 5:22 and 23. Which character qualities are the same? Which are different?
2. From Philippians 2:1–16, make a list of godly character qualities that a mom's life should evidence.
3. Read John 14:27. Sometimes the thought of raising children in our wicked society can frighten us! What promises does this verse make?
4. Read Proverbs 15:1. List some times during the day when you might need to remember this verse.

Being a Godly Mother   137

5. After reading Psalm 141:3, list some ways you have failed to guard your words. According to the verse, how could you prevent these sins the next time?
6. Read Hebrews 11:1 and list some ways God has proven His faithfulness to you and your family.
7. According to Proverbs 25:28, what consequences could result from a mother's lack of self-control?

GROUP PROJECT

If any "crafty" women are in your group, ask them to design a wall decoration that lists the fruit of the Spirit. Then as a group, have fun making one for each of you. How does this activity fulfill God's command in Deuteronomy 6:6–9?

EXTRA READING

✔ Dengler, Sandy. *Susanna Wesley*. Chicago: Moody Press, 1987. An excellent biography for young readers. Your children might benefit from your reading it aloud to them.
✔ Elliot, Elisabeth. *The Shaping of a Christian Family*. Nashville: Thomas Nelson Publishers, 1992. In this wise book Elliot tells how her parents taught her from an early age to love and honor God.
✔ Fleming, Jean. *A Mother's Heart*. Colorado Springs: NavPress, 1982. A favorite book of mine. Fleming shows us how to love our children and how to be the mothers we should be.
✔ Schaeffer, Edith. *What Is a Family?* Grand Rapids: Baker Book House, 1975. A classic that uses various pictures to describe what a family should be.

NOTES

1. Marvin J. Gersh, *How to Raise Children at Home in Your Spare Time* (New York: Stein and Day Publishers, 1966), 79.

CHAPTER *10* TEN

Filtering the Parenting Advice

POINT TO PONDER

"There is none righteous, no, not one; there is none who understands; there is none who seeks after God. They have all turned aside; they have together become unprofitable; there is none who does good, no, not one. . . . Destruction and misery are in their ways; and the way of peace they have not known. There is no fear of God before their eyes"
(Romans 3:10–12, 16–18).

In God's eyes, who are sinners? The heathen? criminals in big cities? crooked politicians? hateful murderers? Yes . . . and no! All of us are sinners in God's eyes! Even those who have given their hearts and lives to the Lord Jesus have trouble with their flesh, which continually wars against God (Rom. 7; 2 Cor. 10:3; James 4:1, 2; 1 Pet. 2:11).

My Own Experience

My husband and I both gave our lives to Christ as young children. We were both trained from an early age to know the Scriptures, and we were encouraged to practice them in every aspect of our lives. Perhaps this wonderful training resulted in a sort of pride, a feeling that we were "untouchable" and unable to fall prey to worldly philosophies (1 Cor. 10:12). So when I became pregnant with our first child, I never doubted for a moment that we would just *know* how to be wonderful parents.

However, as the pregnancy progressed, the feelings of confidence slid into feelings of doubt and fear. I observed other children (and other parents) and tried to pinpoint exactly which behaviors I wanted my child to copy and which behaviors I hoped he or she would never try! My job gave me access to a wonderful library, so I began to read everything I could on parenting. I didn't think it made much difference who the author was, as long as the principles made sense and seemed workable. I began to stockpile a set of philosophies that would help me be a great parent. My confidence began to return.

I remember reading a book on the practical matter of feeding my new baby. The book began by telling how we humans are creatures of instinct, able to respond to the needs of our children because of many years of evolution. I knew the Bible denies the philosophy of evolution. I believed God created us in His image, with a reasoning mind not a set of animal instincts. However, I dismissed the chapter because it was written by an unbeliever, and I accepted the rest of the book because it made sense in my eyes and seemed logical, even scientific.

Other advice encouraged my feelings of self-esteem and happiness, placing more emphasis on my emotions than on standards of right or wrong. I read that "a child who feels right acts right and is a joy to parent."[1] Also, "as with any feature of a parenting style, if it is not working and does not feel right, then drop it."[2] Many of the authors claimed to be Christians, and although their words did not match Scripture, I trusted their advice.

Our son was born. Then came weeks of frustration. He cried for hours at a time! The experts promised we would feel lovingly bonded to our son. We hated being parents! (We were too

Filtering the Parenting Advice

proud to admit it to anyone else, but my husband and I looked desperately at each other and said, "Is this what parenting is going to be like?") The advice said we should respond to our baby's every cry. Following that advice left us feeling exhausted and depressed, and we agonized as we held him constantly, took him into our bed, and fed him nearly around the clock.

> The way of peace they have not known, and there is no justice in their ways; they have made themselves crooked paths; whoever takes that way shall not know peace (Isa. 59:8).

I reached the end of my rope one night when our son screamed for five hours straight. I laid him in his crib and let him cry. I felt horribly guilty for leaving him alone in his room, but I was afraid I might do something violent if I continued to hold him any longer. I had fed him several times, rocked him, changed him, tried *everything*. My husband was working the night shift, and I had no one I felt I could turn to for help. (I could have called several people, but I was embarrassed to admit defeat.)

In tears, I turned on my computer and began searching the Internet for answers. Around 3:00 A.M., deaf by now to the continuing screams of my baby, I began to talk to another mother in a chat room. She willingly listened to my story (it was late for her too), and she gave me some practical advice. As she lovingly suggested some changes to what we were doing, I began to notice something about what she said. Although she never once told me she was a Christian, as she counseled me, memory verses I had learned began to parallel her advice. She later suggested some reading for me, and as I read books by authors who unashamedly followed Biblical principles, I asked God to forgive me. Finally, the philosophies I was reading matched God's Word, and my husband and I determined this time to obey.

The result—which happened almost overnight in our case—was a peaceful home. Our baby stopped crying, and people later commented repeatedly on what a happy child he was. We were again filled with confidence, yet this confidence was based upon God's Word and not our feelings. We were well rested. We began to fall in love with our son.

Where Advice Comes From

Since then we have observed that at each major junction in our lives, both good advice and bad advice have come our way. Each time we have taken what we've heard and compared it to Biblical principles. God has been faithful to give us godly friends and mentors who have willingly opened their homes to us. As we observed their obedient children, it was easy to see that they were practicing their advice to us in their own lives.

Do you remember what I said about Psalm 1 being my favorite passage of Scripture? It says,

> Blessed is the man who walks not in the counsel of the ungodly, nor stands in the path of sinners, nor sits in the seat of the scornful; but his delight is in the law of the LORD, and in His law he meditates day and night. He shall be like a tree planted by the rivers of water, that brings forth its fruit in its season, whose leaf also shall not wither; and whatever he does shall prosper. The ungodly are not so, but are like the chaff which the wind drives away. Therefore the ungodly shall not stand in the judgment, nor sinners in the congregation of the righteous. For the LORD knows the way of the righteous, but the way of the ungodly shall perish.

Many parenting philosophies have come and gone over the years. In the middle of the last century, some Christians fell prey to the philosophy that parents should rule their children with a rod of iron, never teaching their children to think but forcing them to adapt to the ways of the parents. As a result, many teens rebelled as soon as they were able to leave home. Some saw their parents as hypocrites, people who enforced one thing yet lived another. These young people determined to act differently toward their own children.

Filtering the Parenting Advice **143**

An even more dangerous philosophy is prevalent in the current generation of parents: that children are basically good. Decisions revolve around the emotional health of the parent and the child. Helping a child "feel good" and helping the parent and child develop a "positive relationship" are the ultimate goals. The children quickly learn that the world revolves around them. Their happiness is more important than their holiness.

Parents are also told to provide "realistic" standards for their children so that every child can succeed regardless of his or her true ability. In this environment everyone will feel happy; everyone will be loving and kind. Yet in reality, children learn they can have their own way. They become wise, or right, in their own eyes (see Proverbs 12:15). They do not learn to submit to parental authority; consequently, they are unprepared to submit to the authority of their teachers, their government, or their God.

Do you know children who consistently get their own way? Do the kids in the Sunday School at your church rule their parents? Are your public schools and day-care centers filled with children who feel that the world revolves around them?

Is this philosophy Biblical? Not according to God's Word.

Children are not basically good. "For all have sinned and fall short of the glory of God" (Rom. 3:23).

The goal of Biblical parenting is not solely to help our children feel good. Feelings can deceive. "The heart is deceitful above all things, and desperately wicked; who can know it?" (Jer. 17:9). "There is a way that seems right to a man, but its end is the way of death" (Prov. 16:25).

God is a holy God. He wants us to live holy lives and to train our children in righteousness. Our lives should revolve around Him. "Because it is written, 'Be holy, for I am holy' " (1 Pet. 1:16).

The Lord wants parents to have a working knowledge of His Word. We need to hide His commands in our hearts, apply them to our lives, and recall them often (another reason why we must diligently study and memorize Bible verses). Use Scripture to answer the tough questions of life. Thoroughly understand doctrine. Know God's opinion on every matter.

> Hear, O Israel: The LORD our God, the LORD is one! You shall love the LORD your God with all your heart, with all your soul, and with all your might. And these words which I command you today shall be in your heart. You shall teach them diligently to your children (Deut. 6:4–7).

The burdens of parental responsibility are lifted when we realize we are holding our children to God's standard, not our own. When our children ask why they must behave in a certain way, we are free to take them to the Bible and show them from God's Word what He requires. Therefore, our children answer to God for their actions. However, we are responsible before God to teach them diligently.

God wants us to teach our children consistently. Use every moment as a teaching opportunity.

> And shall talk of them when you sit in your house, when you walk by the way, when you lie down, and when you rise up. You shall bind them as a sign on your hand, and they shall be as frontlets between your eyes. You shall write them on the doorposts of your house and on your gates (Deut. 6:7–9).

As your children learn to apply Scripture to every situation, they will begin to grasp not only *what* the Lord commands them to do but *why*. The Word of God will begin to take root in their hearts. They will learn to think Biblically.

And because your behavior before them is a consistent example, they will see living proof that following God works!

IN SUMMARY

Let me give you a few suggestions that may help you apply a Biblical philosophy of child training in your home. Parents

Filtering the Parenting Advice **145**

must know God's Word before they can teach it effectively, and many resources are available to help you learn God's Word. Your church is the first place you should turn. In part 5 we will talk about how you should link up with other believers in Christ. I also suggest that you begin to study Proverbs for excellent parenting advice. Finally, take advantage of the wonderful books available to Christians today. Many godly parents have compiled lists and helpful hints for parents based on Scripture. Just remember that you have the responsibility of comparing what you read with the Bible.

Your role as a mother will stretch you as no other, showing you the glaring character flaws in your own life. Allow God to mold and shape you into His image, and thank Him for the privilege of shaping the next generation for His glory.

> Turn away my eyes from looking at worthless things, and revive me in Your way. Establish Your word to Your servant, who is devoted to fearing You (Ps.119:37, 38).

EXTRA CREDIT ASSIGNMENT

Memorize this passage of Scripture by learning one verse at a time; then recite the passage to a minimum of five women.

> "Hear, O Israel: The LORD our God, the LORD is one! You shall love the LORD your God with all your heart, with all your soul, and with all your might. And these words which I command you today shall be in your heart. You shall teach them diligently to your children, and shall talk of them when you sit in your house, when you walk by the way, when you lie down, and when you rise up. You shall bind them as a sign on your hand, and they shall be as frontlets between your eyes. You shall write them on the doorposts of your house and on your gates" (Deuteronomy 6:4–9).

STUDY GUIDE

1. According to 1 Corinthians 10:12, how can we cultivate humility in our hearts?
2. According to Isaiah 59:8, what are some symptoms that our lives displease God?
3. Read Psalm 1:1 and 2. How can you know you're receiving bad advice? How can you know you're receiving good advice?
4. After reading Proverbs 12:15, tell how the principles of this verse could be taught to children. Why is it urgent to teach these things to them?
5. Read Deuteronomy 6:4 and 5. What do you think it means to love God with all your heart, soul, and strength?
6. Read Psalm 119:37 and 38. What are some "worthless things" to look at in our culture? According to these verses, how can we be "revived" in God's way?

GROUP PROJECT

Read Deuteronomy 6:7–9 and discuss how you could implement these verses in your homes. How is this similar to the group project in chapter 9? Make a list of some important things that your children need to learn. Now plan creative ways to teach them, using ideas from Deuteronomy 6.

EXTRA READING

✔ Decker, Barbara. *Proverbs for Parenting.* Boise, ID: Lynn's Bookshelf, 1991. This book classifies different Proverbs according to needs that you might have as a parent. What an excellent way to know God's opinion on your parenting!
✔ Ezzo, Gary, and Anne Marie Ezzo. 5th ed. *Growing Kids God's Way: Biblical Ethics for Parenting.* Simi Valley, CA: Growing Families International, 1998. An eighteen-week course in parenting that you can enroll in at a local church. You can also order the book with audiotapes for learning at home.

Filtering the Parenting Advice   **147**

✔ Forster, Pam. *For Instruction in Righteousness: A Topical Reference Guide for Biblical Child Training*. Rev. ed. Gaston, OR: Doorposts, 1995. I highly recommend this book. Doorposts publishes many other practical tools to help you develop your parenting skills. Order a catalog at 1-888-433-4749 or www.doorposts.net.

✔ Tripp, Tedd. *Shepherding a Child's Heart*. Wapwallopen, PA: Shepherd Press, 1995. A great tool to help you evaluate how to train your child's heart and not just change his outward behavior.

NOTES

1. William Sears, *Nighttime Parenting: How to Get Your Baby and Child to Sleep* (New York: Penguin Books, Plume, 1985), 1.

2. Ibid., 2.

CHAPTER *11* ELEVEN

Realizing That Children Are a Blessing

POINT TO PONDER
"He grants the barren woman a home, like a joyful mother of children. Praise the LORD!" (Psalm 113:9).

Nothing is as wonderful as holding a newborn baby . . . or as scary . . . or as overwhelming and emotional. I am thankful for the role of mothering God has given to us women. I still remember being a little girl and playing with dolls, pretending each baby doll was real and needed me! Then marriage brought excitement as I dreamed of the day God would bless our home with a baby.

The desire to have a child is healthy, placed in the hearts of women by God Himself! But just like every other role God has given us, Satan is doing what he can to sidetrack women, to deceive them, and to discourage them from participating in the blessing of God.

Women in their childbearing years have many decisions to make, yet controversies have clouded the issues. Some experts even claim to base their opinions on the Word of God. I see a great need for checking the context of Scripture, for praying for wisdom, for considering your motives, and for accepting that differing opinions exist. Let's examine some of the issues you might face personally—or that older women should know about as they counsel young moms.

Family Planning

I play the piano for the congregational singing at my church, and one Sunday I was reflecting on the words of the hymns while I played. I thought about how great God's love is as we sang "Great is thy faithfulness, / O God, my Father, / There is no shadow of turning with Thee"[1] and "To God be the glory—great things He hath done! / So loved He the world that He gave us His Son, / Who yielded His life an atonement for sin / And opened the Lifegate that all may go in."[2]

The same God Who created Adam and Eve also knew they would turn in rebellion from Him. He knew He would have to give His Son—to die in a horrible way—before He even said, "Let there be light." When Jesus Christ fashioned Eve from Adam's rib, He already knew the agony He would face on the cross because of their sin and their descendants' sin (Col.1:16).

This same God commanded Adam and Eve to "be fruitful and multiply; fill the earth and subdue it" (Gen. 1:28). God knew what misery would follow their sin; yet *before they sinned,* He gave them this command to fill the earth. Years later, after God had destroyed most of humankind in the worldwide flood, He repeated His command to Noah and his family: "Be fruitful and multiply, and fill the earth" (Gen. 9:1, 7). He promised to make Abram and his descendants fruitful so that the nation of Israel would be large and strong (Gen. 16:10; 17:2, 20).

God's people have always seen children as a blessing. Indeed, children are a unique part of God's plan. But we must remember that *God* is the author and giver of life. "All things were made through Him, and without Him nothing was made that was made" (John 1:3).

Realizing That Children Are a Blessing **151**

> For You formed my inward parts; You covered me in my mother's womb. I will praise You, for I am fearfully and wonderfully made; marvelous are Your works, and that my soul knows very well. My frame was not hidden from You, when I was made in secret, and skillfully wrought in the lowest parts of the earth. Your eyes saw my substance, being yet unformed. And in Your book they all were written, the days fashioned for me, when as yet there were none of them (Ps. 139:13–16).

Some people believe that the world is overpopulated and that people should limit the number of children they have. I do not see this principle supported in Scripture, for God is greater than any scheme we have. He has made a wonderful world capable of supporting the command He gave to Adam and his descendants. However, we must not become proud and think we are able to control our own destinies, either by limiting the number of children we have or by choosing to have an unlimited number. "Unless the LORD builds the house, they labor in vain who build it; unless the LORD guards the city, the watchman stays awake in vain" (Ps. 127:1).

Many times we think we are wise enough to "plan our families" without God's help. How ridiculous we must look in His eyes! The conception of a child is a miracle, no matter how well-educated we are. No child can be conceived without God's hand, and no child can be "prevented" without the permission of God. In my opinion, it is best not to worry, plot, or plan—but to simply trust in the sovereignty of God for your children.

What a delight it is to begin to see children as a gift from God! "Behold, children are a heritage from the LORD, the fruit of the womb is a reward" (Ps. 127:3). As any woman who cannot have children will tell you, the ability to conceive is not to be thought of lightly.

So does the Bible tell us how many children we should have? No, it doesn't. We live in an age where knowledge about how our bodies function and accessibility to technology to help us conceive force us to make decisions that never before had to be thought about. Throughout most of the history of the world, the ability to conceive was regarded as a great mystery. Women in Bible times knew that God opened the womb. Today we often don't think about God's opening the womb but only about "timing it right" to get pregnant or using various methods to prevent conception.

> Identifying what is morally right has been complicated by the development of medical technology. Today's generation is faced with decisions that did not exist even ten years ago. For one thing, a child can have up to five parents by the time he gets to the crib: Father A supplies the sperm. Mother B supplies the egg. The embryo is implanted in Mother C. And the child is raised by Father D and Mother E.[3]

I am *not* saying technology is bad. Only the improper use of technology is bad. With greater knowledge comes greater responsibility. This area is definitely a gray one in Scripture, but think about the following things when "planning" your family.

1. The issue of controlling conception is never mentioned in Scripture. Therefore, you and your husband need to think about why you want either a small or a large family, and then compare your motives to Biblical principles.

2. If you feel obligated to limit the size of your family, is it for selfish reasons? For instance, if you are waiting to have children until you are older so you can pursue a career, are you sure this goal is God's will for you, or is it a selfish desire for money, acclaim, or self-fulfillment? Do you not want any more children because the ones you already have are unruly and obnoxious? Are babies too much trouble? These are tough questions, and I don't presume to tell you what decision to make. I ask only that you search your heart and your motives. What role does God want you to play at this season in your life?

Realizing That Children Are a Blessing

3. Many people use Psalm 127:4 and 5 as a reason to have a large family: "Like arrows in the hand of a warrior, so are the children of one's youth. Happy is the man who has his quiver full of them." While the psalmist is obviously saying that a father of many children has the potential for much joy, consider the following:

> Be warned that selfishness comes in more subtle forms, such as a woman having baby after baby just because she likes cuddling infants. God wants infants to grow up to be responsible men and women. They must never be regarded as playthings. Psalm 127 teaches that a good marksman has his quiver filled only with as many arrows as he can deliver to the mark. The application to parenthood is for a couple not to have any more children than they can raise and provide for in a godly way. This is a serious matter. Preventing conception has no eternal consequences, whereas raising ungodly, undisciplined individuals can lead to their eventual damnation.[4]

Again, this controversial subject is not addressed directly in Scripture. The Word of God gives us freedom in some of these matters as we depend upon the Holy Spirit and as we seek God's direction through prayer. I know many believers who choose to camp on one side of the issue or the other.

4. Obviously abortion is not an option for a believer in Christ. Have you, therefore, researched the method of birth control you might be using to be sure it is not abortive? Use caution and educate yourself so you do not unwittingly harm a tiny child.

5. Consider your health. What are the long-term risks associated with using certain methods of birth control? For example, medical books warn that taking birth control pills increases the risk of heart attack, stroke, and blood clots in certain women. More commonly, birth control pills can have side effects that might leave you feeling less than your best much of the time. Will you be able to maintain a joyful spirit (which God commands) while using a product that can make you moody? Of course, pregnancy has its own similar side effects, yet the biggest "side effect" of pregnancy, a new baby, is certainly worth any discomfort you may face!

Commit this area of your life to the Lord, as you do every portion of your life. Bring all decisions to the Lord in prayer, and trust Him to guide you.

Pregnancy and Childbirth

It is not a mistake that pregnancy lasts nine months. We have so much to do! Yet when I consider the miracle of life that is forming, I am humbled again by the power and might of God.

Pregnancy is a time when we can witness the creative abilities of God firsthand. On my daughter's second birthday, I thought about how quickly her first two years had passed. It seemed that just yesterday she was a newborn.

Yet when I compared her to my six-month-old son, I was amazed! She was so much bigger than he was! His fingers and toes were so much smaller; his ability to move and to communicate so much less. He had so much growing to do before his second birthday!

But how much growing he had already done! When he was conceived, he was no larger than the period at the end of this sentence. Our family has always enjoyed learning how big an unborn baby is at each stage of development. At six weeks, our baby was about one-seventeenth of an inch long and had a heartbeat. At twelve weeks, fingers and toes had separated, and hair and nails were beginning to grow. At eighteen weeks, he weighed about half a pound, and I had already felt him move. At twenty-four weeks, babies gain six ounces in one week alone as their muscles, bones, and organs mature quickly. At thirty weeks, an unborn child may weigh three pounds and can blink his eyes. At thirty-six weeks, a baby is near his birth size and is starting to get dimples of fat around his elbows and knees. At birth, a baby

Realizing That Children Are a Blessing

can fit through his mother's pelvis, yet only weeks later he will be too long to cradle with one arm. By four months, as I held my baby, his head would bump one arm of my chair and his feet would push against the other. And in only a few short years, my son will be "as big as Daddy."

All of this tremendous growth takes place quietly, simply, and without our notice, without our permission. What a mighty God we serve! "For by Him all things were created that are in heaven and that are on earth, visible and invisible" (Col. 1:16).

As you reflect on the power and love of God, be reminded that God will sustain you through your pregnancy and the work of childbirth to come. Worry is a normal human emotion, but do not allow yourself to worry for nine months. Use the time as an opportunity to learn to trust God. And remember,

> Are not two sparrows sold for a copper coin? And not one of them falls to the ground apart from your Father's will. But the very hairs of your head are all numbered. Do not fear therefore; you are of more value than many sparrows (Matt. 10:29–31).

Juanita Purcell, the author of several books, including *Joyous Journeys around the Detours,* spoke on the topic of worry at a ladies' retreat I attended. She said that in her journal she has a page titled "Why Sink When You Can Swim." On this page she has written Bible verses that comfort her and turn her attention back to God when her mind is frozen with fear. Pregnancy gives us a great opportunity to begin to memorize God's Word and to apply it to our circumstances.

God created pregnancy, just as He created everything else. It is a normal process of life. Pregnancy is a physiological event, not a state of illness. By "physiological," I mean that pregnancy is a normal function of a woman's body. Just as your teeth are meant to chew and your fingers are meant to wiggle, your womb is designed to grow a child. If you continually focus on the problems that happen to a small percentage of pregnant women, you may tend to worry and fret and fear. It is true that because of the sin of Adam and Eve, all creation is now in a fallen state. Disease does happen. Death is inevitable. Labor can be sweaty, hard work with some pain thrown in, yet anxiety and fear displease God.

No matter what, pregnancy is a time to prepare. Dr. Robert Bradley, the famous obstetrician who pioneered the ideas of having fathers as coaches in delivery rooms and using natural methods of pain relief during labor, has compared labor to a swimming event. If you know that nine months from now you are going to be thrown into a lake and asked to swim for shore and you don't know how to swim, you would be foolish to worry and fret during the nine months. A wise woman would learn to swim! Childbirth is a strenuous physical event that takes definite preparation, not only mentally but physically as well. Parenting is a tough job that also requires physical and spiritual preparation. Use your time wisely by researching the various options available to you, reading, sharing with other mothers, and praying.

Physically prepare your body by eating well. Tom Brewer, M.D., coauthor of *What Every Pregnant Woman Should Know,* recommends that you eat 80–100 grams of protein a day, obtained from healthy sources such as milk, eggs, cheese, meat, and whole grains. You should also eat at least two servings a day of dark green, leafy vegetables, as well as yellow and orange-colored fruits and vegetables and sources of vitamin C. Salt your food to taste and drink a half gallon *or more* of water each day. Get your carbohydrates from healthy whole grains instead of nutrient-robbed white flours. Your baby cannot obtain nutrients that are not first in your own body. Your body cannot grow a healthy child if it is struggling first to keep you well!

You also need to prepare your body by exercising. Take a daily walk in some fresh air. Learn how to do exercises that will prepare your muscles for the process of childbirth, such as pelvic

Realizing That Children Are a Blessing

rocks, squatting, tailor sitting, and Kegel exercises. Learn how to relax your muscles voluntarily so that during labor your uterus (a muscular organ) can work unhindered.

Prepare mentally by learning all you can about the process of childbirth. Carefully choose the books you read and classes you attend. Is the author or instructor concerned about your health or about maintaining hospital policy? Learn about the history of childbirth so you clearly understand the issues. Find a health-care provider who will support the choices you make.

Just as necessary, use the nine months of pregnancy to prepare emotionally and spiritually. Begin to gather around you a group of supportive people who will help you during the busy days ahead. Can people in your church watch your other children, prepare some meals for you, or do your grocery shopping after the new baby arrives? Maybe you should begin saving money for a short-term housekeeper or for a doula, also called a labor assistant, who can support you and your husband at the hospital during labor (see resources for more information).

Begin to memorize verses of Scripture that will help calm you when moments of anxiety arise during your pregnancy and especially during labor. For instance, "You will keep him in perfect peace, whose mind is stayed on You, because he trusts in You" (Isa. 26:3).

Pray often during your pregnancy. Ask the Lord to help you in your role as a mother. Pray for your husband, for your other children, for your marriage, for unity in your decisions, for love for your little one. Pray that your new baby will be a blessing to everyone and that you will have wisdom in caring for him or her. Pray for your health-care providers. Pray for courage to make difficult decisions. Pray for health and safety.

One of my high school teachers told us that she prayed during her entire pregnancy that she wouldn't use bad language if the pain of labor became too great! She was concerned that her testimony for the Lord not be compromised in that way. I have heard many other stories about nurses asking women how they were able to remain calm and sweet at a time when many mothers scream and strike out in anger. Imagine the joy of being able to share Christ with someone as you welcome a new child into your family!

Many other preparations must be made, so use your time wisely. Consider the resources at the end of this chapter for further suggestions.

IN SUMMARY

Many controversies arise when it comes to pregnancy, labor, and infant care. You need to research the various issues, pray about each decision, and use godly wisdom. Remember that each baby is an individual with a unique personality. Therefore, don't compare your new baby with the children at your church or in your neighborhood or with your previous children (2 Cor. 10:12). Also, be careful about judging other parents and condemning their parenting decisions. Even if you are sure you are right, you will never be able to help others if your attitude is unloving or unkind.

However, as you prepare for the rest of your parenting years, remember that the decisions you make now will affect the remainder of your children's lives. Don't set habits that must be broken later. It is always easier to parent with an eye on the future than to continuously try to correct habits that have been formed. Use your early parenting years to grow in wisdom and knowledge.

EXTRA CREDIT ASSIGNMENT

Memorize this passage of Scripture by learning one verse at a time; then recite the passage to a minimum of five women.

> "For You formed my inward parts; You covered me in my mother's womb. I will praise You, for I am fearfully and wonderfully made; marvelous are Your works, and that my soul knows very well. My frame was not hidden from You, when I was made in secret, and skillfully wrought in the lowest parts of the earth. Your eyes saw my substance, being yet unformed. And in Your book they all were written, the days fashioned for me, when as yet there were none of them. How precious also are Your thoughts to me, O God! How great is the sum of them!" (Psalm 139:13–17).

STUDY GUIDE

1. Read John 1:3. In an age of technology and medical knowledge, how can the truths of this verse keep our perspective correct?
2. According to Psalm 127:1, what actions show we are not trusting God?
3. According to Proverbs 3:24–26, why should we not be afraid?
4. How could Romans 8:28 comfort a pregnant woman, a mother who has lost her child, or a tired new mom?
5. After reading Philippians 4:6 and 7, list some practical ways to overcome anxiety in our lives.

GROUP PROJECT

Discuss how you could begin an encouragement ministry to pregnant women, new mothers, and women struggling with infertility. List some practical ways to help them. How will your plan of action be different if you are ministering to unsaved moms as well as women in your church? Plan how to help someone this week!

EXTRA READING

✔ Augustson, Sharon, Diane Dirks, Anne Marie Ezzo, Carol Gurrola, Pam Harer, Kathy Hoefke, and Sharon Nelson. *Birth by Design: The Expectant Parent's Handbook*. Simi Valley, CA: Growing Families International, 1999. A training manual for Christian childbirth educators that covers many topics relating to pregnancy, childbirth, and postpartum. I especially appreciate this manual's emphasis on Scripture and the benefits of "renewing your mind" with God's Word during pregnancy and childbirth. Order at 1-800-474-6264 or www.gfi.org.

✔ Bradley, Robert A. *Husband-Coached Childbirth*. Rev. ed. New York: Bantam Books, 1996. I heartily recommend this book.

✔ Brewer, Gail Sforza with Tom Brewer. *What Every Pregnant Woman Should Know: The Truth about Diet and Drugs in Pregnancy*. Rev. ed. New York: Viking Penguin Inc., 1985. Helpful advice for women who want the best possible nutritional start for their pregnancy and their unborn child. This book has my highest recommendation!

✔ The Center for Biblical Bioethics, a ministry division of Baptists for Life, offers free consultation services about bioethical situations that individuals may face, as well as a helpful Web site (www.bfl.org/cbb/index.htm) and a catalog of resources designed to help you make tough decisions. Write to the Center for Biblical Bioethics at P.O. Box 3158, Grand Rapids, MI 49501 or call 1-616-257-6800.

✔ Ezzo, Gary, and Anne Marie Ezzo. *Let the Children Come Along the Infant Way*. Louisiana, MO: Growing Families International, 2002. One of the most controversial books I recommend. Yet I argue that the authors' views on infant care deserve careful review by all Christian parents. Order the book and accompanying audiotapes at 1-800-474-6264 or www.gfi.org.

✔ Klaus, Marshall H., John H. Kennell, and Phyllis H. Klaus. *Mothering the Mother: How a Doula Can Help You Have a*

Realizing That Children Are a Blessing

Shorter, Easier, and Healthier Birth. New York: Addison-Wesley Publishing Co., 1993. According to the authors' research, the presence of a doula shortens labor by an average of two hours, decreases cesarean sections by over 50 percent, decreases the need for pain medication, helps fathers participate, and more.

✔ McCutcheon, Susan. *Natural Childbirth the Bradley Way*. Rev. ed. New York: Penguin Books, 1996. I heartily recommend this classic on preparing for childbirth.

✔ Parker, Shonda. *The Naturally Healthy Pregnancy*. Sisters, OR: Loyal Publishing, 1998. An in-depth nutritional guide for women's health, especially during the childbearing years. I love how Parker gives advice for naturally calming many of the common symptoms that women experience during pregnancy.

✔ Pride, Mary. *All the Way Home: Power for Your Family to Be Its Best*. Wheaton, IL: Crossway Books, 1989. Pride delves into the matter of family planning and other key issues. While she takes a stronger stand against conception control than many Christians, her viewpoint will help you think through these issues and determine what God's Word says.

✔ Sears, William, and Martha Sears. *The Birth Book*. New York: Little, Brown and Company, 1994. While I do not personally agree with Dr. Sears on many of his parenting views, this book is well researched, simple to understand, and full of helpful advice.

✔ Weschler, Toni. *Taking Charge of Your Fertility*. New York: HarperCollins Publishers, Perennial, 1995. An excellent resource for those who wish to be wise as they plan their families yet desire to use a reliable natural family-planning method.

NOTES

1. Excerpt from "Great Is Thy Faithfulness" by Thomas Chisholm (Carol Stream, IL: Hope Publishing Co., © renewal 1951).

2. Excerpt from "To God Be the Glory" by Fanny Crosby.

3. Sharon Augustson et al., *Birth by Design: The Expectant Parent's Handbook, 2d ed.* (Simi Valley, CA: Growing Families International, 1999), 173.

4. Ibid., 177.

CHAPTER *12* TWELVE

Loving and Teaching Your Children

POINT TO PONDER
*"I have no greater joy than to hear that
my children walk in truth"
(3 John 4).*

When God designed women and planned our roles in the world, He must have smiled as He thought of all the fun we would have. Yes, He knew being a woman would be hard work at times, yet in His sovereignty He designed our hearts to "tick" best when fulfilling God's plans for us.

This statement is never truer than in the area of motherhood. God's will for you as a mother is for you to love your job! How can I say this so confidently? Because God's Word teaches us so!

Loving Our Children

Young women are admonished to "love their children," and older women in the church are to teach us how to love them (Titus 2:4). In this case, the word "love" in the original Greek language means "to be very fond of and to have great delight in."

Learning to love and delight in your children may take practice, but the effort will give you joy and fulfillment.

The times for you to love your children are numerous. You can show love to a tiny infant by cuddling, singing, rubbing his back, and rocking him. A toddler needs your love when she repeatedly falls and scrapes her knee. You can show a talkative kindergartener love by lending a listening ear. You can show love to a struggling eight-year-old by looking in his eyes and reassuring him of your confidence in his abilities. All the way through the teen years (and beyond!), the children of our culture are desperately crying out for love from their parents.

During the different seasons of life, the ebb and flow of days and nights, in times of sickness and discouragement as well as triumph, the most important job God has given you as a mother is to love your children. Love takes work. It takes effort and selflessness to love a crabby child . . . or an infant who constantly needs your care . . . or a pair of siblings who can't seem to get along. Some days the job won't be easy, so stay close to those older and wiser women in your church. Learn from their mistakes and seek their prayer support (more on this topic in part 5).

Begin to plan concrete ways you can show your love to your children. The possibilities are limited only by your creativity. A half hour of Play-Doh has the potential to communicate more love than words ever could. Maybe you could plan a special "Mommy Time" with each child at least once a week. During this time you could make paper dolls, go to the park, have an ice cream treat, take a nature walk, splash in puddles, pet animals at a farm, shop for a new toy, or visit a shut-in from your church. At home, with your children gathered around you, try out a new cookie recipe, plan a scavenger hunt, play miniature golf with straws and marshmallows, work a puzzle together, pick wildflowers, read a psalm together (or set it to music), play hide-and-seek, make a tent with blankets over the kitchen table, or make matching T-shirts with fabric paint.

Be generous with praise and enthusiasm. Commit to encour-

Loving and Teaching Your Children 165

aging your kids twice as often as you scold them. If you aren't sure you praise them enough, ask your husband. He'll know!

Shower your children with plenty of physical love as well. Because of our corrupt society, workers at schools, churches, and clubs are warned not to touch children, except maybe to pat their heads or shoulders. Make up for our sinful culture by cuddling with your kids on a Saturday morning, holding them on your lap, spreading on lots of hugs and kisses, roughhousing with them, and linking arms often. Never let a day go by without verbalizing your love and a S.W.A.K (Sealed With A Kiss)!

Why does God want us to love our children so much? Because God's view of our children is different from the world's view. In the Gospels we read how Jesus welcomed the children into His company, rebuking His disciples when they attempted to turn the children away (Matt. 19:13–15). When His disciples argued about who was the greatest in God's kingdom, Jesus responded:

> "If anyone desires to be first, he shall be last of all and servant of all." Then He took a little child and set him in the midst of them. And when He had taken him in His arms, He said to them, "Whoever receives one of these little children in My name receives Me; and whoever receives Me, receives not Me but Him who sent Me" (Mark 9:35–37).

God's Word teaches that children are to hold a special place in our hearts. They are small for only a short time. Use these fleeting years carefully! Love your children—not just when they're young but throughout their lives.

Teaching Our Children

Scripture also admonishes women to be teachers to their children. The book of Proverbs holds much advice for parents and gives all of us mothers insights on to how to do our job.

1. Scripture implies that both the father and the mother should give instruction and "laws" to their children. "My son, hear the instruction of your father, and do not forsake the law of your mother; for they will be a graceful ornament on your head, and chains about your neck" (Prov. 1:8, 9).

2. A mother who doesn't teach her children to fear the Lord will have many sorrows. A fool is someone who does not acknowledge God in his life (Ps. 14:1; 53:1). "A wise son makes a glad father, but a foolish son is the grief of his mother" (Prov. 10:1). "A wise son makes a father glad, but a foolish man despises his mother" (Prov. 15:20).

3. A mother who has taught her child to be wise will have great joy. "The father of the righteous will greatly rejoice, and he who begets a wise child will delight in him. Let your father and your mother be glad, and let her who bore you rejoice" (Prov. 23:24, 25).

4. Teaching children takes effort, commitment, and direct involvement in their lives. "The rod and rebuke give wisdom, but a child left to himself brings shame to his mother" (Prov. 29:15).

Our first responsibility is to train our children to obey. As Samuel said to Saul, "To obey is better than sacrifice" (1 Sam. 15:22). Try this instructive study: Using a concordance, look up each use of the word "obey" in the Bible. You will quickly see the high level of importance that God places on obedience.

In fact, if you simply train your child to obey, most other things will fall into place. Train your baby to obey you when you say, "No throwing peas!" Then she will be ready to obey you when you say, "Do not touch the glass dish" or "Do not run into the street."

A mother named Elizabeth offered these basic rules for moms on her Web site: "(1) Be reasonable and fair in your requests. (2) Say what you mean, and mean what you say. [In my opinion, this suggestion is the most important one to remember!] (3) Be vigilant. [Elizabeth suggests keeping your little ones with you, a proactive way to head off problems before they even start.] (4) Be just in your discipline. (5) An immediate, negative consequence is usually best because it is easily understood and free from psychological repercussions. [No nagging or threatening required.] (6) Be merciful in overlooking genuine accidents, as well as when you observe genuine repentance.] (7) Be consistent. (8) Be loving always and especially so when your child is behaving well."[1]

It is of utmost importance that you teach your children about God. I have mentioned often how children learn best by our example. Yet I also realize I will never be a perfect mother. I have many areas that need work! But this weakness does not excuse me from actively teaching my children *now*. I can't wait until my own life is perfect. I have found that it's helpful to plan multiple times each *day* for teaching my children about the Lord.

Howard Bixby presented six "Projects for Profit and Pleasure"[2] in a seminar I attended. I'm listing all six, with his permission, and adding my comments.

1. Keep a family devotions calendar. As a family, develop a month's schedule of activities and/or topics to cover in family devotions.

The resource section at the end of this chapter lists books that will give you ideas to help you get started. The best learning, however, will probably come when you teach your children what God has been teaching *you* in your own private devotional time. Nevertheless, set aside an hour or so to plan ahead for the coming month. This discipline alone will help you be consistent!

2. Use a "We Ask, God Answers" notebook. Purchase a loose-leaf notebook and paper; make columns on each page. Allow your family to write down specific prayer requests and God's answers when they come.

Pam Forster, author of *For Instruction in Righteousness* and other helpful parenting books, suggests making "memorials" for your family as well. She asked,

> Has God delivered members of your family from death? Celebrate that event each year. We annually remember the day of our Benjamin's appendectomy, when we discovered that our little 2½ year-old toddler had miraculously survived for over a week with an undiagnosed ruptured appendix. We talk about God's guidance, our church family's prayers and support, the miraculous way that God caused his body to seal off the infection from the rest of his body. It is a reminder to our entire family that God is our faithful protector; we can trust in Him.[3]

Forster recommends using baby books, journals, picture albums, or at least a box of photos to review occasionally.

3. Design a missionary prayer bulletin board. Collect and display missionary prayer cards, artifacts, and photos to encourage your children to pray for missionaries.

My grandparents had a large bulletin board hanging on their kitchen wall. When we visited them, my grandfather gathered all of us at 10:00 A.M. each day to read the Bible and pray for each of the missionaries displayed on the wall. I wonder what great deeds God performed through the lives of His servants because of the faithful, daily prayers of my grandparents! I do know that this consistent example planted a love for missionaries in my own heart, and I intend to do the same for my children.

4. Develop a church prayer card file. Cut prayer and praise items from your church's weekly bulletin or prayer prompter. Glue them onto 3" x 5" cards. Choose an item to pray for at each mealtime.

Recently a godly older woman from our church passed away. At her funeral the pastor shared how she had prayed *daily* for every member of our church. He asked who would take her place now that she had gone on to Heaven. What a ministry for you and your kids!

Loving and Teaching Your Children

5. Create a file of Bible story recordings. Purchase (or make) cassette tapes or CDs of stories for use in your family devotions. On busy days we play a tape for the kids at bedtime, after the lights have been turned out. See the list of resources at the end of this chapter for suggestions.

6. Play Bible application games. You might try "Bible Story Charades." Take turns pantomiming a favorite Bible story or Bible character. The rest of the family gets three guesses. Another good game is "Bible Memory Concentration." Choose eight Bible verses and references that everyone has memorized. Write the verses on eight square cards. Write the eight references on eight more square cards. Number the opposite sides of cards from 1 to 16 in random order, and place the cards in a grid as in the example below. Take turns matching verses and references.

1	2	3	4
5	6	7	8
9	10	11	12
13	14	15	16

As a parent, you also have the responsibility of teaching your children about the world we live in. John Holzmann, publisher of Sonlight Curriculum, stated,

> In the supportive environment of their parents' home, with their parents' help, children should be made aware

> of false beliefs and foolish ideas. They should be made
> aware of these ideas and then carefully instructed about
> why the ideas are false, foolish, or wrong. Moreover, they
> should be taught how to respond to false and foolish ideas.[4]

When your children are very young, you do much of the thinking for them, choosing to mold their behavior to beliefs you know are right according to the Bible. The priority is teaching them to obey. However, as your sons and daughters mature, do not neglect teaching them *why* they must obey you! Allow them to question you, in a respectful manner, and to discover your heart for God. You need to be their coach, allowing them to think for themselves in the shelter of your home, teaching them to bring every idea and philosophy into subjection to God's Word. It is vitally important that they learn to think *before* they leave home!

My own parents had many short nights, giving up some sleep and choosing instead to spend time with me, answering my tough questions about life. Their best contribution was a listening ear, allowing me some time on my "soap box," then showing me how to find the answers myself in the Bible. My parents taught me how to use Bible reference tools to find answers. They took me along with them as they visited in the homes of unbelievers—members of cults and atheists, as well as sincere seekers of the Lord. They allowed me to sit around the dining room table and participate in discussions with visiting pastors, missionaries, and evangelists. As the conversations strayed into matters of theological debate, God's Word became real to me and applicable to every area of my life. What a heritage!

You must also pass this heritage on to your children. In most homes the mother spends more time with the children and is their primary caregiver. For that reason, moms must accept the responsibility of "teacher" to their children. Many families homeschool so they will have even more hours to spend teach-

Loving and Teaching Your Children   **171**

ing and instructing their kids. Whether you choose this route for yourself or not, make the training of your children *your* responsibility—not the church's, the school's, or the government's.

God has entrusted your children into your care. What a joy and privilege to watch as your child's foolishness is gradually exchanged for wisdom! Teaching your children *can be* enjoyable!

IN SUMMARY

If teaching your kids sounds like a cruel form of torture, if you believe spending too much time with a toddler is equivalent to getting a bad case of the hives, then there is hope for you! First of all, begin to see your children as God sees them. Ask God to help you learn to love them! He will answer your prayer in a multitude of miraculous ways if you ask with a sincere desire to change.

Then continue reading into part 4, where we will discuss how to make your home a place of joy and contentment—where you, your husband, and your children will be glad to spend time together!

EXTRA CREDIT ASSIGNMENT

Memorize this passage of Scripture by learning one verse at a time; then recite the passage to a minimum of five women.

> "How can a young man cleanse his way? By taking heed according to Your word. With my whole heart I have sought You; oh, let me not wander from Your commandments! Your word I have hidden in my heart, that I might not sin against You" (Psalm 119:9–11).

JUGGLING LIFE'S RESPONSIBILITIES

STUDY GUIDE

1. In Matthew 19:13–15 the disciples had a different opinion of children than Jesus did. Why do you think the disciples felt this way? Have you ever observed a similar situation?
2. Read and think about Mark 9:36 and 37. How can we show we have received God in our lives? What are some practical ways to do this?
3. According to Proverbs 1:8 and 9, what benefits come to our children when we teach them to obey?
4. According to Psalm 14:1 and 53:1, what is the Biblical definition of a fool? How are some fools taught by example?
5. According to Proverbs 29:15, how does a child become wise? Whose responsibility is this?
6. Read the story of Moses and his mother in Exodus 1:1—2:10. What are some specific things Moses' mother must have had to teach him before she weaned him? How does this example show us the importance of training our children while they are still very young?

GROUP PROJECT

Choose and make one of the six projects listed in this chapter that will help you teach your children about God. You may decide to break into small groups, each group doing a different project. Strategize together on how you will implement this teaching tool in your individual home situations.

EXTRA READING

✔ The Children's Bible Hour is a good resource for Bible story tapes and CDs, Christian music recordings, and a daily devotional for children called *Keys for Kids*. Order online at www .cbhministries.org or call 1-888-224-2324.
✔ Fawcett, Cheryl, and Robert C. Newman. *Kids' Questions about God and Jesus*. Schaumburg, IL: Regular Baptist Press,

Loving and Teaching Your Children   **173**

2003 (formerly published as part of *I Have a Question about God*). Three other books are in this series of devotional books for children ages 4–10: *Kids' Questions about the Bible and Creation; Kids' Questions about Sin and Salvation;* and *Kids' Questions about Church and the Future.* Order at www.rbp store.org or 1-800-727-4440.

✔ Forster, Pam. *For Instruction in Righteousness.* Rev. ed. Gaston, OR: Doorposts, 1995. This resource is just one of many I highly recommend for every family! Doorposts also sells great charts that you can hang on your wall to remind you of how God wants parents to act. The chart "If . . . Then" is a visual reminder that "If you lie, then you will pay this consequence," etc. It is extremely helpful for parents who are trying to be consistently just in their discipline! Order a catalog at 1-888-433-4749 or www.doorposts.net.

✔ Hadidian, Allen, Connie Hadidian, Will Wilson, and Lindy Wilson. *Creative Family Times.* Chicago: Moody Press, 1989. This little book is short on theory and long on ideas for building character in your preschoolers.

✔ Martin, Gail. *What Every Child Should Know along the Way: Teaching Practical Life Skills in Every Stage of Life.* Mt Pleasant, SC: Parent-Wise Solutions, Inc., 1988. This helpful book includes advice on family devotions, family unity, character development, personal safety, and using our God-given talents.

✔ Ortlund, Anne. *Children Are Wet Cement.* Grand Rapids: Baker Book House, Fleming H. Revell, 1981. My favorite author shares practical advice for imparting Biblical truth to children while they are still open to receiving it.

✔ Schoolland, Marian M. *Leading Little Ones to God: A Child's Book of Bible Teachings.* Rev. ed. Grand Rapids: Wm. B. Eerdmans Publishing Co., 1981. A great devotional book for children who are kindergartners or older.

174 JUGGLING LIFE'S RESPONSIBILITIES

✔ Stormer, John A. *Growing Up God's Way*. Florissant, MO: Liberty Bell Press, 1984. A step-by-step guide for getting children ready for school and life from birth on.

✔ Taylor, Kenneth N. *The New Bible in Pictures for Little Eyes*. Rev. ed. Chicago: Moody Press, 2002. An excellent Bible story book for your little ones.

NOTES

1. For more practical ideas on teaching your children to obey, visit www.atriptothewoodshed.com.

2. Howard Bixby, "Family Devotions: Projects for Profit and Pleasure" (lecture, Baptist Bible College, Clarks Summit, PA, n.d.).

3. Pam Forster, *For Instruction in Righteousness*, rev. ed. (Gaston, OR: Doorposts, 1995), 11.

4. John Holzmann, "Questions and Answers" (Littleton, CO: Sonlight Curriculum, 2000–2001 catalog), 104.

PART *4* FOUR

Your Home

POINT TO PONDER
"And whatever you do in word or deed, do all
in the name of the Lord Jesus, giving thanks to
God the Father through Him"
(Colossians 3:17).

I will never forget the day I discovered that making my home pretty was part of the will of God for my life! With the dishes stacked high in the sink and on every available kitchen surface, with unfolded laundry piled on the living room floor, with toys scattered upstairs and down, and with overdue bills waiting to be paid, I turned in desperation to the Word of God. I searched for every Scripture passage that spoke about a wife's responsibilities, and I made a list that covered the front and back of a piece of notebook paper.

What I read made me tremble! I realized all my dreams for my life hinged upon my success as a homemaker, for my very reputation was at stake. I determined to make a change, and, grabbing a piece of tape, I hung my list on the kitchen cabinet over the sink. I plunged into the dishes and attacked stuck-on grime as I read the verses I had written. Halfway through, I turned the sheet over and read the other side of my list. Later, as my kitchen shone with cleanliness, I realized that not only was my reputation at stake, my joy and happiness were as well. My great discovery was that

> Every wise woman builds her house, but the foolish pulls it down with her hands (Prov. 14:1).

Evidently I'm not the only woman who has made this discovery. As I browse through a popular Christian bookseller's catalog, I see scores of resources designed to bring women to the realization that a skillful housewife is a needed commodity. Christian women worldwide are heeding the call of Titus 2:3–5 and training the younger women around them to be "homemakers." A lucrative business awaits those who are savvy enough to take heed to this trend and add training materials, tools, and seminars to the market. Curriculum series help mothers train their daughters in the skills of keeping a home. Obviously many talented women excel in homemaking!

I'm not one of them, but I have a strong desire to become one. The Bible teaches that "an excellent wife is the crown of her husband" (Prov. 12:4). That idea appeals to me! Scripture also very clearly teaches that keeping a home is primarily the responsibility of the wife (1 Tim. 5:14; Titus 2:3–5).

God has been gracious enough to outline some of the duties of an excellent wife in the well-known poetry of Proverbs 31. If you, like me, desire improvement in this area, maybe you should read this portion of Scripture, then grab a piece of notebook paper and some tape and display your own list of qualities that you'd like to see in your life. You will find that this list is immensely practical, for an excellent wife is . . . a hard worker . . . enterprising . . . diligent . . . wise with her money . . . conscious of the future . . . skillful in her home . . . kind and hospitable . . . attentive to her appearance.

You could probably add many more things to the list. Here, in part 4, let's discuss three main areas of household management that are addressed in Scripture: our finances, managing our homes, and creating a peaceful atmosphere in our homes.

If God can change my heart, what can He do in yours?

CHAPTER *13* THIRTEEN

Being a Faithful Steward

POINT TO PONDER

"Trust in Him at all times, you people; pour out your heart before Him; God is a refuge for us"
(Psalm 62:8).

If your husband has delegated to you the day-to-day financial operations in your home, a basic understanding of wise money management is crucial. But even if he handles most of the paperwork, you undoubtedly have many opportunities to *spend* money. Some day you may be on your own as a widow, and you'll need to know how to make your money last.

Does God really care about your money? Oh yes! Sixteen of Jesus' thirty-eight parables mention the important subject of money. But God is also concerned with your heart. Jesus said, "For where your treasure is, there your heart will be also" (Luke 12:34). If I could peek into your checkbook today and glance at your spending habits for the last six months, I would immediately know where your heart is.

Learning to handle money wisely can be boiled down to a handful of principles. As you master these principles, you will begin to see the results in a more peaceful home. Like many

177

178 JUGGLING LIFE'S RESPONSIBILITIES

families, my husband and I have made some financial mistakes. The pressures that money puts on you can make you feel like all the air has been squeezed out of your lungs. But when you begin to follow God's principles for money, that huge burden is lifted.

What Is the Source of Your Income?

Anne Ortlund shared this thought in one of her books: "The source of your money is never your job." I remember the day I highlighted that phrase in her book. I shut the book and then closed my eyes. I thought about what a strange concept that is in our world! Then I opened the book and continued to read.

> The source of your money is never your job. If it were and you lost your job, you might have a nervous collapse. No, the source of your money is God. He owns it all; he distributes it as he pleases; and he has promised over and over to take care of the physical needs of every one of his children. . . . God is always our source! Now, from tending the Garden of Eden on, people have always been given important, meaningful things to do in life. These things are his will for us, and they may or may not cover our physical needs in reimbursement. Never mind. We're still to do them with all our hearts. Even Jesus said, "My food is to do the will of Him Who sent Me" (John 4:34)—and his own needs in turn were met.[1]

Think about how freeing this concept is! God is the source of your income. Period. After all, He owns it all. "The earth is the LORD's, and all its fullness, the world and those who dwell therein" (Ps. 24:1).

As the nation of Israel gave toward the building of God's house, King David proclaimed:

> Yours, O LORD, is the greatness, the power and the glory, the victory and the majesty; for all that is in heaven and in earth is Yours; Yours is the kingdom, O LORD, and You are exalted as head over all. Both riches and honor come from You, and You reign over all. In Your hand is power

Being a Faithful Steward

> and might; in Your hand it is to make great and to give strength to all (1 Chron. 29:11, 12).

One day at our house when we were low on cash and didn't have enough milk for breakfast, our son asked the Lord for a cow! I laughed out loud, but then I remembered that God has said, "For every beast of the forest is Mine, and the cattle on a thousand hills" (Ps. 50:10).

Down through history, great saints of God have acknowledged God's ownership of everything and have gone to Him in faith, asking Him to provide for their needs. Indeed, God not only owns all things, but He has direct control of them as well. He is able, therefore, to bless us and care for us.

As God meets our needs, He makes us His stewards—managers—of the resources He has given us. "Moreover it is required in stewards that one be found faithful" (1 Cor. 4:2). Faithfulness is the basic requirement for using God's money. Being faithful means we need to be steadfast, reliable, and loyal. Also, we must not worry about where tomorrow's money will come from. That is up to our Master. Our responsibility is to oversee the careful use of the resources already entrusted to us.

Remember that God has given us stewardship of other resources as well. We are to be faithful in using our time, for it belongs to God. Our possessions are not ours but His, and we must use them for His glory. Our health is given to us by God, and we should wisely guard it so we can be most effective for Him. Our children belong to God; they have been placed into our families for us to guide, teach, and love. Most importantly, the good news of Jesus Christ is a message that has been placed in our hands. In each area we can either ignore God and live for self, or we can go to the other extreme of fretting and worrying.

Our spending habits also affect each of these responsibilities. We use money to purchase possessions. Our health can be enhanced by the wise use of money (and by not worrying about money!). Caring for our children requires money. Even our use of time may determine how we spend our money (e.g., taking time to fix a meal at home instead of eating out). Money is also sometimes needed to share the gospel with others.

I would like to remind you of an important Biblical principle. The love of *anything* else but Jesus Christ leads to evil, greed, and sorrow. Our attitude makes all the difference.

> For the *love* of money is a root of all kinds of evil, for which some have strayed from the faith in their greediness, and pierced themselves through with many sorrows (1 Tim. 6:10, emphasis added).

> Now godliness with contentment is great gain. For we brought nothing into this world, and it is certain we can carry nothing out. And having food and clothing, with these we shall be content (1 Tim. 6:6–8).

When we see God as the source of all we are and have, we can be content with everything He has given us. It is not our duty to worry about *where* the money comes from, for all of it comes from His hand. It is our duty only to be content with what He has given us—and to use it faithfully!

We can stop trying to juggle everything ourselves. Rather, we become content to hand the responsibilities to God. We allow Him to handle things for us.

Contentment frees us to concentrate on our purpose of glorifying God in each area of our lives. Contentment allows us to keep God as our first priority, freeing us to concentrate on Him instead of our circumstances. Our second and third priorities, caring for our husbands and children, will be easier, since we will be focusing on pleasing God in each aspect of these relationships.

Should a Wife Work?

Thinking about our priorities brings up a controversial question, one that doesn't have an easy answer: Should a wife work?

Being a Faithful Steward 181

This issue is one that each husband and wife should answer after much prayer and consideration. Let me share some conclusions my husband and I have reached for *our* family.

I have found that I am unable to love God, my husband, and my children the way I should while working outside my home. Fatigue alone makes it impossible to accomplish all the tasks that are necessary if I'm going to treat my family right. I tend to shove my devotions aside as other concerns crowd my schedule. When I'm tired, I find it is tough to be submissive and loving to my husband the way I should. Since the hours I have to spend with my children are limited, I cannot oversee their training. The only option is to delegate their care to others.

While some women may be more capable managers than I am, many financial experts have questioned whether having two incomes helps a family in any measurable way. The Microsoft Network placed an article on its home page that discussed whether second incomes cost more than they produce. By the time job-related expenses are figured in, many women are working with no financial gains. These expenses include taxes, which because of a higher tax bracket can consume almost half of a second salary, commuting, and child care.

Child care, according to the MSN article, "can easily wipe out whatever's left of a second income after taxes. Sue Sharp, a singer and voice teacher who has two children, says she gave up teaching when she realized she was 'working just to pay for day care. It just was not worth it.' "[2]

I checked the cost of child care in my small town, and I found Sharp's statement is generally true, even though most things are less expensive here than in bigger cities.

Two-income couples also need to allow for commuting costs: "Figure on about 30 cents a mile if you drive (to cover fuel, maintenance and wear and tear)."[3]

Calculate the cost of lunches for everyone, as well as dinner out on the busy days when you are too tired to prepare it yourself. Many jobs for women require expensive business clothing as well as dry cleaning, and possibly hiring someone to do your laundry, since you'll be busy. You may also need a maid to clean your home.

Finally, the excessive busyness of your life may tempt you to overspend in many ways. You may also find yourself buying little (and big) presents for your children, hoping to give them as many material comforts as you can in exchange for the lack of time you can spend with them.

I could cite many reasons why moms should be home with their children, especially when they are young. When your children are older, remember that simply staying home to manage your home will free you to minister to your husband and to others in a multitude of wonderful ways. In fact, the MSN article stated that a wife's decision to stay at home can give "her husband's career a boost because he's now free to work longer and not worry about home matters that she can attend to. This is no mere rationale; there is evidence that executives with stay-at-home wives on average earn more than their colleagues in two-career households."[4]

Remember your God-given role of being a helper to your husband? *He* is an excellent reason to stay home!

Many women have chosen to begin home-based businesses to relieve the financial strains of their lives while still being able to stay at home with their families. I have been able to choose this route as well. For five years I taught piano lessons in my living room on an almost full-time basis. Without this income, staying home with my toddlers would have been more difficult.

However, I want to warn you that working at home will not solve all your problems. Many expenses that apply to out-of-the-home workers will also apply to you. Expenses for your home business will eat up a substantial amount of your income. Taxes

Being a Faithful Steward

183

are even higher for a self-employed individual, and you must be disciplined enough to deduct them on your own. If you or your children are ill and you are unable to work, you will lose a large chunk of income. You may not have health insurance or other benefits of a full-time job. Finally, you may find you are exhausted most of the time, and you may begin to rely on take-out and convenience foods, which are expensive. I was nervous about quitting my at-home job, but afterward I found *only a slight difference* in our ability to pay the bills!

I am firmly convinced that, for me, contentment was the number one factor that determined if I needed to work. Contentment allowed me to enjoy my children enough to want to be their primary caregiver. Contentment made me happy with my cooking skills and eager to improve them. Contentment provided peace when my friends had professionally manicured nails, expensive cars, and bigger homes. Contentment continues to give me joy when I open the window blinds in the morning and remember that today I can *stay home*!

We have chosen to keep me home, and I have discovered that great fulfillment comes in being an available helper to my husband, a ready teacher to my children, and an able minister to those in my church with needs. No career has ever provided such benefits!

Learning to live on your husband's salary will require two things: determination and discipline. You will need determination as you begin mapping out a plan of action to make one-income living possible. You may not be able to make the switch overnight. Many months of planning and careful oversight may be needed. After you have come home to stay, determination will be needed to control excess spending. You may also need determination as your children get accustomed to having you around more! You might get on each other's nerves! Determination, with a generous helping of love, is essential.

What Are Your Options for Using Money?

Discipline is the other requirement. Keep in mind, though, that discipline is needed for *every* family that wants to manage its finances responsibly. Remember that the first concern of a steward is faithfulness. You must learn to use your money wisely.

What Are Your Options for Using Money?

There are only three things you can do with your money: "share it, spend it, or save it."[5] Of those three choices, I believe sharing is the top priority. You may think my opinion is strange, since it's important to spend our money for necessities such as food and housing. However, I believe the Bible teaches that one of our primary responsibilities as Christians and as wise stewards of our money is first to share it.

The first way we can share our money is by giving a portion of it back to God. Proverbs 3:9 says, "Honor the LORD with your possessions, and with the firstfruits of all your increase."

Notice that as God gives us increase, we are to give the *first* fruits back to Him as a way to honor Him. Usually this portion was referred to as a tithe, since God commanded the nation of Israel to give a *minimum* of 10 percent of their crops, their animals, and any financial increase to God as an offering (Lev. 27:30). However, before this command was given, before the nation of Israel even existed, we see the example of Abraham offering a tithe to Melchizedek (Gen. 14:20).

Why did God require a tithe from the *first* fruits of Israel's increase? Why should we give to the Lord before spending our money in any other way? First of all, tithing demonstrates trust. You have no way of seeing into the future to be sure your needs will be met until the next paycheck. Your gift tells God you are willing to honor Him even though you can't see how it's all going to work out.

A lovely couple we know shared with us how they never used to tithe because, on paper, they just couldn't see how they could

Being a Faithful Steward   185

afford to! Numerous debts and medical bills had piled up, and they felt that paying their bills before tithing was the ethical thing to do. However, they could never seem to make ends meet.

The Holy Spirit began to convict them, through His Word, about honoring and trusting the Lord by giving to Him first. One Sunday the husband and wife were both so convicted that when the offering plate was passed, he looked at her with tears streaming down his cheeks. Her eyes were moist as well, and she nodded her assent as he took out his checkbook. That day was the first time they tithed, and they have been tithing faithfully ever since. God richly provided in numerous ways; not only are their debts paid, but their home and car are paid for as well.

I could tell you many other similar stories! I know in our own home, this principle has never been wrong.

God promised to meet the needs of His people as they surrendered in obedience to Him. "Honor the LORD with your possessions, and with the firstfruits of all your increase; so your barns will be filled with plenty, and your vats will overflow with new wine" (Prov. 3:9, 10).

God also warned Israel about disobedience.

> Will a man rob God? Yet you have robbed Me! But you say, "In what way have we robbed You?" In tithes and offerings. You are cursed with a curse, for you have robbed Me, even this whole nation. Bring all the tithes into the storehouse, that there may be food in My house, and prove Me now in this, says the LORD of hosts, If I will not open for you the windows of heaven and pour out for you such blessing that there will not be room enough to receive it (Mal. 3:8–10).

I believe God also wants us to go a step further in our trust of Him by sharing our money in other ways. For example, you may want to support your church in additional ways, perhaps with love gifts for your pastor or gifts to missionaries. A ministry in your town may need your help. The Lord may lead you to give to individuals who are hurting financially.

Share in these ways *before* you spend your money on yourself. You may think that you cannot afford to take this step, but let me remind you that a few dollars given cheerfully is worth much more to God than great wealth.

I also encourage you to read 2 Corinthians 9, where the apostle Paul reminded the Corinthian believers that God had great plans to accomplish through them as they gave freely to others. He reminded them, "He who sows sparingly will also reap sparingly, and he who sows bountifully will also reap bountifully. So let each one give as he purposes in his heart, not grudgingly or of necessity; for God loves a cheerful giver" (2 Cor. 9:6, 7).

No matter how much you give, you cannot give more than God. Paul went on to say, "And God is able to make all grace abound toward you, that you, always having all sufficiency in all things, may have an abundance for every good work" (2 Cor. 9:8).

Why does God bless us with money? So that we will have an abundance of opportunities to do good. And as we do good with the money entrusted to us, God will sufficiently meet our needs (2 Cor. 9:8). Jesus reminded His disciples, "Give, and it will be given to you: good measure, pressed down, shaken together, and running over will be put into your bosom. For with the same measure that you use, it will be measured back to you" (Luke 6:38). (This is a great verse to memorize and to teach your children. Think of the fun hand motions you could use to help learn it! Think of the lessons children can learn as they begin to share with each other.)

Now let's look at a practical plan for spending your money, ensuring that you are able to share with others. Before you spend anything, you need a plan of action, otherwise called a budget. A budget will help you evaluate your priorities for your money.

Determine, first of all, your expenses. Then prioritize your expenses according to several categories. Is it a need? "And having food and clothing, with these we shall be content" (1 Tim.

Being a Faithful Steward   **187**

6:8). Is it just a want or a desire? Use caution! "Do not love the world or the things in the world. If anyone loves the world, the love of the Father is not in him. For all that is in the world—the lust of the flesh, the lust of the eyes, and the pride of life—is not of the Father but is of the world. And the world is passing away, and the lust of it; but he who does the will of God abides forever" (1 John 2:15–17).

For instance, tithes and offerings are a *need* in our house. We tithe our income and give another percentage as various offerings. This additional figure is an amount that we prayed about and decided was appropriate for us. You may feel led of the Lord to give a different amount. The point is, this amount is not optional for us. We give it first, as soon as we receive our paycheck, before we have an opportunity to spend it on something else.

Other necessities include housing, transportation, food, clothing, health care, and education. You will need to make your own list. However, some necessities may overlap into the "wants" category. You need a place to sleep and eat (you may not need such a large or fashionable home). You need some way to get places (you may not need the latest car or several cars). You need healthy food (you may not need to eat out several times a week). You need adequate clothing (you may not need closets overflowing with designer labels).

Be a wise steward of your money, and determine to be content. Allowing yourself some wants and even desires is not wrong. The danger is in pursuing material things so much that you are trapped by their power. Do you feel that God wants you to stay home with your family? Prayerfully look at your budget and analyze your spending habits.

Making a plan is important, but working the plan in everyday living is the difficult part. Robert Mundy suggested that you ask three questions before major purchases: "Do I need it? Can I afford it? Is it the best buy?"[6]

As you carefully spend your money, keep your plan in the forefront of your mind. Two areas that are trouble spots to me are overspending with small purchases and not keeping careful records. Carrying cash is a huge temptation to me. I hardly ever buy something large on impulse, but it's harder for me to resist a quick soda at the convenience store or a fast trip to McDonald's. Therefore, I keep careful track of every penny we spend, whether it's a large purchase or fifty cents on bubble gum for my kids.

My husband and I have also found it is dangerous to use plastic money in the form of credit cards. I'd recommend that you abide by these rules if you decide to use credit cards:

1. Always pay the entire amount each month. Never carry a balance on your credit card.

2. Use a credit card only if you are absolutely certain you can repay the full amount. Few things in life are certain. "Come now, you who say, 'Today or tomorrow we will go to such and such a city, spend a year there, buy and sell, and make a profit'; whereas you do not know what will happen tomorrow. For what is your life? It is even a vapor that appears for a little time and then vanishes away. Instead you ought to say, 'If the Lord wills, we shall live and do this or that' " (James 4:13–15).

3. Never use a credit card for impulse purchases. "The plans of the diligent lead surely to plenty, but those of everyone who is hasty, surely to poverty" (Prov. 21:5).

4. Make using a credit card inconvenient. I heard one time that if you feel vulnerable to impulse buying with a credit card, place your card inside a ziplock bag. Place the bag inside another bag, fill it with water, and place it in the freezer. You will need to defrost your credit card before you can use it, which will give you time to carefully think through your purchase!

5. Keep careful records of everything you spend with your credit card. Some experts recommend subtracting each purchase in your checkbook so you won't be tempted to spend that

Being a Faithful Steward   189

money at another time during the month. This method also
ensures you will have enough money to pay the balance in full
when it is due.

Many people find that using a debit card is much simpler
than a credit card, since each purchase is automatically deducted
from your checking account immediately. If you choose this option, be sure to keep good records so that you don't overdraw
your account.

Be careful of debt in all its forms. The Bible warns that "the
rich rules over the poor, and the borrower is servant to the lend-
er" (Prov. 22:7). Getting too far into debt leads to many pitfalls. If
you are unable to repay what you have borrowed, your testimony
can be ruined. The strain of ever-increasing bills can lead to
marriage and health problems. Most importantly, debt can hamper your freedom to serve God. If God calls you to move so you
can more effectively serve Him, your debt could make it hard to
follow His leading.

The Word of God gives many instructions about money and
debt:

> No one can serve two masters; for either he will hate the
> one and love the other, or else he will be loyal to the one
> and despise the other. You cannot serve God and mammon
> [money] (Matt. 6:24).

> No one engaged in warfare entangles himself with the
> affairs of this life, that he may please him who enlisted him
> as a soldier (2 Tim. 2:4).

> Owe no one anything except to love one another, for he
> who loves another has fulfilled the law (Rom. 13:8).

> And my God shall supply all your need according to His
> riches in glory by Christ Jesus (Phil. 4:19).

What are some warning signs that you have allowed your
debt to get out of control?

1. You have borrowed to the maximum of your credit limit.

2. The amount you owe increases each month.

3. You are barely able to make the minimum monthly payments.

4. You are using a credit card for essential living expenses.

5. You are taking cash advances on your credit cards to make other credit card payments.

6. You are spending 15 percent or more of your monthly income on credit card payments.

What should you do if you find that your family's debt has mushroomed out of control? First of all, don't hide the problem from your loved ones. They may be able to help you; in addition, they can provide godly counsel and emotional support. "He who covers his sins will not prosper, but whoever confesses and forsakes them will have mercy" (Prov. 28:13).

Second, you need to face your creditors. Ignoring the problem or failing to return your creditors' calls and letters is a big mistake. Before contacting them, however, carefully analyze your situation and determine exactly how much you can afford to pay each month. As a Christian, your testimony is at stake. If you promise to pay, you are morally obligated to do so.

> When you make a vow to God, do not delay to pay it; for He has no pleasure in fools. Pay what you have vowed—better not to vow than to vow and not pay (Eccles. 5:4, 5).

> For which of you, intending to build a tower, does not sit down first and count the cost, whether he has enough to finish it—lest, after he has laid the foundation, and is not able to finish, all who see it begin to mock him, saying, "This man began to build and was not able to finish" (Luke 14:28–30).

As you figure out exactly how much you can afford to pay, contact each of your creditors in writing and explain your situation. According to Terry Austin and Bobby L. Eklund, coauthors of a financial workbook for church members,

Being a Faithful Steward

> The majority of time they will work with you if you indicate you want to be fair with all your creditors and that you are going to operate on a cash basis rather than a credit basis. In other words, you will not go further into debt.... When it comes time to make the payment[,] send in what you said you could afford—not the contract amount—and do so without fail every month thereafter until the account is paid in full.... If your situation is serious enough, get a lawyer or a licensed financial counselor to work with you. Often they can get the people involved to cancel or reduce the interest and allow you to pay off the principle only. Sometimes they can also keep your credit from being "red-flagged."[7]

You may also be able to have your monthly payment automatically withdrawn from your account each payday. This plan will help you pay your required payment before accidentally spending the money on other things.

To protect yourself against the unknowns of life, you need to carefully save a portion of your income each month. Maybe debt isn't a problem for you. Or maybe you would like to ensure that you never have to borrow for "emergencies," such as when your car inevitably breaks down or when illnesses rob you of your income.

The first purpose of saving is for emergency funds. Many financial counselors advise that you have three to six months' worth of income in a savings or money market account collecting interest. If a sudden expense arises, you can borrow from yourself (always being sure to repay it!) rather than using a credit card or borrowing from relatives. Discipline is required to squirrel away this amount of money, but emergencies are a fact of life that we need to plan for. Again, I would advise that you save a portion *first* each month before spending anything. We have a set amount transferred from our checking account to our savings account each month so we don't have to remember or worry about using it for something else.

When you have an adequate emergency fund set aside, you should begin planning for your retirement or for other major expenses, such as your children's education or paying off your mortgage. If you were to start saving for retirement at age twenty-five, any small amount you could set aside would probably be adequate. If you wait until age thirty-five, you will need to set aside 5 to 8 percent of your income each month. If you wait until you are forty-five, even 15 percent of your monthly income might not be enough! A smart goal would be to completely pay for your home by retirement. You may be able to do this by paying a small additional amount each month on your mortgage. You will save yourself hundreds of thousands of dollars in interest and assure a home for yourself in your older years.

The final way you should save is by sharing with others. Remember, your money does not really belong to you. As a wise steward of all God has given you, be sure to prepare an up-to-date will. In your final preparations, remember the work of the Lord through your church and other worthy causes.

IN SUMMARY

If money has been a source of heartache for you or you are struggling to see how you could stay at home with your family, make changing your financial priorities a top goal. "For where your treasure is, there your heart will be also" (Luke 12:34). Be especially wary of the "Ten Worst Financial Mistakes" that Robert Mundy presented in a financial seminar: "(1) Falling short in tithes and offerings. (2) Not having a budget (a budget is simply a plan for your money). (3) Not saving for emergencies. (4) Buying on credit and paying interest (with the possible exception of your house). (5) Not paying extra on mortgage. (6) Too much savings in a regular passbook account or too large a balance in checking. (7) Buying a car too expensive for your budget. (8) Little or no investment planning. (9) Cosigning a loan for a friend

Being a Faithful Steward　　　　　　　　　　　　　　193

or relative. (10) Impulse buying (don't need it, no comparison [shopping], pay too much, etc.)."[8]

God calls us to wisdom, to contentment, and to alignment of our lives with His priorities. As you begin to gain control over the area of money, you will also notice yourself becoming more disciplined in your time, health, and character. Strive to live so that every purchase you make, every dollar you share, and every plan you conceive brings glory to God. "But seek first the kingdom of God and His righteousness, and all these things shall be added to you" (Matt. 6:33).

EXTRA CREDIT ASSIGNMENT

Memorize this passage of Scripture by learning one verse at a time; then recite the passage to a minimum of five women.

> "Yours, O LORD, is the greatness, the power and the glory, the victory and the majesty; for all that is in heaven and in earth is Yours; Yours is the kingdom, O LORD, and You are exalted as head over all. Both riches and honor come from You, and You reign over all. In Your hand is power and might; in Your hand it is to make great and to give strength to all" (1 Chronicles 29:11, 12).

STUDY GUIDE

1. Read Psalm 24:1. Name some of your favorite material possessions. Remind yourself that these really belong to God, to use or to take away as He desires.
2. Read 1 Corinthians 4:2. If you hired a servant to be in charge of *your* money, what character qualities would you want this servant to have?

3. According to 1 Timothy 6:10, what is the root of evil? Is it wrong to be rich? Why or why not?
4. According to 1 Timothy 6:6–8, why should we be content? What are your only true needs? How do Americans often show they are not content, even in the areas of food and clothing?
5. According to Proverbs 3:9, how can we honor the Lord? Why is it important to do this first? Is a paycheck the only thing we should honor God with? What other things? What promise is given in verse 10?
6. After reading Proverbs 21:5, think of some times in your life when you have violated the principle in this verse. What was the result?
7. According to Luke 12:34, how does God measure where your heart is? According to Matthew 6:33, where does He want your heart? Where is *your* heart?

GROUP PROJECT

Find a local organization that could use some extra money or help right now. Help each other plan how you can share with this organization. For those whose budgets are tight, how could they help without giving money? What will be the rewards of helping in these ways?

EXTRA READING

✔ Burkett, Larry. *The Family Financial Workbook: A Practical Budgeting Guide*. Rev. ed. Chicago: Moody Press, 2000. This workbook is full of simple explanations for applying Biblical principles to your money management. I love the helpful worksheet and charts. Other books by Burkett include *Debt-Free Living: How to Get Out of Debt and Stay Out* (Moody Press, 2000) and *Women Leaving the Workplace: How to Make the Transition from Work to Home* (Moody Press, 1999).

✔ Forster, Pam. *Stewardship Street*. Gaston, OR: Doorposts,

1992. An excellent tool to teach your children about the wise use of money.

✔ Wellwood, Jackie. *The Busy Mom's Guide to Simple Living*. Wheaton, IL: Crossway Books, 1997. Written for families who are trying to simplify their lives. This book is helpful in many categories, such as health and nutrition, but I especially love the author's money-saving ideas.

✔ Yates, Cynthia. *Living Well on One Income in a Two-Income World*. Eugene, OR: Harvest House, 2003. I learned about this book when I heard the author interviewed on the radio. She believes that *everyone* can cut their expenses by at least 25 percent.

NOTES

1. Anne Ortlund, *The Gentle Ways of the Beautiful Woman: A Practical Guide to Spiritual Beauty* (reprint, 3 vols. in 1, New York: Inspirational Press, 1998), 32.

2. Dan Akst, "Second incomes: twice the work, half the return," www.moneycentral.msn.com/articles/family/wed/1440.asp?special=msn; accessed March 27, 2004.

3. Ibid.

4. Ibid.

5. Robert A. Mundy, "Personal Finance Seminar" (lecture notes, n.d.), 3.

6. Ibid., 6.

7. Terry Austin and Bobby L. Eklund, *Spiritual Preparation* (Dallas: Baptist General Convention of Texas, 1977), 35.

8. Mundy, 2.

CHAPTER *14* FOURTEEN

Wisely Building Your Home

POINT TO PONDER
"With eternity's values in view, Lord, / With eternity's values in view. / May I do each day's work for Jesus, / With eternity's values in view"
(Alfred B. Smith).[1]

When I got married, I didn't know how to manage a home. Until that point in my life, I focused my energies on pursuing a career and finishing college, so I had no motivation to learn the skills of homemaking. Then I met Kraig—and thoughts of careers and grand ambitions turned more domestic.

While I probably will never have the skills of Martha Stewart, the Lord has sent many capable people across my path to help me improve my homemaking skills. Some of these were authors who visited me in the pages of books, which I checked out of the library by the armload. My husband simply smiled at me when he caught me snuggled under a quilt in my rocking chair reading *How to Clean Practically Anything*—and forgetting to start supper! His patience has been fabulous!

Others were capable women I knew: my mother and mother-in-law, friends and sisters-in-law, grandmothers and aunts. These women have no pretend ideals about who I am; instead of nagging me to do better, they have consistently been my examples and motivators.

My closest friends and I have learned about housekeeping together. One of my friends probably fell over laughing when she learned I was going to include a chapter on homemaking in this book. After all, it was she who came over one night shortly after I married and helped me set up a filing system. I had simply begun stacking paperwork around the living room, afraid to throw anything away, yet horrified by how it was taking over the house and helpless to know what to do about it. Within half an hour she had worked miracles in my home and taught me much about organization.

Maybe you feel the same way about your home. It's a wonderful place and you'd love for it to look its best, but your skills are sadly lacking.

If you're nodding your head and loudly sighing, you need to think about *why* you want to change. Without the proper motivation, your home may sparkle for a day or a week, but soon you'll revert to your old habits. Homemaking takes discipline, which isn't fun, and discipline requires great motivation.

Motivation is based on the same priorities we've been discussing all along. Most importantly, you are aiming to bring glory to God. You also want to please your husband. You want to train your children and set a good example for them. You want to have time left over to do good for others.

If you're a list-maker like me, I suggest you grab a piece of paper and a pencil. Begin by listing the ways a clean home can bring glory to God. For me, that meant having a clean home for my husband. He is naturally neat, and I am naturally not! However, I have discovered his brain just doesn't function as efficiently when surrounded by chaos. I would probably never

Wisely Building Your Home 199

notice clutter, but he needs peaceful surroundings in order to think clearly. So one beautiful way in which I can bring glory to God is to help my husband by keeping the house neat.

You will need your own motivations. Search the Scriptures to add Biblical backup to each of your reasons. I believe God is a God of order. We have His example throughout Scripture, and we can see His handiwork in creation around us. So find out what it will take to stir yourself up, and strive to bring glory to God in your home!

When you've made your "Here's Why" list, tack it up in a prominent place. Remember my list over the kitchen sink? You have your own place where you spend a substantial amount of time. Allow your brain to begin to change by hanging your list there and looking at it often.

Just as your priorities affect your motivation, your priorities also influence how you spend your time. For me, sometimes my home is messy, not because I don't know *how* to clean, but because I have chosen to do other things. I spend my time on things I feel are important, and I suspect you do the same.

Again, know *why* you want a well-kept home, and your time will begin to match your mission.

No matter what your priorities, you need to remember that you are as much a steward of your time as you are of your money. God owns all time and has given you a portion to use wisely. "The day is Yours, the night also is Yours" (Ps. 74:16). Therefore, we must use our time to glorify God. "This is the day the LORD has made; we will rejoice and be glad in it" (Ps. 118:24). "Every day I will bless You, and I will praise Your name forever and ever" (Ps. 145:2).

Time, like wealth, is so uncertain. The great and wise king Solomon wrote the book of Ecclesiastes to show us that time is out of our control and that living to please ourselves is a futile endeavor. If you struggle with the use of your time, I suggest you study this interesting book!

God's Word reminds us that life is fleeting. "Do not boast about tomorrow, for you do not know what a day may bring forth" (Prov. 27:1). Use your time, therefore, to God's glory! "See then that you walk circumspectly, not as fools but as wise, redeeming the time, because the days are evil. Therefore do not be unwise, but understand what the will of the Lord is" (Eph. 5:15–17).

When I was a teenager, my Sunday School teacher gave me the following quote, which I posted on my bedroom wall:

> This is the beginning of a new day. God has given me this day to use as I will. I can waste it—or use it for good, but what I do today is important, because I am exchanging a day of my life for it! When tomorrow comes, this day will be gone forever, leaving in its place something that I have traded for it. I want it to be gain, and not loss; good, and not evil; success, and not failure; in order that I shall not regret the price I have paid for it.[2]

Five Secrets of the Model Wife

Competent housekeepers always include certain things in their day. As you begin to think about shaping your daily living to your most important priorities, look with me at the model wife in Proverbs 31.

1. She rises early. "Who can find a virtuous wife? For her worth is far above rubies. . . . She also rises while it is yet night, and provides food for her household, and a portion for her maid-servants" (Prov. 31:10, 15).

A wise wife knows not to waste those early morning hours by sleeping in too long. It seems to be a universal truth that those who discipline themselves to rise early in the morning usually accomplish the most. Note that our Biblical model did not waste this early morning time. Instead she prepared a good breakfast for her family and created a list of things to do.

By rising early, before other activities crowd into your schedule, you can spend some time in the kitchen making a wholesome and nourishing breakfast. I know that when I repeatedly hit the snooze button on my alarm clock, breakfast tends to be dry toast or Pop Tarts. Making good meals definitely requires more time than serving convenience foods. However, the returns are increased energy for the morning, a brightly burning metabolism that helps to burn excess calories, and steady blood-sugar levels and moods.

As well as eating properly, the smart wife thinks through each step of the coming day. I would encourage you to put your "housekeeping brain" into a central location, such as a daily planner, a clipboard, an index-card filing box, or your computer. Each morning you can access your "brain" and plan your day in a concrete way. Remember, sometimes even the best-planned days go awry, so don't feel tied to a schedule. However, you will accomplish more if you have a plan of action.

2. She carefully manages her home. "She considers a field and buys it; from her profits she plants a vineyard. . . . She watches over the ways of her household, and does not eat the bread of idleness" (Prov. 31:16, 27).

A wise wife realizes that as the manager of a home, she is responsible to see that everything gets done. This job description doesn't mean she must do all the work herself! In fact, we see that the Proverbs 31 woman delegated much of her work to servant girls, and she imported food from faraway places (Prov. 31:14, 15). However, she kept a watchful eye on everything that happened in her home and adjusted her plans accordingly.

If you're not wealthy enough to hire a group of servant girls, may I remind you that your children are quite capable of helping around the home? One of your great privileges and responsibilities is to train your children how to become competent adults.

Gail Martin, author of *What Every Child Should Know along the Way,* offered this excellent counsel: "Mastery of any skill will come at different times for different children. Endeavor to work

202 JUGGLING LIFE'S RESPONSIBILITIES

alongside your child as you begin to introduce new skills—remembering that training takes patience and learning takes time and repetition."[3]

Here are some of the skills she suggested we teach our children.

Age	Skill
Age 2	• Undress self
	• Put away own pajamas
	• Wash face and hands
	• Comb or brush own hair (with help)
	• Brush teeth (with help)
	• Pick up toys
	• Tidy up bedroom
	• Clear off own place at table
Age 3	• Dress self (with help)
	• Make own bed (use comforter)
	• Wipe up own spills
	• Help set table
	• Help clear table
	• Snap, zipper, and button
	• Put dirty clothes in hamper
Age 4	• Help gather laundry
	• Pick up outside toys
	• Shake out area rugs
	• Dust and clean TV screen
	• Empty wastebaskets
	• Know own phone number
	• Know own address
	• Help empty dishwasher
	• Help bring in groceries
	• Tie own shoes
	• Sit quietly in church (looking at books or drawing okay)

Wisely Building Your Home

	• Know how to make emergency phone call (911)
Age 5	• Put away clean clothes neatly
	• Clean own fingernails
	• Leave bathroom clean after use
	• Clean toilet
	• Feed and water pets
	• Begin to understand the differences and value of money
	• Receive a small allowance (if used)
	• Begin learning about saving, spending, and giving
	• Dust low shelves and objects (consider using a feather duster)
	• Empty kitchen trash

Martin lists many other practical life skills for children through the age of sixteen, but you can see how much even very young children are capable of doing if their mothers train them from an early age.[4]

John Holzmann, an educator, recommended four steps whenever you teach a new skill to your kids: modeling, teaching, supervising, and inspecting.[5] I've paraphrased his material and added some of my thoughts below.

Modeling. Take a week to observe yourself as you do the chore. Not only will you serve as a role model for your child, never asking him to do something you are not also willing to do, but you will have a chance to notice the steps involved in each project.

Teaching. Instead of assuming your child will automatically know how to do something, spend the second week doing the chore in front of your child, allowing him to observe. Talk him through each step and literally show him how it's done.

Supervising. Take a third week to help your child perform the new task as you watch him. Encourage him and show him ways he can improve, rather than criticizing him for a job not done to your standards.

Inspecting. The fourth week, assign him a task and step back. Then kindly evaluate the finished product. Try to encourage your child as much as possible, even if you must ask him to do it over again. Rewards such as sticker charts tend to be useful this week as you teach your child to incorporate his new task into his daily routine.

Taking the time (and it *is* time-consuming!) to teach your children practical life skills will eventually pay you back in rich dividends of time. In the meantime, think of the patience you are learning and the joy of accomplishment you are passing on to your kids.

A wise housewife also oversees the household income, much as we talked about in the last chapter. Notice that the Biblical wife did indeed work a second job to supplement her husband's income (Prov. 31:16, 24). If you have ever had a home-based business, you realize just how much oversight is needed to make it profitable!

Finally, notice that our model wife was not lazy. The Bible has so much to say about laziness. If you find you have tendencies toward laziness, you may want to add the following verses to your memory work:

Proverbs 6:6	Ecclesiastes 9:10
Proverbs 10:26	Luke 16:10
Proverbs 14:23	1 Corinthians 9:27
Proverbs 18:9	Galatians 6:9
Proverbs 21:5	Ephesians 4:28
Proverbs 21:17	2 Thessalonians 3:11, 12
Proverbs 22:13	James 4:17
Proverbs 26:16	

3. She is a hard worker. "She girds herself with strength, and strengthens her arms. She perceives that her merchandise is

Wisely Building Your Home

205

good, and her lamp does not go out by night" (Prov. 31:17, 18).

The Bible teaches us to do our best in whatever we do. "Whatever your hand finds to do, do it with your might" (Eccles. 9:10). This teaching does not mean you should never rest, for God wisely set an example for us by resting on the seventh day of Creation. You need to be sure to schedule into your life times of rest and to replenish yourself physically and spiritually. However, when you aren't resting, work hard!

For those times when you must keep going and bedtime is hours away, try the following tips to refill your energy level:

- Get up and get moving!
- Play some lively music.
- Eat a snack that includes both a protein and a carbohydrate (maybe some whole-wheat bread and almond butter).
- Sip a cold drink as you work.
- Promise yourself a reward for completing your tasks.
- Race the clock.

4. She plans ahead so she can reach her goals. "She stretches out her hands to the distaff, and her hand holds the spindle. She extends her hand to the poor, yes, she reaches out her hands to the needy. She is not afraid of snow for her household, for all her household is clothed with scarlet" (Prov. 31:19–21).

It is easy to see that this wise woman's goals included helping others and providing for her family's needs. Notice that the things she did required advanced planning and much time. I am not a good seamstress, so I suppose it would take me twice as long to sew clothing for the poor as it probably did this skillful woman. However, no matter who is doing the sewing, the seamstress must plan ahead by choosing a pattern and material, finding time in her very busy day to sew, and then delivering the garment to the poor and generously helping them in other ways.

When winter comes, this mother is prepared. Her children's dressers and closets are already full of warm clothes, made ahead of time when thick, warm fabrics were on sale. When emergencies arise, she is prepared. She thinks through the possibilities ahead of time. I'm impressed—aren't you?

What are your goals in life? Have you listed the practical, everyday steps that you must take to reach your goals? I have already stated that my priorities are in this order: God first, then my husband, then my children, then serving in my church, and finally, reaching my "world" for Christ. In the front of my planning notebook, I have a "Daily To-Do" list that tells me what I must do each day so I can reach my goals.

__ Have I read my Bible?

__ Have I had a shower (and prayer time)?

__ Am I dressed for the day?

__ Are the kids dressed?

__ Are the beds made?

__ Is the house neat?

__ Have we had a nutritious breakfast?

__ Is the kitchen clean?

__ Have I done my daily cleaning chores?

__ Have I read a book to the kids?

__ Have I planned the day's meals?

__ Am I prepared for church activities?

__ Have I written encouraging notes to people who need them?

__ Have I worked on my writing assignments?

You can see that my tasks for the day are arranged according to priority. This list helps ensure that my relationship with God comes before cleaning my house and that I have spent time with my children before preparing for church activities.

5. She is a skillful worker. "She makes tapestry for herself; her clothing is fine linen and purple. . . . She makes linen garments and sells them, And supplies sashes for the merchants" (Prov. 31:22, 24).

Our model wife in Proverbs 31 was obviously a skillful worker. Not only did she wisely use her skills to adorn herself with fine clothing, but she also marketed her skills and brought in extra money for the family.

Excellence should be the hallmark of a Christian. "An excellent wife is the crown of her husband" (Prov. 12:4). While most references to excellence in Scripture refer to our inner character (see Philippians 1:10, for instance), God is pleased when we do our work "heartily" to please Him (Col. 3:23).

Our everyday work should be a reflection of the character of God. The word "skillful" is used twenty-two times in Scripture, and each time it refers to the quality work men or women did. For example, when Solomon began to construct the great temple for God in Jerusalem, he was careful to find only the most skillful artisans so God's dwelling place would be greater than those of all the other gods (2 Chron. 2). In the same way, let the work of your hands reflect God's greatness in everything you do.

Life Is Full of Cycles

As you contemplate the type of housewife God wants you to be, and as you think about aligning your time with your priorities, remember that life is full of cycles. Your days repeat each other, one after another. You may work better during one time of day than you do during another. For instance, my brain remains foggy until well into the day, and I just don't move very quickly in the morning. So I have made it my goal to have my house tidied up and ready for the morning before I go to bed. That way I can muddle through my morning routine without too much thought. I reserve work that requires more mental effort for the afternoon and evening.

You may also find it easier to maintain order and stay consistent if you follow a weekly cycle. Many of our grandmothers and great-grandmothers assigned a major household chore to each day of the week, and they followed this routine religiously: washing on Monday, ironing on Tuesday, sewing on Wednesday, shopping on Thursday, cleaning on Friday, and baking on Saturday. Sunday was a day of rest. I have found that following a similar routine has been the key to keeping my home clean!

As you think about housekeeping routines, don't forget monthly and yearly cycles. As the Bible says, "To everything there is a season, a time for every purpose under heaven: a time to be born, and a time to die; a time to plant, and a time to pluck what is planted; . . . a time to gain, and a time to lose; a time to keep, and a time to throw away" (Eccles. 3:1, 2, 6).

There is a time for spring cleaning and a time to organize recipes, a time to turn the mattresses and a time to air out the closets, a time to prepare for a new school year and a time to do income taxes, a time to bake Christmas cookies and a time to barbecue outdoors.

Our lives follow seasons. If you have a new baby, you will not have the same housekeeping standards as a stay-at-home mother with two teenage daughters. God is not glorified when we don't rest; neither is He glorified when we are lazy and uncaring. Strive to balance your standards, and learn to be content with this season in your life.

I'm so embarrassed to admit that I failed a course called "The Ministry of Marriage and Motherhood." I took the course my sophomore year of college, when I was a newlywed and excited about my new role as a wife. However, I had not learned the benefits of keeping order in my life. I loved the class, but I procrastinated and ran out of time to complete the numerous assignments.

The "F" on my report card provided the catalyst I needed.

Wisely Building Your Home 209

Sometimes God has to allow us to see the cobwebs in our hearts before we realize how much we need cleansing. The same is sometimes true in our homes. Often we don't realize how low our housekeeping standards have sunk until the doorbell rings unexpectedly—or until there is no clean underwear in the drawer.

Sarah Phillips, a guest speaker in the marriage and motherhood class, shared with us twenty-one pointers for a better household routine. Now I would like to share them with you.

1. Get organized!
2. Don't begin today doing yesterday's work.
3. Get a good start in the morning. Work when you are alert and at your best.
4. Do the hardest jobs first. Don't procrastinate.
5. Never handle anything twice that you can handle once. Avoid the "for now" syndrome.
6. Use a calendar for all family members.
7. Have a pen and paper handy. Writing down reminders and ideas helps us keep track of things better and helps us not to forget.
8. Do routine tasks quickly.
9. Concentrate on one thing at a time. Avoid getting sidetracked.
10. Use waiting time wisely.
11. Use travel time wisely.
12. Delegate. Also teach children responsibility.
13. Avoid time wasters such as the telephone, TV, and Internet.
14. When shopping, use a list. Shop at off-peak hours; grocery shop biweekly; Christmas shop early.
15. Make two things at once; e.g., casseroles (only one "get ready" and one "clean up" for two meals).
16. As a family activity, use assembly lines; e.g., cookie baking, Christmas cards.

210   JUGGLING LIFE'S RESPONSIBILITIES

17. Use the Swiss cheese method: punch holes in big jobs.

18. Use small time segments to do small jobs; e.g., water plants, empty dishwasher.

19. Make your kitchen efficient—will save steps and time.

20. Time-saving gadgets—some are not really that great and just add to the clutter. (I once had an appliance that, after a complicated assembly for each use, would peel my potatoes. Then I had to carefully remove the blades and wash them by hand.)

21. Work on developing a mix-and-match wardrobe.[6]

Organization and Clutter

Arranging your time and your priorities to match the example of the Proverbs 31 woman sounds easy. Yet nothing could be further from the truth! The day I searched the Scriptures for God's viewpoint on homemaking, I discovered new motivation and methods. But I am still stuck inside the same disorganized body. This shell, this old nature, continues to torment me.

I have been accused of being a pack rat, and while I resent the connotations, I know it's the truth. Daily I fight a war against clutter and disorganization in my home. While I feel somewhat like the proverbial blind man who leads other blind men around, I offer some "de-cluttering" suggestions that, while not eliminating my natural tendencies, do help me keep my home a little neater.

To conquer clutter in my life, I must first realize the true value of my possessions. In fact, my possessions are worth very little. Yet I am a steward of my possessions. God has given me many things to care for, to maintain, and to use wisely for His service. However, the danger comes when I attach such great importance to *things* that I am not willing to let them go.

My children have been blessed with many toys. Some of their toys were gifts from grandparents, aunts and uncles, and dear friends. Some were purchased by Mommy and Daddy. Some were twenty-five cent garage-sale finds. My husband is amazed,

Wisely Building Your Home

though, that I can become more attached to a toy than my kids can! As a result, at times their bedrooms can overflow (literally!) with toys I am unwilling to either pack away for a later time or give to those who need them more.

The same thing can happen with collections, old magazines, kitchen appliances, baby clothes, pictures that never made it into a scrapbook, and income tax returns. Fear, pride, and sentimental feelings make my heart lurch, my brow sweat, and my fingers grip tighter onto the possessions I have.

Anne Ortlund offered many suggestions in her helpful books. One of her best ideas is to "eliminate and concentrate."[7] Eliminate those things that cause distraction. Concentrate on things that help you reach your goals.

For instance, if I were to work on organizing my children's toys, I would first think about our priorities. We want them to be able to play. Yet it is important to us to teach our children to take care of their things. We also want our children to play with wholesome toys that teach them to be creative and imaginative. So . . . eliminate broken toys; concentrate on easy storage solutions. Eliminate useless toys from fast-food restaurants; concentrate on standbys like blocks and Legos.

Here's another way to say it: simplify things. Our lives are too busy. Our schedules are cluttered. Our living rooms are cluttered. We have more options than resources. We have too many choices! "All things are lawful for me, but not all things are helpful; all things are lawful for me, but not all things edify" (1 Cor. 10:23).

We used to live close to a large Amish community. When the kids and I started to feel housebound, we loved to drive out to the Amish country and observe the people. We'd stop at a big farmhouse and buy homemade candy, chat with the farmers' wives, and pet the horses. We felt as if we'd been transported to another time. Amish living is peaceful. The pace is simpler. Yet it is truly a way of life. While we do not choose to copy their lifestyle, we can learn much from their ways.

Finally, we can alter our clutter-collecting mentality by learning to be content. The apostle Paul, while sitting in a Roman prison, wrote, "I have learned in whatever state I am, to be content" (Phil. 4:11). Contentment is easier for a woman who is satisfied with Christ alone. If you realize that He is your sole source of peace and joy, that He loves you and will do only what's best for you, and that He will provide for your every need, you can be content! When you are in that joyful state of mind, *things* will not hold the same appeal. Yes, you may admire the beautiful centerpiece on your friend's table, but you don't need one just like it to be happy. You simply rest in the Lord and allow Him to delight and surprise you.

Observe your life this week. Note those areas where the clutter of things and a frantic pace have taken over. Consider your motives and your priorities. Ask God to show you where you can simplify so you are a wiser steward of all He has given you.

Now you've decided to remove the clutter from your home and *get organized*. How?! If you're like me, the desire to change may be strong, but you may lack the know-how.

I've discovered as many methods exist to organize your home as there are homes! You may find a helpful how-to book at the library and throw it down in disgust when its author offers you no help whatsoever. However, your best friend may pick up the same book and revolutionize her housekeeping. The same holds true for advice from mothers-in-law and pastors' wives. God did not create us as cookie cutters of each other, and our strengths and weaknesses differ greatly. What works for one may not work so well for another.

Keep that thought in mind as I tell you what has helped me. It is more important that you determine to change and follow through on your determination. We don't both have to alphabetize our spices in green jars.

Wisely Building Your Home

My favorite book on the topic of organization is Julie Morgenstern's *Organizing from the Inside Out: The Foolproof System for Organizing Your Home, Your Office, and Your Life*. She devoted a major portion of her book to analyzing why a present situation isn't working. This section was extremely helpful to me because I had desired to be organized, but I wasn't able to make it work. Once I discovered *why* my home looked so cluttered, I was able to fix the problem more easily.

The other important point she helped me realize was the age-old maxim: "A place for everything and everything in its place." For me that means labeling containers so I won't forget where I put something. I learned to store things at their point of use (which meant purchasing cleaning supplies for *each* bathroom and a pair of scissors for *each* place I might want to use them). Kraig and I even had fun rearranging some furniture and rethinking the use of some of our rooms.

I'm sure some women never have to learn these principles. They are simply *born* neat! But for the rest of us, learning simple techniques from authors, experts, and experienced homemakers makes the difference between frustration and the freedom to go beyond housework and begin ministering to our families and communities.

IN SUMMARY

Let's conclude this discussion by listing *five keys to good housekeeping.*

First, always be willing to learn! A teachable spirit will take you far. When your husband criticizes your ability, don't take offense. Be wise and learn from your mistakes. Be humble. Change!

Here is *the second key:* Be skillful! Determine to have a spirit of excellence in all you do. Don't scrub the toilets because you *have* to, because you're just a lowly housewife and no one else around this place will do it, grumble, grumble, grumble. No! "Whatever your hand finds to do, do it with your might" (Eccles. 9:10).

I don't consider myself a very good cook, but one of my goals is to become one! Because of this goal, I collect cookbooks, both old and new. My family chuckles at my growing collection, and they willingly swallow the concoctions I make. But I have made it my goal to become a good cook! I have decided to *learn* to enjoy the kitchen!

However, I must remember *the third key* to good housekeeping: I must do all for God's glory, not my own pride. "By pride comes nothing but strife, but with the well-advised is wisdom" (Prov. 13:10). When my motive for mopping is pride, I will react in anger if my toddler spills sugar all over my freshly cleaned floor. When my motive for making my bed with crisp, hospital corners is pride, I will have a haughty spirit toward my husband's "quick-tuck-the corners-in" method. Proverbs 21:19 reminds me that it is "better to dwell in the wilderness, than with a contentious and angry woman."

The fourth key to good housekeeping is ageless: Never look down on the value of old-fashioned hard work. Some of us who would otherwise succeed in our homes fail because we're lazy. When you are tempted to procrastinate, remember that the work must be done sometime! It is much easier to scrub the dishes right away than to wait until the food has hardened. Or, as Proverbs 12:24 says, "The hand of the diligent will rule, but the lazy man will be put to forced labor."

Finally, *number five,* know when to stop! It's certainly truthful to say that "a woman's work is never done." On many mornings I feel like I'm an assembly-line worker, constantly repeating the tasks I have just finished. A mom I know put this message on her answering machine: "I'm not here. I'm playing with my daughter before she grows up because, as you know, cleaning

Wisely Building Your Home

your house while the children are growing is like shoveling the snow while it's still snowing!"

It is important for you to finish what you start, but you also need to learn to rest. One reason I love schedules is that they help me work when it's time to work and play when it's time to play. Otherwise I tend to get uptight and stressed. Things become more important to me than relationships. My housework becomes more urgent than a living, vibrant walk with God.

So determine to rest. Of course, resting is much easier if the confusion of clutter has been put away. Balance is needed.

You will continue to learn, and I will continue to learn, and we will all strive to make our homes places of beauty, rest, and peace. Learning takes time, so we need to be patient with each other.

Now, having written this chapter, I can relate to the apostle Paul when he wrote, "But I discipline my body and bring it into subjection, lest, when I have preached to others, I myself should become disqualified" (1 Cor. 9:27).

If you visit me, you'll call first—right?

EXTRA CREDIT ASSIGNMENT

Memorize this passage of Scripture by learning one verse at a time; then recite the passage to a minimum of five women.

> "See then that you walk circumspectly, not as fools but as wise, redeeming the time, because the days are evil. Therefore do not be unwise, but understand what the will of the Lord is" (Ephesians 5:15–17).

JUGGLING LIFE'S RESPONSIBILITIES

STUDY GUIDE

1. Read Colossians 3:17. How can a clean home bring glory to God? Can you think of any other Scripture verses to support your view?
2. According to Psalm 74:16, how can you know God is a "God of order"?
3. How can Psalm 118:24 and Psalm 145:2 help you on a day when you don't *feel* like cleaning your house?
4. What does Ecclesiastes 9:10 teach us about the importance of our time?
5. Read Proverbs 12:4. In what ways could your homemaking skills bring shame to your husband?
6. How can 1 Corinthians 10:23 help you choose which items you should keep and which you should toss when you're "decluttering" your house?
7. Read Philippians 4:8 and list some things we should think about to help us keep our attitudes right at home.

GROUP PROJECT

Make a list of the womanly qualities in Proverbs 31 for your group. Photocopy this list and give one to each woman. Everyone should place a smiley face by her strengths and a frown by her weaknesses. Then allow the women with strengths in certain categories to share helpful hints with those who need help. Keep it fun! You might even want to compile your own housekeeping book!

EXTRA READING

✔ Aslett, Don. *Is There Life After Housework?* Rev. ed. Cincinnati: Writer's Digest Books, 1992. Books by Don Aslett are bestsellers for a reason. He knows how to clean!

✔ _____. *Not for Packrats Only.* New York: Penguin Books, 1991.

Wisely Building Your Home 217

✔ _____. *No Time to Clean!* Pocatello, ID: Marsh Creek Press, 2000.

✔ Campbell, Jeff, and the Clean Team Staff. *Speed Cleaning*. 3rd ed. New York: Dell Publishing, 1991. As one of the first books I ever read on *how* to clean my house, I greatly admire its commonsense advice. The author explains what tools work best, in what order to clean a room, and even how to know if a room does *not* need to be cleaned!

✔ Forster, Pam. *Plants Grown Up*. Gaston, OR: Doorposts, 1995.

✔ _____. *Polished Cornerstones*. Gaston, OR: Doorposts, 1997. If teaching your children how to care for the home is your goal, you will enjoy these books. *Polished Cornerstones* is written for teaching daughters and *Plants Grown Up* for sons.

✔ Maxwell, Steven, and Teri Maxwell. *Managers of Their Homes*. Leavenworth, KS: Communication Concepts, Inc., 2001. A helpful book for families who would like to try a schedule to help them "get it all done." This book is intended for home-schooling families, but anyone can benefit from its advice. Also see www.titus2.com.

✔ Mendelson, Cheryl. *Home Comforts: The Art and Science of Keeping House*. New York: Simon & Schuster, 1999. This book is an encyclopedia of housekeeping for those women just starting out.

✔ Morgenstern, Julie. *Organizing from the Inside Out: The Foolproof System for Organizing Your Home, Your Office, and Your Life*. New York: Henry Holt and Company, 1998. This book fits my personality, and I love the author's system for getting organized.

✔ Schofield, Deniece. *Confessions of an Organized Homemaker*. Rev. ed. Cincinnati: Betterway Books, 1994. This book is a favorite of a friend of mine. By looking at all the organizational books listed here, you should be able to find one that fits *your* style.

218   JUGGLING LIFE'S RESPONSIBILITIES

✔ Young, Pam, and Peggy Jones. *Sidetracked Home Executives: From Pigpen to Paradise.* Rev. ed. New York: Warner Books, 2001. This book is funny and motivational. The authors recommend a system of 3" x 5" cards to keep you organized. You can also check out www.flylady.com for a Web site that will send you daily housekeeping reminders.

NOTES

1. Alfred Smith, "With Eternity's Values in View" (Nashville: Zondervan Music Group, © renewal 1969).

2. Source unknown.

3. Gail Martin, *What Every Child Should Know along the Way: Teaching Practical Life Skills in Every Stage of Life* (Mt. Pleasant, SC: Parent-Wise Solutions, 1988), 87.

4. Ibid., 87–90.

5. John Holzmann, Sarita Holzmann, and Rebecca W. Lewis, *Studying God's World ("K") Basic Course Guide and Teacher's Manual,* rev. ed. (Littleton, CO: Sonlight Curriculum, 2000), 38.

6. Sarah Phillips, "Priorities" (lecture, Baptist Bible College, Clarks Summit, PA, n.d.).

7. Anne Ortlund, *The Gentle Ways of the Beautiful Woman: A Practical Guide to Spiritual Beauty* (reprint, 3 vols. in 1, New York: Inspirational Press, 1998), 38.

CHAPTER *15* FIFTEEN

Creating a Peaceful Sanctuary

POINT TO PONDER
"Each of us is an innkeeper who decides if there is room for Jesus."[1]

I want to invite you to travel to an imaginary home. It's a rainy day in November. You are walking through the storm. Your clothes and hair are wet, and you are cold. You are hungry. You are tired. Yet up ahead you see the lights of a home. Someone took the time to light a candle in each window. The lights twinkle through the downpour as if to say, "Welcome! Hurry up! We're waiting for you!"

The front door is clean and bright, and the hostess answers as soon as you knock. You smell fresh bread as she opens the door and wraps a warm towel around you. A little girl takes your shoes and gives you soft slippers instead. A young boy smiles and invites you to sit in the best chair. A black-and-white fluff-ball of a dog greets you, its whole body shaking in friendliness.

Ahhh. . . . Don't you feel better already? Isn't it amazing what shelters our homes can be? You see, life *is* stormy! People are cold. We all get tired.

But we can come home! You may not have warm memories of growing up, and you may still struggle with the effects of living in a dysfunctional society. Yet "if anyone is in Christ, he is a new creation; old things have passed away; behold, all things have become new" (2 Cor. 5:17). Jesus offers hope for your family and new life for your home.

We have talked about the outward trappings of keeping a home, but let's pause for just a minute to ponder how to keep the heart of our home calm, serene, and peaceful.

"If I keep my house immaculately clean, and am envied by all for my interior decorating, but do not show love in my family—I'm just another housewife.

"If I'm always producing lovely things—sewing, art, macramé; if I always look attractive, and speak intelligently, but am not loving to my family—I am nothing.

"If I'm busy in community affairs, teach Sunday school, and drive in the carpool, but fail to give adequate love to my family—I gain nothing.

"Love changes diapers, cleans up messes, and ties shoes—over and over again.

"Love is kind, though tired and frazzled.

"Love doesn't envy another wife—one whose children are 'spaced' better, or in school so she has time to pursue her own interests.

"Love doesn't try to impress others with my abilities or knowledge as a mother.

"Love doesn't scream at the kids.

"Love doesn't feel cheated because I didn't get to do what *I* wanted to do today—sew, read, soak in a hot tub.

"Love doesn't lose my temper easily.

"Love doesn't assume that my children are being naughty just because their noise level is irritating.

"Love doesn't rejoice when other people's children misbehave and make mine look good. Love is genuinely happy when others are honored by their children."[2]

Why Should a Wife Care about Her Home's Atmosphere?

It should matter greatly to you that your home is a sanctuary and a refuge. First of all, you are a reflection of all that makes up your home. Have you seen women who look like they just crawled out of bed? Did you wonder what their homes look like? Do you wish you could live there? How about the women you've seen hollering at their kids? Do you think their homes are peaceful retreats filled with loving words? You can usually tell what the home is like by observing the woman who lives there.

A woman sets the tone for all that happens in the home. I saw a T-shirt that said, "If momma ain't happy, ain't nobody happy!" It is crucial for you, as the pacesetter in your home, to fill it with loving words, forgiving hugs, kind smiles, and heavenly scents.

As you set the standard, you also provide motivation for others in your family to follow your example—especially your children. Everyone begins to get along better together. Everyone learns the give-and-take that's necessary for healthy family relationships. Everyone begins to desire to spend time together as a family instead of trying to *escape* the family.

And a happy wife, leading a happy home, is great to come home to!

As you learn to adjust the atmosphere of your home by adjusting the attitudes of your heart, you will become more effective in each of your roles as a woman. Do you want to be a better wife? In my husband's humble opinion, home is much nicer if it is clean, I'm looking pretty for him, and a yummy meal is on the table. I have a feeling your husband might say the same!

My son thinks home is a great place if he can play games with Mommy and Daddy, read books with us, and do special activities with us.

I can be a better friend if my home is always in order. Maybe that means I have some soothing teas in my pantry or a few favorite flowers to snip and share or an easy-to-find list of my friends' birthdays. Maybe I even have a guest room that stands ready (and comfortable) for anyone who might like a few days' retreat.

No matter what I am doing, my home should stand waiting to be used—as always, for the glory of God.

What Can Be Done to Change Your Home's Atmosphere?

Let me help you get your creative juices flowing. Try looking at your home the way a stranger would. What's her first impression?

Enter your front door and take a deep breath. Does your home *smell* refreshing? If not, it may be time to invest in some lovely candles or in some scented sachets. Maybe a new air filter would do the trick. Plan your baking so the comforting fragrance of fresh bread greets your husband when he comes home from work.

Look around you. What's out of place? As Anne Ortlund wrote, "I've always figured if I could make a room look *pretty,* pride would force me to keep it passably vacuumed and dusted! What has disciplined me is the philosophy that you can't see a daisy in a bud vase if there's a sock in the middle of the floor."[3]

As you're looking around, don't forget to glance in the mirror to see if you're looking your best for your family—and remember your smile!

What does your home *sound* like? Music is a pleasure we continually enjoy in our home. We each have our favorites, and we're sure to listen to a little of everyone's. Except for after lunch, when we each have a quiet time of rest, you will probably hear music coming from our stereo system or tunes from our piano. We unashamedly sing in the shower, sing when we make lunch, and gather together on Saturday nights to sing our favorite songs.

Colossians 3 talks about the atmosphere in a Christian home as it reminds us to

> seek those things which are above. . . . Put off all these: anger, wrath, malice, blasphemy, filthy language out of

Creating a Peaceful Sanctuary

> your mouth. . . . Put on tender mercies, kindness, humility, meekness, longsuffering; bearing with one another, and forgiving one another. . . . Let the peace of God rule in your hearts, to which also you were called in one body; and be thankful (Col. 3:1, 8, 12, 13, 15).

Then my favorite passage of all admonishes,

> Let the word of Christ dwell in you richly in all wisdom, teaching and admonishing one another in psalms and hymns and spiritual songs, singing with grace in your hearts to the Lord. And whatever you do in word or deed, do all in the name of the Lord Jesus, giving thanks to God the Father through Him (Col. 3:16, 17).

Music is crucial to the health of your family. If you can't carry a tune, *listen* to good music! Choose music that will allow "the word of Christ to dwell in you richly," music that will teach and admonish you. As you fill your heart with His Word through music, you will find your attitudes are more thankful, and you'll find it easier to obey God. As a result, your home will be blessed.

As you continue to follow the instructions of Colossians 3 (submission, obedience, and more), you will be surprised to hear sounds of laughter in your home! Why not? You are all friends, fellow-servants of Jesus Christ, and lovers of God.

You can help the fun along by providing board games and popcorn. You might want to institute a family game night each week. Joke books are a great addition to any mealtime. Make up fun names for each family member, names that are special to just your family (such as, "Rasca-Nagel Bagel" or "Anna Banana").

Speaking of mealtime, I read an article by Mimi Wilson and Mary Beth Lagerborg in which they share some secrets of making mealtime the best time of your day. Here are seven pointers they include:

"1. Sit down together at the table and keep distractions, especially the television and telephone, at a minimum.

"2. Treat each family member with respect.

"3. Establish some basic rules concerning acceptable table language, behavior, and topics.

"4. Children should ask to be excused and should learn to sit at the table for a reasonable length of time, according to their age and personality, after they have finished eating.

"5. Steer the conversation away from criticizing other people, whether present or absent.

"6. Ask questions at the table for which anyone seated will have an answer, and which cannot be answered with a simple yes or no.

"7. Remember what Colossians 4:6 says: 'Let your speech always be with grace, seasoned, as it were, with salt, so that you may know how you should respond to each person.' "[4]

Not only should the mealtime conversations be wholesome, but the food you serve should be too! Your attitude toward cooking should reflect God's attitude of excellence, of love for your husband and children, and of being a careful manager of your home. This task will be much easier to accomplish, perhaps, if you plan ahead with a weekly menu and certainly by thinking about supper early enough in the day. Even leftovers can be special if you follow my mother-in-law's advice and have a weekly "Refrigerator Smorgasbord" night. (Empty out the fridge and allow each member of your family to make their own feast.) Make some meals more pleasant than others by using candles, soft music, and pretty place settings to set the mood. Finally, educate yourself on nutritional basics so that not only do you fill your family's tummies, but you also fuel their bodies for proper growth and health. (See recommended books at the end of the chapter.)

Not only should you consider how your home smells, looks, sounds, and, yes, even tastes, you should also plan for a home that *feels* good. Providing a soft seat in a secluded spot, some-

Creating a Peaceful Sanctuary 225

where perfect for reading or daydreaming, may be just the trick for soothing an uptight teenage girl. Sheets that are crispy clean help little ones relax. Crystal goblets can cheer up a dreary day.

Don't forget to include the feel of loving hugs! A squeeze around your son's shoulders . . . a back rub . . . gently braiding someone's hair . . . these all have a place in a loving home. And what kid wouldn't benefit from a playful puppy or a tiny kitten?

You are the wife, the mom, the builder of a home. God has created you in His image, and He has given you a touch of the creative genius He holds.

> We are created in the likeness of *the Creator*. We are created in the image of a *Creator*.
>
> So we are, on a finite level, people who can create. Why does man have creativity? Why can man think of many things in his mind, and choose, and then bring forth something that other people can taste, smell, feel, hear and see? Because man was created in the image of a Creator. Man was created that he might create. It is not a waste of man's time to be creative. It is not a waste to pursue artistic or scientific pursuits in creativity, because this is what man was *made* to be able to do. He was made in the image of a Creator, and given the capacity to create—on a finite level of course, needing to use the materials already created—but he is still the creature of a Creator.[5]

Therefore, it is your privilege and your blessed responsibility to create a refuge of peace and beauty in your home. How you go about doing that will differ from the other women around you, but what is important is that you purpose in your heart to make your home a priority.

Don't wait! I love to browse in the mall or at home improvement stores, dreaming of all the possibilities for my home. But if I added up how much it would cost to make all of those improvements *today,* I'd be too discouraged to ever start.

I've learned, instead, to use a few dollars from the grocery budget to buy new potholders for my kitchen. It's amazing how clean potholders can make me feel transformed! A new houseplant, a cleaned-out refrigerator, or a fresh coat of paint on the front door can do the same for my attitude.

As a mom, I've also discovered that money will never provide as much happiness for my family as memories can. A simple picnic will mean more to your children than a new toy. Reading a book together on a snowy evening will bind you closer than you ever thought possible. "Better is a dry morsel with quietness, than a house full of feasting with strife" (Prov. 17:1).

Preserving traditions together will bind you close together as a family. Strive to make Christmas, birthdays, hot summer barbecues, and even restful Sunday afternoons a time that you spend *together* as a family. A little planning ahead will do wonders for your enjoyment of a special day. Prepare a favorite meal, give simple gifts, and keep your camera handy.

Allow your memory-making to honor God as well. As God commanded the nation of Israel, "These words which I command you today shall be in your heart. You shall teach them diligently to your children, and shall talk of them when you sit in your house, when you walk by the way, when you lie down, and when you rise up" (Deut. 6:6, 7). Has God blessed your family in a special way, maybe by providing for a need or answering a request? Make a memory of that blessing in a concrete, visible way, such as in a scrapbook, in a photo collage, or with a yearly family holiday.

IN SUMMARY

Do you want a home filled with peace? Then follow God's prescription: "You will keep him in perfect peace, whose mind is stayed on You, because he trusts in You" (Isa. 26:3). Continuously point the hearts and minds of your family toward God. God has given you your home as a tool to use for His glory. By

Creating a Peaceful Sanctuary 227

walking intimately with God, by graciously submitting to your husband's leadership, by wisely training your children in obedience, and by filling your home with God's beauty, you can have an unimaginable impact on the world for Christ.

> Now to Him who is able to do exceedingly abundantly above all that we ask or think, according to the power that works in us, to Him be glory in the church by Christ Jesus to all generations, forever and ever. Amen (Eph. 3:20, 21).

EXTRA CREDIT ASSIGNMENT

Memorize this passage of Scripture by learning one verse at a time; then recite the passage to a minimum of five women.

"Therefore, as the elect of God, holy and beloved, put on tender mercies, kindness, humility, meekness, longsuffering; bearing with one another, and forgiving one another, if anyone has a complaint against another; even as Christ forgave you, so you also must do. But above all these things put on love, which is the bond of perfection. And let the peace of God rule in your hearts, to which also you were called in one body; and be thankful. Let the word of Christ dwell in you richly in all wisdom, teaching and admonishing one another in psalms and hymns and spiritual songs, singing with grace in your hearts to the Lord. And whatever you do in word or deed, do all in the name of the Lord Jesus, giving thanks to God the Father through Him" (Colossians 3:12–17).

STUDY GUIDE

1. Read 2 Corinthians 5:17. How is your idea of home life different now from before you were saved?
2. According to Colossians 4:6, how should members of a family speak to one another? What speech difficulties do *you* have?
3. According to Genesis 1:27, in whose pattern (or "image") were you made? What special homemaking abilities could you improve upon?
4. Proverbs 17:1 talks about the value of a peaceful home. When are you most likely to be disagreeable in your home? According to Isaiah 26:3, what steps could you take to improve the atmosphere (or your attitude)?

GROUP PROJECT

Hold a tea party with your group to help you try out new homemaking ideas. Strategize ways to include all five senses (taste, smell, touch, sound, and sight) at your tea party. Be sure each group member has a part so that one person is not burdened with all the preparations.

Ask each woman to bring an object for a memory "show and tell." Using her object, she can tell about a memory that is special to her and how she can create memories for her family now.

EXTRA READING

✔ Arterburn, Stephen, and Carl Dreizler, *52 Simple Ways to Say "I Love You"* Nashville: Thomas Nelson Publishers, 1991. Here is a fun little book to help you plan special ways to show your husband, kids, and friends how much you love them.
✔ Barnes, Emilie. *15 Minute Family Traditions and Memories*. Eugene, OR: Harvest House Publishers, 1995. This book is full of ideas to help you enjoy holidays and special occasions with your family while you focus their attention on the Lord.
✔ Fallon, Sally, with Mary G. Enig. *Nourishing Traditions: The*

Cookbook That Challenges Politically Correct Nutrition and the Diet Dictocrats. Washington, D.C.: NewTrends Publishing, 1999. This cookbook with delicious recipes also includes answers to common nutritional questions. For me, it finally answered my questions with documented studies and common-sense reasoning. I highly recommend this book!

✔ Schaeffer, Edith. *The Hidden Art of Homemaking*. Wheaton, IL: Tyndale House, 1971. Here is a classic by a woman who made it her goal to live for God's glory. In this book she discusses how to incorporate music, painting and sculpture, gardening, food, drama, clothing, and more into your family life in creative ways.

✔ Willits, Terry. *Creating a SenseSational Home*. Grand Rapids: Zondervan Publishing House, 1996. This book is one of my favorites. Willits walks you through each room of your home and shows you how to create beauty for each of your senses. Through it all, she teaches you how to do it all for the Lord! Not only is this book about beauty, it's also a book you will be proud to display on your coffee table.

✔ Wurzbacher, Linda, Kevin Miller, and Ed Strauss. *More Mealtime Moments: 164 Faith-filled Ideas for Family Discussion*. Wheaton, IL: Tyndale House, 2001. You can set this handy spiral-bound book on your table during meals. Each page includes activities built around themes to help your family members communicate better with each other and with the Lord.

NOTES

1. Source unknown.

2. Jean Fleming, *A Mother's Heart* (Colorado Springs: NavPress, 1982), 142–43.

3. Anne Ortlund, *The Gentle Ways of the Beautiful Woman: A Practical Guide to Spiritual Beauty* (reprint, 3 vols. in 1, New York: Inspirational Press, 1998), 59.

4. Mimi Wilson and Mary Beth Lagerborg, "The Best Part of Dinner?" *Focus on the Family* (August 1994), 13

5. Edith Schaeffer, *The Hidden Art of Homemaking* (Wheaton, IL: Tyndale House, 1971), 24.

PART 5 FIVE

Your World

POINT TO PONDER

"Can a woman forget her nursing child, and not have compassion on the son of her womb? Surely they may forget, yet I will not forget you. See, I have inscribed you on the palms of My hands"
(Isaiah 49:15, 16).

I t is easy to become discouraged about the world we live in. Our society has become ever more antagonistic toward God and toward us, His children. While just a generation ago morals were commonly accepted, today absolutes have vanished and have been replaced by a terrifying abyss of tolerance for beliefs and lifestyles. Not only is God's design for the family obsolete—God seems to be obsolete as well!

Chin up, dear woman! God is still on the throne, and "blessed are all those who put their trust in Him" (Ps. 2:12). Nothing surprises Him or catches Him off guard. You can be sure that the events of our world are entirely within God's plan and purpose.

Even more amazing is the fact that *you* are part of His plan. God has a strategy to *change* this world, and His strategy includes you.

You see, no matter how much the world around us rejects God, He continues to love it. The apostle Paul explained it this way:

> And you He made alive, who were dead in trespasses and sins, *in which you once walked* according to the course of this world, according to the prince of the power of the air, the spirit who now works in the sons of disobedience, among whom also we all once conducted ourselves in the lusts of our flesh, fulfilling the desires of the flesh and of the mind, and were by nature children of wrath, just as the others. But God, who is rich in mercy, *because of His great love with which He loved us,* even when we were dead in trespasses, made us alive together with Christ (by grace you have been saved), and raised us up together, and made us sit together in the heavenly places in Christ Jesus, that in the ages to come He might show the exceeding riches of His grace in His kindness toward us in Christ Jesus (Eph. 2:1–7, emphasis added).

God has done all this for us, yet we often become comfortable and proud in God's grace, forgetting *from what* He has saved us and forgetting *why* He has saved us—and that He loves others just as much as He loves us.

The magnificence of God's plan is that He wants us to *love* others, to show mercy as we have been shown mercy from God. The Bible speaks more about how we are to love others than it does about God's love for us! We must never forget our purpose.

> For we are His workmanship, created in Christ Jesus for good works, which God prepared beforehand that we should walk in them" (Eph. 2:10).

> And *walk in love,* as *Christ also has loved us* and given Himself for us (Eph. 5:2, emphasis added).

> Therefore if there is any consolation in Christ, if any comfort of love, if any fellowship of the Spirit, if any affection and mercy, fulfill my joy by *being like-minded, having the same love,* being of one accord, of one mind. Let nothing be done through selfish ambition or conceit, but in lowliness of mind let each esteem others better than himself. Let each of you look out not only for his own interests, but also for the interests of others. Let this mind be in you

Your World 233

which was also in Christ Jesus (Phil. 2:1–5, emphasis added).

> In this the love of God was manifested toward us, that
> God has sent His only begotten Son into the world, that
> we might live through Him. In this is love, not that we
> loved God, but that He loved us and sent His Son to be the
> propitiation for our sins. Beloved, *if God so loved us, we also
> ought to love one another* (1 John 4:9–11, emphasis added).

In John 17 we read that God's design is for believers to be one with each other, just as Jesus, God the Son, is one with God the Father (v. 11). We are to be cleansed and made new by the truth, which is God's Word (v. 17). And then we are to go into the world to share God's love, just as God sent Jesus into our world to show us the Father's love (v. 18).

God is a God of order, and His orderly plan includes the church. In the book of Acts we see how He orchestrated the sending of the gospel into all the known world. Obedient believers who worked *together* for the advancement of the gospel demonstrated His love.

The same holds true today. Imagine the impact on the world if every Christian had a close relationship to God, if every wife submitted to her husband, if every parent taught his or her children loving obedience, if every home was a refuge of peace and harmony, and if all these proper relationships overflowed into our churches. Obedience to God in the *little things* can make a *huge difference*!

The "world" around *you* is watching you. Jesus said,

> You are the light of the world. A city that is set on a hill
> cannot be hidden. Nor do they light a lamp and put it under
> a basket, but on a lampstand, and it gives light to all who
> are in the house. Let your light so shine before men, that
> they may see your good works and glorify your Father in
> heaven (Matt. 5:14–16).

While traveling in southern France, my husband and I drove by a village set on a hill. It was almost dusk, and the homes built on the hillside were still dark. Yet an old church at the top of the hill had lights we could see from miles away.

Imagine with me what would happen if Christian families lit up the spiritual darkness around them. What if one godly woman showed Biblical respect to her husband and love to her children? What if her good works overflowed to her neighbors in the community? What a light she would be in a land filled with disbelief in God!

Exactly *how* does a Christian woman fulfill her role in influencing the world for Christ? What part can she play, especially when the demands of home and motherhood may leave her with little time or energy for anything else? In this final section, let's discuss what God's Word has to say about being a godly woman in the midst of a godless society.

CHAPTER *16* SIXTEEN

Contributing to the Body of Christ

POINT TO PONDER
"Now to Him who is able to do exceedingly abundantly above all that we ask or think, according to the power that works in us, to Him be glory in the church by Christ Jesus to all generations, forever and ever. Amen"
(Ephesians 3:20, 21).

My dad is a pastor. When I was growing up, we were expected to be present every time the church doors were open (unless we were ill, of course). Sunday School and Sunday morning worship—we were there. Potlucks—we were there. Sunday night services, midweek prayer and Bible studies, youth group, children's meetings, visitation, you name it—we were there. I memorized many Bible verses and could recite the books of the Bible in order. I learned to pray out loud. I learned to sing the great hymns and worship choruses of the church. I knew how to operate the copier in the church office. I knew how to lead a child to the Lord. I saw kids throw pies in my dad's face at the end of Vacation Bible School contests. I chased a greased pig around an empty lot. I giggled when my brother reflected

236   JUGGLING LIFE'S RESPONSIBILITIES

sunlight off the face of his watch onto the bald head of a man in our congregation. I sang with my friends around campfires. To me, all of this is part of fellowship.

My husband also grew up in a parsonage. When we married, we began attending a large church near our college campus. No longer were we the pastors' kids. We hadn't grown up with these people. We didn't know the names of the people in our Sunday School class, let alone know how to operate the copier in the church office. The songs in the worship service were unfamiliar. Instead of sharing special times with friends in the church foyer on Sunday nights, we slipped out of the service after the last "Amen."

After a couple weeks of following this routine, one Sunday morning we rolled over in bed and just looked at each other.

"I wonder if anyone would notice if we just didn't go to church today."

"Probably not. . . . But we *should* go. . . ."

"Yeah, we should." Silence. "Have you ever skipped church before?"

"No. Have you?"

"No. Wanna see what it's like?"

"Sure, I guess."

It was fun for an hour or so. We went to Denny's in our jeans and T-shirts and ate a big breakfast with all the other church-skippers. But we didn't pray out loud before we ate. We were too ashamed to admit we were Christians who weren't in church. We were even more lonely than we'd been at church!

You see, we missed the fellowship. That day we decided we had two options if we wanted to regain the fellowship we so dearly needed. We could either find a new church, maybe a smaller one, and try again with a new bunch of worshipers, or we could make an effort to become involved in the ministries of this large church, to become known, and to minister where we could. We chose the second option, and the Lord has allowed us to fellowship with His

Contributing to the Body of Christ   237

saints in several churches across the country since then.

Fellowship. What is it? Why do we need it? How do we know when we've found it? What can we contribute?

Fellowship requires having the same purposes and feelings as someone else. Fellowship with believers includes confessing sin, building each other up, encouraging each other in good works, remembering Christ's work for us on the cross, caring for each other's needs, and showing Biblical love to each other.

> But if we walk in the light as He is in the light, we have fellowship with one another, and the blood of Jesus Christ His Son cleanses us from all sin (1 John 1:7).

> Let us consider one another in order to stir up love and good works, not forsaking the assembling of ourselves together, as is the manner of some, but exhorting one another, and so much the more as you see the Day [of Christ's return] approaching (Heb. 10:24, 25).

We *need* the regular encouragement of our fellow believers so that we are continually "stirred up" to love and good works.

When I make pasta, I regularly stir the pasta in the boiling water. Otherwise, it sits and starts to harden, sticks to the sides of the pan, and eventually becomes burnt and crispy. In the same way, we *need* our fellow believers to stir up our lives, to inspire us by their example, to convict us by their teaching, and to jostle us by their reprimands.

Choosing a Biblical church with which to fellowship should be a decision jointly made by you and your husband. But how do you find a church that is Biblical? Just *what is* a Biblical church? And when you've found it, what role should you as a woman have to contribute to that particular body of believers?

A Biblical Church

The primary characteristic of a Biblical church is its loyalty to God's Word. While this requirement seems obvious, it can be

238   JUGGLING LIFE'S RESPONSIBILITIES

difficult, nevertheless, to find a church that has remained faithful to Scripture.

The church might hear God's Word from the pulpit but fail to apply its principles to concrete, everyday situations.

The church may surrender to pressure from individuals who are hungry for power.

The church may surrender its decision-making ability to governing organizations instead of being governed by the Bible.

Of course, Satan is always busy trying to deceive the minds of Christians and trying to distract us from our true purpose. He does not want churches to succeed!

Let's get practical. If you are looking for a church that is Biblical in doctrine and practice, you first need to know what the Bible says. That takes study! If you aren't sure what the Bible teaches about basic truths, then you might ask a pastor's wife or some other knowledgeable woman to meet with you regularly to explain to you what the Bible says and what the church believes. Of course, it will be your responsibility not to just accept what she says but also to search it out for yourself afterward. Remember that the Holy Spirit will teach you through the Word of God (John 16:13; 17:17; 1 Cor. 2:9–12). Ask God for wisdom (James 1:5).

The church in Berea, a small town that Paul and Silas visited on their missionary journeys, has become famous for its members' eagerness to compare all they learned to the standard of the Scriptures.

> When [Paul and Silas] arrived, they went into the synagogue of the Jews. These were more fair-minded than those in Thessalonica, in that they received the word with all readiness, and *searched the Scriptures daily* to find out whether these things were so. Therefore *many of them believed*, and also not a few of the Greeks, *prominent women as well as men* (Acts 17:10–12, emphasis added).

One of the first things you'll notice about a church is the

Contributing to the Body of Christ

quality of its preaching. As you listen to the Word of God being explained to you—oh, wait! That's an important point! Does the pastor actually *explain* the Word of God to you? Or does he just comment on various issues, philosophies, and current events, adding his own opinion to the pool of thought? He should do more than just mention a key verse. A wise pastor will guide you through a passage of Scripture, keeping his emphasis on what the Bible says. Verse by verse he'll teach you, comparing one Scripture with another, and encouraging you to follow along and learn.

Another sign of a Biblical church is that the members bring and use their Bibles. If no one carries a Bible, then Bibles must not be too important in the service.

Do the teachers and leaders of the church encourage independent study of the Bible? Will they help you obtain study aids, and will they teach you how to learn at home? Do they encourage you to take notes so that you can do further study later? Do small groups frequently meet to discuss what the Bible says? All of these attributes characterize a Bible-honoring church.

Of course, methods and programs vary from church to church. Some methods are based on Scripture, but often they are a matter of individual interpretation. If you question a church's method, determine the reasoning behind it before you criticize. Seek a church where you feel comfortable, but remember that tastes in music, styles of worship, and methods for training vary not only from town to town but from year to year. Keep your emphasis on God's Word, and allow God to *use* your church in your life.

Notice that I've said nothing about whether the church is friendly, about whether someone visited you right away, or about the range of programs it offers for your children. It is my belief that you should attend church *to minister* and not *to be ministered to*. As a woman who loves God and His Word, you have a vital role in your church.

A Biblical Role

As I read in Scripture, I find several important roles for a woman to fill as a member of her local church. These roles are open to some debate, for various churches interpret Scripture verses in different ways. Women, as well as men, have pondered their talents, trying to figure out what their spiritual gifts might be. However, the Bible makes it clear that some spiritual gifts are to be used exclusively by men. For instance, while the concept is unpopular in some circles, the Bible teaches that women are not to be pastors or deacons (1 Tim. 3:2, 12; Titus 1:6). Likewise, women are not to teach or hold authority over men (1 Tim. 2:9–15).

However, this concept of not teaching men doesn't mean women should not *teach*! Remember that Titus 2 instructs the older women to teach the younger women. Also, Scripture does not prohibit women from teaching children, although it does seem to indicate that men have an important responsibility to teach children as well. Many women have had a huge impact on children by faithfully teaching them, whether in Sunday School and church programs or from their homes, kitchen tables, and backyards.

Many women also spend hours in prayer for their fellow believers. Without this faithful prayer, much that has been accomplished would never have happened.

Some women are helpers, always finding a job that needs to be done and doing it. Others bring mercy, giving comfort and hope to those who are discouraged and needy. Some are generous, contributing to the needs of others without any thought of reward or praise. Some are experts in hospitality, helping strangers feel comfortable and sharing good works with all. Many fulfill a quiet role in the church, sweetly working behind the scenes. In many ways it is similar to how a wife is a helper to her husband. Each is dependent upon the other.

IN SUMMARY

The important thing is that you *find* a ministry role and then work to *fulfill* it. Your church is your family—brothers and sisters who are growing together, helping each other, loving one another, and serving together. Make your church a priority in your own heart, and carry over that priority into your time management. Your marriage will be stronger because of your church involvement. Your children will benefit from their participation in your church (but remember that they learn more from your actions than your words; be sure church is a priority over fishing trips and Little League games!). Most importantly, your walk with God will be stronger and your fellowship with Him sweeter when you contribute to His body, the church.

EXTRA CREDIT ASSIGNMENT

Memorize this passage of Scripture by learning one verse at a time; then recite the passage to a minimum of five women.

> "One thing I have desired of the LORD; that will I seek: that I may dwell in the house of the LORD[1] all the days of my life, to behold the beauty of the LORD, and to inquire in His temple. For in the time of trouble He shall hide me in His pavilion; in the secret place of His tabernacle He shall hide me; He shall set me high upon a rock" (Psalm 27:4, 5).

STUDY GUIDE

1. According to Hebrews 10:24, what is your job as a church member?
2. Psalm 135:1–3 lists some things we should incorporate into

242 JUGGLING LIFE'S RESPONSIBILITIES

public worship. How can you personally add to the worship of your local church, even if you have no particular musical talents?

3. What can you learn from Acts 17:10–12 to help you find a church that is faithful to the truth?

GROUP PROJECT

As a group, go to the Scriptures and make a list of some key elements of a church. For instance, you may want to study Acts 2:41–47, 1 Timothy 2 and 3, or 1 Peter 5. This project requires a lot more "brainwork" than some of the other projects, but it will bind you closer together as you learn how to function well together in your local church.

EXTRA READING

✔ Heald, Cynthia. *Becoming a Woman of Prayer*. Colorado Springs: NavPress, 1996. All of Cynthia Heald's studies are helpful, but this one will guide women who are interested in ministering in the local church through prayer.

✔ Jackson, Paul R. *The Doctrine and Administration of the Church*. Schaumburg, IL: Regular Baptist Press, 1980. This easy-to-read book presents all phases of a local Baptist church: its organization, government, ministry, doctrine, and outreach.

✔ Ortlund, Anne. *Love Me with Tough Love: Disciplines for Living Together in the Body of Christ*. Waco, TX: Word Books, 1979. This book is out of print, but you may be able to find a copy at a bookstore or www.amazon.com.

✔ Ortlund, Anne. *Up with Worship: How to Quit Playing Church*. Rev. ed. Nashville: Broadman & Holman, 2001. This book deals with how to practice the presence of God during a church service instead of just passively being a spectator on Sunday mornings.

Contributing to the Body of Christ   **243**

✔ For further study in the Bible regarding the church, read the books of Acts, 1 and 2 Corinthians, Philippians, 1 and 2 Timothy, and Titus. Many other portions of Scripture reference the church, but these will get you started.

NOTES

1. The phrase "house of the LORD" is an Old Testament reference to the temple, the gathering place for public worship. While the Lord now inhabits our bodies as His temple (1 Cor. 6:19), public worship is still essential for a vibrant walk with God.

CHAPTER *17* SEVENTEEN

Learning from Older Women

POINT TO PONDER
"He has made His wonderful works to be remembered; the LORD is gracious and full of compassion" (Psalm 111:4).

The first 120 disciples were gathered in an upstairs room when the power of the Holy Spirit came upon them. It had been fifty days since Jesus' death. They had been through the agony of seeing Him crucified and buried. They had felt the fear—and then the wonder—when He arose from the dead. They had been with Him ten days earlier, when He ascended out of their sight into the clouds. He had left them a promise: even though He would not reveal the Father's plans for kingdoms and politics, He would give them the power of the Holy Spirit. This promise must have been reassuring to those guys left standing behind—alone, without Jesus!

The Holy Spirit wasn't only a reassuring presence and comfort, though. His coming had a specific purpose. The disciples were to become witnesses of what Christ had done. They were to witness first in Jerusalem, then in the surrounding areas of Samaria and Judea, and finally to "the end of the earth" (Acts 1:8).

245

If I had been in their shoes, I know I would have felt a little intimidated at such a grand idea! *No way, God,* I would have thought, *will I ever be able to tell every single person in Jerusalem about Jesus, even if they DO want to hear! I guess we could form a committee and assign areas of Jerusalem to each person. Then we'll have to spread out to the rest of the world. Let's see . . . divide the world's population by 120 disciples . . . O Lord! It's too big of a job!*

But as Jesus had already told the disciples, "The things which are impossible with men are possible with God" (Luke 18:27). The Holy Spirit would perform a miracle so big that no one could ever attribute it to humanity.

Sure enough, by the end of the day three thousand people who believed were baptized (Acts 2:41), and the numbers continued to grow. "The Lord added to the church daily those who were being saved" (Acts 2:47).

The paradox is that God could have used angels to broadcast His message to the inhabitants of Jerusalem, similar to what He did at Jesus' birth. He chose, instead, to use garden-variety people—people just like us—who were filled with *His* power.

His good news continues to spread throughout the world today, and in the wake of the precious carriers of His Word are people who need to be taught (discipled) in the ways of God. God could use supernatural means to help baby Christians grow, but He has chosen to use us. He has made all His children part of a family that stretches around the globe. In communities large and small, His church is alive and growing. What is His plan to grow His church and ground believers? *His plan is to use ordinary people.*

The same was true with the nation of Israel. Moses commanded the fathers,

> Only take heed to yourself, and diligently keep yourself, lest you forget the things your eyes have seen, and

Learning from Older Women

> lest they depart from your heart all the days of your life. And teach them to your children and your grandchildren . . . . The LORD said to me, "Gather the people to Me, and I will let them hear My words, that they may learn to fear Me all the days they live on the earth, and that they may teach their children" (Deut. 4:9, 10).

To help fathers pass on to their children the accounts of God's mighty deeds, God told them to build memorials that would trigger their memories for generations. One time He even instructed them to blow trumpets to help them remember the Lord their God (see Numbers 10:10).

Now we live in the age of the church, and God has provided a way for us to learn what He wants us to know. Again He could have used supernatural means, but He has chosen to use people instead. Of course, He has given us the Bible, which for most of us is conveniently written in our own languages, but He still desires for people to hear His Word through people (Rom. 10:14, 15).

Many times in our postmodern society we turn to informational sources that we can access easily in the comfort of our homes—books, magazines, radio, TV, the Internet. Yet these impersonal resources lack one of the most important elements in God's plan: a living, breathing example.

God doesn't want just anyone to teach you how to live as a follower of Christ. He has given the older women in your church the great opportunity and grave responsibility to teach younger women.

One example God instituted for the church is that of deacons and their wives. He gave exacting character qualities for the church to look for when selecting deacons. He also included a list for their wives. "Likewise, their wives must be reverent, not slanderers, temperate [having a sound, sober mind], faithful in all things" (1 Tim. 3:11). How can a deacon be an effective servant to the people in his fellowship if his wife does not walk with God and live above reproach in every way?

Widows are also called upon to be examples to the church. The list of qualities for a godly older widow includes that "she has been the wife of one man, well reported for good works: if she has brought up children, if she has lodged strangers, if she has washed the saints' feet, if she has relieved the afflicted, if she has diligently followed every good work" (1 Tim. 5:9, 10).

These practical lists are full of concrete explanations of the type of character God requires in a woman. God knows we need a visible, walking-around person who will live out God's Word in everyday life. Just as our children need to *see* us follow Christ— and not just *hear* us talk about Him—we need the examples of wiser, more experienced, older women living near us where we can watch them.

If you sincerely desire to put into practice the things we have been discussing in this book, it is essential that you find a wise, older believer in your church, a woman whose life exemplifies all that we know is right and good. Do you want a close walk with God? Do you desire a sweet relationship with your husband? Do you want to do a first-class job of raising your kids? Do you want a home that is filled with an aura of godliness? Then find a woman for whom these qualities are a reality!

> But as for you, speak the things which are proper for sound doctrine: that the older men be sober, reverent, temperate, sound in faith, in love, in patience; the older women likewise, that they be reverent in behavior, not slanderers, not given to much wine, teachers of good things—that they admonish the young women to love their husbands, to love their children, to be discreet, chaste, homemakers, good, obedient to their own husbands, that the word of God may not be blasphemed (Titus 2:1–5).

So what should you look for in a godly example? Let's examine the apostle Paul's directions to Titus.

1. A godly woman has "sound doctrine" as a firm foundation in her life. What is sound doctrine? "Doctrine" is another word for "teaching," or "instruction." To be "sound" means to be "healthy and pure." The standard for "pure teaching" is God's Word. So find an older woman who is interested in teaching you what *God* says, not an agenda of her own.

2. A godly woman is "reverent in behavior." Her actions are fitting and proper for a woman who professes to follow Christ. God and His ways are so important to her that every area of her life has been affected.

3. A godly woman is not a "slanderer." She does not accuse others falsely. Satan has been called a false accuser. He loves to harm our reputations. He even stands before God, trying to accuse us before Him and prove to God that we are unworthy of eternal life with Him in Heaven, even though we have been clothed with the righteousness of Christ and are perfect in God's eyes. In the same way, some women will go to any length to harm someone else's reputation. A godly woman has learned to control her tongue!

4. A godly woman is "not given to much wine." Throughout the Bible God warns us not to allow ourselves to give over the control of our minds to alcohol. A person who drinks loses the ability to make decisions, to think rationally, and to choose right from wrong. Interestingly, Ephesians says that instead of being drunk with wine, we should be "drunk," in a sense, or *filled,* with the Holy Spirit (Eph. 5:18). In other words, the only One to Whom we should surrender our ability to make decisions is God Himself, in the person of the Holy Spirit. He should control our lives as thoroughly as wine controls an alcoholic. Make sure the older woman who mentors you is controlled by God, not by any substance such as alcohol, drugs, food, or anything else that can control our thoughts and lives.

5. A godly woman is a "[teacher] of good things." Teaching is an active occupation. It implies a woman who is up and doing, at least at heart! In all honesty, many older women are content to sit down and rest. They may feel that this is the time of their lives when they deserve a break. Or maybe they feel outdated or tired. They figure that the younger, more energetic women should teach and work in the church. However, younger women should be busy at home, caring for their husbands and children, while the older women should be busy *teaching* them how, within the limitations of their circumstances.

You may have to hunt to find a wonderful older woman who matches these descriptions. However, when you find her, you'll be amazed at the gem you've discovered! She'll be able to guide you, to help you learn how to have a great marriage, to lend advice for those tricky parenting dilemmas, and to teach you how to manage your home.

God could just appear in all His glory, right there in your living room. Or imagine if He zapped your family so everyone would be immediately holy! He could personally teach you everything you need to know. But He has a better plan, a plan in which He uses (through the Holy Spirit) willing and surrendered lives of experienced saints.

Why does He care if His ways are passed on from one generation to the next, from older women to younger women? Because God doesn't want His words to be blasphemed or spoken of with evil.

I know a lady who has lived a hard life. She was a pastor's wife, and she and her husband served for many years in small Baptist churches. However, some of the people in their congregations had hurt her feelings. The little things over the years had bruised her, and instead of digging into God's Word and learning to forgive and love, she held all of her feelings inside. By the time she reached her later years, she had become bitter, angry, and outspoken.

Learning from Older Women

Today she is a widow. She frequently eats out, and while seated at her table waiting for her food to be served, she studies the diners at the tables around her. When she sees a wrong behavior, she lashes out at the person. If a child is too noisy, she loudly rebukes the child and his parents. If someone has too much wine with his dinner, this widow is known to get up and snatch his wine glass away, boldly reminding him that he is sinning against God!

And all those who are with her are embarrassed—for the people she has been preaching to, for her, hoping no one will mind this poor little old lady, and for God! We pray that His name will not be brought down by the unkind actions of an embittered woman. Yet we know that many people have been hurt by similar actions of Christians and have since turned away from God.

Women of all ages are capable of bringing down the testimony of God. The Bible is clear that the role women fill is extremely important in not slandering God's name. If older women are known for their godly character and younger women are known for proper behavior in their homes, God will receive the glory.

Let's talk about some practical ways that you can find an older woman to mentor you.

First of all, remember to look for a woman with Biblical characteristics.
- A woman who has sound doctrine
- A woman who is reverent
- A woman who is not a slanderer
- A woman who is not controlled by alcohol or other substances
- A woman who is willing to teach you

Second, review the things she is supposed to teach you.
- To love your husband and children
- To be discreet and chaste
- To be a capable homemaker

- To be morally virtuous and beautiful in character
- To be obedient to your husband

Third, you will need to be humble enough to learn from this wise woman.

> Likewise you younger people, submit yourselves to your elders. Yes, all of you be submissive to one another, and be clothed with humility, for "God resists the proud, but gives grace to the humble" (1 Pet. 5:5).

It is easy to think that just because we're young, we have the answers to all of society's problems. Yet the Bible commands us to respect the wisdom of the older generation. "You shall rise before the gray headed and honor the presence of an old man, and fear your God: I am the LORD" (Lev. 19:32). Again, "Wisdom is with aged men, and with length of days, understanding" (Job 12:12).

Gary and Anne Marie Ezzo, authors of *Growing Kids God's Way*, state,

> One of the first things discarded in a self-oriented independent family structure is respect for the extremes of life, as represented by the callousness of abortion at one end and the absence of respect for the elderly at the other. These collective, social-moral failures are like billboards alerting us that we have moved as a society into the third and final phase of family life—the independent family. By its very nature, the independent family is hostile toward the sanctity of age, resulting in a disregard for the sacred trust between generations.[1]

Honoring age starts out as a heart issue. When you desire to honor those whom God honors, your actions will begin to show honor—as you offer your seat to an older woman or hold a door open for her, as you ask an older woman for her opinion instead of jumping in with your own on a heated topic, as you refrain from telling jokes that might make an older person look bad, and as you humbly seek counsel from a woman who has walked longer with God than you have.

Learning from Older Women   253

Finally, after praying for guidance, you will need to ask a woman for her specific help. Ask her for advice. Take a meal to her and then stay awhile and chat. You might even start a Bible study with her, although I personally don't think it's necessary to be that formal. Just spending time together will allow her to begin to rub off on you. Most likely she will have more time than you do, especially if you have a home and family to care for. However, *you* need to make the relationship a priority! Share concerns with her so she can pray for you. Allow her to hold you accountable for your time spent in the Word, for your marriage, and for your children's behavior. Ask her to teach you how to make luscious strawberry shortcake or how to plant a vegetable garden.

IN SUMMARY

What a privilege we younger women have of learning from the older women in our churches. What a privilege the older ones have of passing on the experience of years to us younger ones. What a joy we'll all have when God's name is exalted and He is glorified by our obedience!

EXTRA CREDIT ASSIGNMENT

Memorize this passage of Scripture by learning one verse at a time; then recite the passage to a minimum of five women.

"But as for you, speak the things which are proper for sound doctrine: that the older men be sober, reverent, temperate, sound in faith, in love, in patience; the older women likewise, that they be reverent in behavior, not slanderers, not given to much wine, teachers of good things—that they admonish the young women to love their husbands, to love their

> children, to be discreet, chaste, homemakers, good, obedient to their own husbands, that the word of God may not be blasphemed" (Titus 2:1–5).

STUDY GUIDE

1. According to Acts 1:8, what was the Holy Spirit's purpose in indwelling believers? Has His purpose changed? How could He fulfill His purpose in you?
2. After reading 1 Timothy 3:11 and 1 Timothy 5:9 and 10, list some qualities you should look for in an older woman who can be your example.
3. According to 1 Peter 5:5, what will you have to do before you can learn from an older woman?

GROUP PROJECT

Plan an "Honor the Aged Night." (If the women in your group are predominantly young, invite some older women from your church.) Serve a simple meal and think of some creative ways to show your appreciation for the things the older women do in your church and community. To add a nice touch, have them bring family photo albums to share with everyone, and allow them to briefly tell their life stories. Through this sharing, each younger woman may more easily be able to pinpoint a suitable mentor.

EXTRA READING

✔ Huizenga, Betty. *Apples of Gold: A Six-Week Nurturing Program for Women.* Colorado Springs: Cook Communications Ministries, Faithful Woman, 2000. In this study you will find helpful advice for starting your own mentoring groups.

✔ Peace, Martha. *Becoming a Titus 2 Woman*. Bemidji, MN: Focus Publishing, 1997. This Bible study guide will be helpful for those who want to study Titus 2 in more depth, either personally or as a group.

NOTES

1. Gary Ezzo and Anne Marie Ezzo, *Growing Kids God's Way: Biblical Ethics for Parenting, 5th ed.* (Simi Valley, CA: Growing Families International, 1998), 138.

CHAPTER *18* EIGHTEEN

Ministering to Lost People

POINT TO PONDER
*"Everyone is trying to accomplish something big,
not realizing that life is made up of little things"
(Doris Greig).*[1]

What would it be like to live in your unbelieving neighbor's house? Imagine thinking their thoughts, having their ambitions, dreaming their dreams. A house just a few blocks from mine reminds me of what it must feel like to be an unbeliever. It has a manicured lawn, a large backyard that is fenced in and full of the latest in kids' play equipment, a driveway filled with several nice cars, and a beautiful walkway to the front door. Yet when I was recently invited inside, I discovered a mess! Nothing was put away. Things were dirty. The blinds were pulled, and the mood repressive. What a surprise!

Most people who live on your street lead lives that are like this house. They are "beautiful people," smiling and well-groomed. Yet inside they are dying. (Actually, the Scripture says they are already dead.) They have no hope, no reason for living. They are surrounded by ruined relationships. They try to cover their pain in an endless number of ways. They try thrill after thrill in an effort to find some measure of satisfaction. But it's no use.

The Bible describes such people as "lost." Have you ever been lost? Have you ever felt your heart tighten in your chest when you realized you didn't know where you were? Worse yet, have you ever been lost and not known it until it was almost too late?

As a woman who is seeking to glorify God in every way, you have the unique privilege of ministering to the "lost" people who live in your town, in your neighborhood, in the house next door. You have a unique circle of influence. These are people God has brought into your life for a specific purpose—so you can minister to them, show them what God has done in your life, and reach them for Jesus Christ.

This job is not glamorous. You probably won't win any awards or get your name published on a list of high achievers. However, God emphasizes reaching the lost. If you want to bring glory to Him, your desires must match His.

Remember that if your walk with God is growing, if your marriage is strong (how rare that is!), if your children are obedient and learning to be like Christ (even rarer!), and if you are caring for the needs of your household (unheard of!), you are in just the spot God needs you to be to reach out to those in your community. Those who don't know God might care for the needy, but they cannot offer true hope. Those with broken marriages have problems of their own to tend. Those with unruly children have nothing unique to offer. Those busy outside their homes have very little extra time to devote to others. Get excited about the possibilities available only to you!

Jesus, the Good Shepherd, offers the only solution for these lost sheep—Himself. And He has given you the opportunity to share His solution with others. In fact, as a woman, the Bible talks about some *special* ways women can impact their world.

A Shining Testimony

The first way you can reach out to those in your neighborhood is so obvious that we often miss it. Yet it can be difficult. Before you can expect to win an audience from the unsaved, you must first *show* them that you are different. When they look at your everyday life, they need to see purpose, joy, peace, and radiance.

Do you remember *why* the older women in your church need to be teaching the younger women "to love their husbands, to love their children, to be discreet, chaste, homemakers, good, obedient to their own husbands"? So that "the word of God may not be blasphemed" (Titus 2:4, 5). Or, as the Amplified Bible states, so that God's Word will not "be exposed to reproach," or discredited.

Your actions as a wife *directly affect* how the unsaved view God's Word. In other words, if you take the Bible's commands seriously, then others will notice and figure that the Bible is useful for everyday living. However, if you attend church faithfully but fail to apply to your life what you learn, then others will assume that the Bible is just a nice book with no application to modern life.

Notice that Titus 2 specifically mentions your relationship to your husband (love and obedience—ouch!), to your children, and to your home. It also mentions your high quality of character. Perhaps some of our most private areas are not as private as we had thought!

The Bible compares everyday works to a light that everyone can see. "You are the light of the world," Jesus said. "A city that is set on a hill cannot be hidden" (Matt. 5:14). People *can* see your works! Therefore, Jesus admonished, "Let your light so shine before men, that they may see your good works and glorify your Father in heaven" (v. 16).

So many times we think that the *words* we say will have more of an impact on the lost than our *works*. We carefully plan what we will say to interest them in the gospel. We debate Scripture verses and doctrines. We may pray earnestly for someone's salvation. Yet it is of no avail if our actions do not match what we are saying. After all, why should a dying person jump from one condemned boat to another? No, we need something radically different. We need a woman whose life matches the Bible's standard—a difficult task, indeed!

You can see this principle in action in the life of a woman who lives with an unsaved husband and wants to witness to him. What a difficult task! After all, she may manage to act like a Christian when she is out of the home; but no one knows her as well as her husband. Home is where she "lets down her hair."

On the other hand, probably no one cares about the lost condition of her husband as much as she does! She *cares deeply* that he doesn't know Christ! She doesn't want him to spend eternity separated from God! Perhaps that is why it's so easy for her to begin "nagging" her husband to Jesus. His salvation is always in her thoughts, her prayers, her hopes, and her worries.

To women in such a situation, the apostle Peter wrote these words:

> Wives, likewise, be submissive to your own husbands, that even if some do not obey the word, they, *without a word, may be won by the conduct of their wives,* when they observe your chaste conduct accompanied by fear. Do not let your adornment be merely outward—arranging the hair, wearing gold, or putting on fine apparel—rather let it be the hidden person of the heart, with the incorruptible beauty of a gentle and quiet spirit, which is very precious in the sight of God. . . . Finally, all of you be of one mind, having compassion for one another; love as brothers, be tenderhearted, be courteous; not returning evil for evil or reviling for reviling, but on the contrary blessing, knowing that you were called to this, that you may inherit a blessing (1 Pet. 3:1–4, 8, 9, emphasis added).

No matter who you want to win to Christ—a husband, an aunt, or an exercise partner—your lifestyle speaks volumes more than your words ever could. Does it seem impossible to live

Ministering to Lost People

without fault, with such a high standard of conduct that others will see a dramatic difference in you? Does it sound far-fetched to be loving, submissive, courteous, and compassionate, even at home? Of course it does! But remember what we discussed in part 1? God's power is greater than all your sin! "Christ *in* you, the hope of glory" (Col. 1:27, emphasis added).

Your responsibility is to walk with Him every day, submitting every area of your life to Him and allowing Him to rule over you and *change* you. As the psalmist said, "I sought the LORD, and He heard me, and delivered me from all my fears. They looked to Him and were *radiant,* and their faces were not ashamed" (Ps. 34:4, 5, emphasis added).

Jesus knew that the only way a watching world will see a difference in you is if they see *Jesus* in you. "Do not be conformed to this world, but be transformed by the renewing of your mind" (Rom. 12:2). Be different. Be transparent. Be open. Be willing to shine your light to those who see you every day.

Loving Hospitality

I love how the Bible is so practical! One of the most widely mentioned ways that women can impact our world for Christ is very ordinary. The Bible simply asks us to show hospitality.

The Greek use of the word "hospitality" in Scripture means "a brotherly love of strangers and foreigners." It implies that we open our homes out of love and friendliness. We don't invite only our close friends or people we want to impress. Rather we invite those who can't necessarily repay us. We show friendship to those with no friends.

Let's take a look at some Scriptural examples of hospitality. One is the excellent wife described in Proverbs 31, who "extends her hand to the poor, yes, she reaches out her hands to the needy" (v. 20). Maybe the writer was thinking about Abigail, the wife of Nabal, a very rich sheep farmer. She brought an abundance of food to David and his men at a time when they needed help the most.

The account goes like this: David's spiritual leader, Samuel, had just died, and King Saul was hunting for David. He wanted to kill him. David and his men had been protecting some of Nabal's property, and now they were hungry and tired, so David sent ten men to ask Nabal for food. Nabal, who was known for being "harsh and evil," lived up to his reputation by blatantly refusing to help David's men. Well, David became so angry that he grabbed his sword and four hundred of his men and set off to destroy Nabal!

Meanwhile Abigail, "a woman of good understanding and beautiful appearance," heard about the trouble brewing between her husband and David. Without saying a word to Nabal, she "made haste and took two hundred loaves of bread, two skins of wine, five sheep already dressed, five seahs of roasted grain, one hundred clusters of raisins, and two hundred cakes of figs, and loaded them on donkeys." Quickly she made her way to David's camp and offered him the food as a peace offering. (See 1 Samuel 25 for the full account.)

Because of Abigail's quick thinking, many lives were saved from bloodshed. A gracious, understanding, humble woman saved the day with her hospitality!

Your love for others can literally save their spiritual lives by demonstrating in a concrete way what Christ has done for you. Love without actions has no meaning, as we all know. Paul reiterated this thought when he wrote, "Let love be without hypocrisy. Abhor what is evil. Cling to what is good" in Romans 12:9.

In verses 10–13 Paul listed some practical ways to put our love into action: (1) Love each other with brotherly affection and take delight in honoring each other. (2) Never be lazy in your work; serve the Lord enthusiastically. (3) Be glad for all God is planning for you; be patient in trouble and prayerful always.

Ministering to Lost People

(4) When God's children are in need, be the one to help them out. Get into the habit of inviting guests home for dinner or, if they need lodging, for the night.

In Hebrews 13:1 and 2 we read, "Let brotherly love continue. Do not forget to entertain strangers, for by so doing some have unwittingly entertained angels." Remember how Abraham unknowingly entertained angels and the Lord Himself in his tent one day? (See Genesis 18.) We should think of hospitality as a privilege, not a burden.

Peter wrote, "And above all things have fervent love for one another, for 'love will cover a multitude of sins.' Be hospitable to one another without grumbling" (1 Pet. 4:8, 9). You see, love must come from the heart. Peter may have been thinking about the time Cornelius, a wealthy Italian commander who was searching for God, invited Peter to his home. At first Peter didn't want to have anything to do with someone of another nationality, but he learned through a vision that "God shows no partiality. But in every nation whoever fears Him and works righteousness is accepted by Him" (Acts 10:34, 35). Though it was difficult, Peter allowed Cornelius and his family to welcome him into his (Cornelius') household, and the gospel began to spread to the uttermost parts of the earth.

In God's eyes a truly great woman opens her arms to the needy around her. God looks with favor on a woman who is "well reported for good works: if she has brought up children, if she has lodged strangers, if she has washed the saints' feet, if she has relieved the afflicted, if she has diligently followed every good work" (1 Tim. 5:10).

One such woman was Tabitha, who lived in the town of Joppa and was known for her "good works and charitable deeds." Then Tabitha "became sick and died," and the believers sent two men for Peter. When God allowed Peter to bring Tabitha back to life again, "it became known throughout all Joppa, and many believed on the Lord" (Acts 9:42). God received the glory!

This incident happened right before the salvation of Cornelius, which I told you about a moment ago. Maybe Peter learned about hospitality by watching it firsthand at Tabitha's house.

Hospitality sounds so simple and unimportant. Sometimes we overlook it for a "more important" job in the church such as teaching a class or leading a Bible study group. Yet hospitality can open doors to hearts, soften those hearts, and make them more receptive to the gospel.

Let's look at some practical characteristics of hospitality in the Bible. These are easy enough to try this week!

1. Hospitality meets people's physical needs. For instance, a woman in the Old Testament provided food and water for Elisha, as well as shelter and privacy in his own bedroom (2 Kings 4:8–37). In the New Testament, Mary and Martha showed hospitality to Jesus by opening their home, giving Him delicious meals and caring for Him (Luke 10:38–42; John 12:1–3). "A way to a man's heart is through his stomach" is often true for your husband, and it's also wise advice for reaching your world for Christ. Your trademark cookies or famous lasagna could open hearts that might otherwise be closed to you.

2. Hospitality should happen often. Again, the woman who cared for Elisha made it a regular part of her life by asking her husband to build a special room for Elisha (2 Kings 4:8–10). If you have a big house, you could have fun fixing up a "prophet's chamber." Then ask God to show you some people with needs that you can help fulfill. Maybe you don't own a home or all your rooms are full of kids. You can still make hospitality a regular part of your life by sharing what you *do* have. You must take the initiative if hospitality is to happen. The best way to do that is to grab your calendar and set aside regular dates for hospitality. Maybe on the first Sunday of every month you could invite a family you don't know very well to come over after church.

Maybe every third Friday you could invite some lonely teenagers for board games and popcorn. If your son plays football, you could invite the team on a Saturday morning for donuts and to watch their game video on your big-screen TV. If the parents of your daughter's friend are having a rough time in their marriage, invite them for a barbecue and some friendship. Schedule it, ask God to give you ideas, and *do* it—regularly.

3. Hospitality includes the "unlovely." Our society is enamored with "beautiful people." We see lovely faces and bodies everywhere we go. Yet Scripture is clear that love includes the unlovely. James tells us that

> pure and undefiled religion before God and the Father is this: to visit orphans and widows in their trouble, and to keep oneself unspotted from the world. . . . If a brother or sister is naked and destitute of daily food, and one of you says to them, "Depart in peace, be warmed and filled," but you do not give them the things which are needed for the body, what does it profit? (James 1:27; 2:15, 16).

Jesus illustrated these thoughts when He told the parable of the Good Samaritan (Luke 10:25–37). Hospitality is not just socializing. It is meeting the needs of others.

4. Hospitality involves listening. Just as Martha quarreled with Mary because Mary sat at the feet of Jesus instead of helping in the kitchen, you may think that hospitality means bustling about and waiting on people (Luke 10:38–42). Sometimes hospitality means simply listening to what your guest has to say.

5. Hospitality is easiest when you have the cooperation of the whole family (even the kids). Mary and Martha never would have quarreled if they had decided ahead of time which duties belonged to whom. Plan ahead, ask your husband for help, and involve your children in the process. Even Jesus employed help—a little boy and twelve disciples—when He showed hospitality to a crowd of five thousand people by feeding them miraculously (John 6:5–14).

6. Hospitality does not need to be elaborate! "K.I.S.S." means "Keep It Simple, Sister." When your husband kindly brings a lonely coworker home for supper, a boring casserole served with love will mean more than a fine dinner served with a grudge. If you try to get too fancy, you might get discouraged and never invite anyone over!

One gracious author wrote,

> Sometimes hospitality means weeping with a friend or a neighbor, or staying up extra late just to listen to the story of the pain in someone's life. It may be watching the neighbor's children when their mother is ill, or taking food to the home of a new neighbor. Hospitality can take many shapes and forms. We need to pray, "God, please make me willing to see, and then grasp, the opportunities you send my way. I trust your Holy Spirit to give me the wisdom and strength I need from you for each opportunity you call me to participate in this day and this week. By the power of Jesus' name, I commit my life to you as your servant."[2]

Personally Sharing Christ

After we build some credibility with the unsaved, we will earn the right to speak to them about our personal relationship with God. What is credibility? It means you are trustworthy and your message is believable. How can you become credible? By building genuine relationships with people so they can see you are *human*—that you still hurt, that you still have feelings, that you can laugh and have fun. Through it all, however, they need to see you relying on the Lord!

In short, becoming credible and building relationships take time. If you follow the principles in this chapter, the people with whom you build friendships will see integrity in your life. They will be amazed at the love you show them. They will be able to relate to you as they see your human side.

Then you can tell them *why* you are different. Now will be

Ministering to Lost People   267

your opportunity to share with them what God has done for you! Dewey Bertolini, a youth pastor and a professor at a Christian college, explained his method of evangelism to teenagers.

> God's power is expressed through our weakness (2 Corinthians 12:9). By sharing out of the context of our own personal pain, we immediately create a common bond with others who are enduring pain of their own. The walls break down. Their fear of sharing with us disappears. Our willingness to be vulnerable before the young people we meet allows them the same luxury in response to us.

> The most effective evangelism takes place when we apply the good news of the Gospel to the specific needs of each young person. We have a God who can meet every need. To those from broken homes He becomes a father to the fatherless (Psalm 68:5). The brokenhearted can read of a Jesus who wept at the tomb of His friend (John 11:35). To the fearful He is the God who holds the future in His hand (Revelation 1:8). To the anxious he offers a peace that passes all understanding (Philippians 4:7). To the guilty He provides forgiveness and cleansing (Isaiah 1:18). No more positive and compelling message exists in the world today than the Gospel of Jesus Christ. Every need of every hurting heart can be met by its truth.[3]

Does that quote give you goose bumps? As you think about the hopelessness of your lost friends, the pointless lives of your acquaintances without Christ, the questions of your unsaved relatives, it is exciting to realize that God can use you to give them the answers they need! Ask God for courage to speak up for Him. As He gives you opportunities (and He will!), use them for His glory.

As the apostle Peter wrote, "But sanctify the Lord God in your hearts, and always be ready to give a defense to everyone who asks you a reason for the hope that is in you, with meekness and fear; having a good conscience" (1 Pet. 3:15, 16).

Notice the order: (1) "Sanctify," or set apart as holy, the Lord

God in your own heart. Your life must be holy first. (2) "Always be ready." (3) "Give a defense." As any lawyer knows, a good defense requires study and preparation. You can be working on this now, preparing yourself to defend the Lord and His Word by memorizing Scripture. (4) They can see "hope" in you. (Can they?) (5) "With meekness and fear." Be humble as you deal with the sin in the world (see Galatians 6:1). Be fearful of God's wrath upon sinners and eager to share His mercy with them. (6) Have "a good conscience." These words bring us back to the subject of a pure testimony before a watching world.

What a privilege we have as women! When we are genuinely different, when the roles we have chosen and the joy with which we live stand in stark contrast to women around us, we will have the opportunity to let our light shine. The homes in our neighborhoods don't have to be dark and hopeless. They can be bright and peaceful!

A Needy World

Just as Jesus reminded His disciples to "lift up their eyes" to the "harvest fields" of lost souls around them (John 4:35), I want to conclude this book by encouraging you to lift your eyes above your ordinary, everyday life and see a *world* that is lost without Christ.

We've already discussed the needs of the people in your circle of influence, those who live in your town, and those who might be your close friends. But for just a minute, consider the faceless people groups who live around the world. Our world is exploding in growth and in the capability to communicate. We are more globally minded. Never before have we had such opportunities to "reach out and touch someone." Travel makes it possible for an ordinary person to visit any place in the world for a reasonably affordable price.

As a woman seeking to follow God, you have the privilege to

Ministering to Lost People   269

fulfill special roles that He has chosen for you. You have the *privilege* of walking closely with God, of making your family a priority in your thinking and your time, and of ministering to your community through your home. I don't want you to forget these roles! They should be the most important things in your life!

Nevertheless, consider the role you might be able to have in furthering the gospel around the world.

A mistaken notion in Christendom is that full-time Christian workers are a more godly breed, that having a pastor or missionary for a husband is superior to being married to a used-car salesman or a garbage man. I simply don't find this view in Scripture. God has called *all* of us to be full-time Christians! Being "ministry minded" does not mean you are in ministry vocationally but that you have the mentality of a servant of God. This mind-set is necessary for all believers.

Having said that, I need to remind you that fewer young people are choosing the pastorate or missions as a career. According to the Barna Research Group, "The United States has so many unchurched people that the nation has become one of the primary missions targets of Christians who live in other countries around the world."[4]

I believe a primary reason fewer children are growing up to choose ministry as a career is that their parents are not teaching them the importance of ministry. Consider this example:

> A couple of summers ago Paul Bubar, Overseas Director for Word of Life, interviewed about 20 kids each week at Word of Life Island, their teen camp. He asked, "If you could be anything you wanted to be, what would you be?" The responses ranged from architects to veterinarians. "Out of the entire summer," said Bubar, "only one said, 'I want to be a youth pastor.' None said, 'I want to be a pastor,' and three said, 'I want to be a missionary.' Each week I asked how many came from homes where both parents were saved. The figure was an astounding 81 per-

> cent. This tells me that Christian parents, in their quest for their children to have financial security in life, have held up all these secular options. Very few are holding up service to the Lord as an option. In my opinion, kids are not being urged to serve the Lord in a full-time capacity."[5]

As a mom, can you see the possibilities that you have for influencing the world? Concern for worldwide evangelism is mostly caught, not taught. Love of missions and ministry should be the norm in your household, so ordinary that your children grow up not knowing anything different. Hold up missionaries and other Christian workers before your children as heroes to be emulated, not poor servants to be pitied. Allow your children to accompany you and your husband as you go on missions trips, as you volunteer for service organizations, and as you go about doing other "good works." Invite missionaries to spend the night in your home so that your children will be able to observe them up close and ask them questions.

Your children must also be trained in *how* to evangelize the world. While many parents leave this responsibility to the church, the Bible says that parents are ultimately responsible. Realize that you need to be teaching your children important Biblical doctrines and how to defend them, what other religions believe and what the Bible says about those beliefs, how to share their own testimonies with people (as well as providing actual *practice* for them), how to be a good neighbor as we discussed previously, and how to maintain a shining testimony by avoiding temptation and learning to walk with God.

The task can seem overwhelming! But don't wait! Make "Learning to Serve God" a daily subject in your home. Have fun quizzes with your kids about Bible stories, Biblical facts, and timeless doctrines. Memorize God's Word with them. Read aloud to them from biographies of great Christians, as well as from Scripture. Help them learn to be consistent in their own Bible

Ministering to Lost People

reading and prayer time. Purposely plan opportunities for them to share their love and faith with others.

I received the following information from Baptist Mid-Missions, a missions agency. It has been helpful to me as I think about instilling a "missions mentality" in my children.

Missions Atmosphere

• Missions education is not confined within the walls of the church. Training in the home and church supplement each other. Our homes need fertile soil where missions-minded children and adults can grow and mature.

• Display missions-related items around the house. These might include curios from various countries, a world globe, a bulletin board with a world map, maps of individual countries, prayer letters, and prayer cards.

Information

• Home libraries should include missions-related books such as missionary biographies, novels, and historical accounts of various mission boards and their missionaries.

• Other sources of information include missionary prayer letters, mission board periodicals, and church missionary bulletins.

• Children might enjoy missionary flashcard stories as well as missions adventure books.

• Try to contact people of another culture who may be living in your town. Meet with them or invite them to your home, if appropriate. This will give you a deeper understanding of the people and may even open a door for you to witness.

Study Together

• Learn about the missionaries and their fields of ministry (language, culture, size, and location of the country, religion, people and dress, time-zone differences). Sources of information include encyclopedias, missionaries (personal conversations and prayer letters), mission board home offices, newspapers, and magazines.

- Memorize a verse and/or song in a foreign language.
- Encourage family members to give reports of mission books they've read.
- Have a time of drama and/or role-playing in which you imagine life in another country and culture. Act out a segment from a missionary biography.
- Using missionary prayer letters or field surveys as a basis, prepare missions-oriented quizzes or games (word searches, crossword puzzles). Play a game that originated in another country.
- Organize a notebook for each missionary in which are listed their names, birthdays, anniversaries, addresses, prayer requests, pictures, and field information.

Service

- As a family, offer to help at a missions headquarters or a special ministry in your area (stuff envelopes, mow lawns, wash windows).
- Visit a mission field. North America offers a tremendous variety of ministries: American Indian, Mormon, Hispanic, church planting.
- Witness to neighbors and friends.

Involvement

- Establish an "Adopt-a-Missionary" program: one missionary per family or each member may adopt a different missionary. Maintain regular contact with the adopted missionary.
- Plan a "Family Missions Night" each month.
  - –Turn off the TV, radio, stereo.
  - –Sing missionary songs.
  - –Plan an ethnic menu.
  - –Introduce a new aspect of missionary life/culture.
  - –Present a book report/drama.
  - –Telephone a missionary.
  - –Make a cassette or videotape.

Ministering to Lost People 273

–Write letters to your missionary. (Note: When writing letters to missionaries, keep in mind that children enjoy hearing from adults and adults appreciate letters from children. At times, the family could combine ideas to write one letter. Other times, various members of the family could write individual letters to several missionaries.)

• What to write: who you are; what you do; facts about your family, sports, pets, hobbies, family outings, or vacations; books read; salvation experience; church news and activities; thoughts from a message; prayer requests.

• What to ask: names of nationals for whom to pray, prayer requests, news about their ministries, family needs, hobbies, special interests, cultural differences.

• Pray regularly for your missionary. It is easier and more personal when you *know* them. Place the world map and prayer cards in an area where they may be easily seen.

• Plan for special missions projects. Write to find out needs and interests.

• Hands-on: Color flashcards, make awards, assemble Gospel Wooly Worms and bracelets.

• Financial: Purchase Christmas gifts or provide a financial gift for a special project. Children may help raise the funds by selling baked goods to family and neighbors, collecting pop cans, or family-approved methods. The family may designate part of its normal Christmas gift budget to go to missions. Check with the missionary regarding the best way to ship parcels.

Open Homes

• Entertain missionaries on a regular basis. Expose the whole family to a quality time of discussion and interaction. It is time well-invested and reaps eternal rewards.

• Look for other opportunities: veteran and retired missionaries, parents of missionaries, missionary kids, international students.

News Media

• TV and newspapers provide world events that may affect missionaries. Clip relevant articles for your missionary notebooks.

• Discuss news events as a family during devotions. How might the latest development affect your missionaries and their ministry?

Surrender

• Ourselves: Adults must first be surrendered to the Word of God in its entirety. We must fully understand the importance of missions, that it is God's plan for carrying the gospel to the lost around the world. We must be willing to be a part of that plan in whatever way God chooses.

• Time: Establishing a "Missions in the Home" program takes time and effort. No family will do all of the suggested activities, and many will come up with their own ideas. The future of missions depends on adults and children taking time to do some "missions homeschooling."

• Children: As children learn about missions and their hearts are sensitive to God's call, some will express an eagerness to serve as missionaries. Children need to know their parents are pleased when they choose to obey God's call, even if it means being physically separated by thousands of miles.[6]

As a godly wife, you also need to see the possibilities for ministry in your husband. As the saying goes, "Behind every great man is a great woman." Most men won't attempt to do great things without the support of their wives.

Remember that you are your husband's helper. Don't try to lead him by coercing him or nagging him or trying to make him feel guilty. Instead, help him serve the Lord in whatever occupation he is involved. Missions begins in our own surroundings. We must share Christ in the workplace before we can legitimately share Christ in a foreign country. We must be involved in the

Ministering to Lost People

"work of the ministry" in our Monday-through-Saturday lives before we can be qualified to be a church leader. Your husband needs your support, your prayers, and your encouragement.

And what if God impresses on your husband's heart the need to leave his job and start a career as a full-time Christian worker? What if God calls your husband to be a pastor? or to leave your comfortable hometown and go to a Bible college or seminary? or to leave your extended family and move to another state (or even a foreign country) to start a church? Follow him with a willing heart. If you are being submissive to your husband, then as God works in your husband's heart, He will also move in yours. Be careful to follow God's leading as He guides you through your husband.

IN SUMMARY

Are you beginning to see the possibilities God has for you? You have the potential to be an instrument in God's hand, effective in changing the world. It starts in the heart, then it radiates into the home. It starts with you.

Consider making a list of those to whom you could minister. Start a section in your prayer journal just for them. Commit these people to the Lord, and ask Him to keep you responsive to Him. Have an older woman in your church hold you accountable for the areas in your life that are weak. Rework your budget, if necessary, so you can afford to be hospitable or to support missionaries or to send your teenagers on a weekend evangelism trip.

I love what Oswald Chambers says about serving God.

> Ministering as opportunity surrounds us does not mean selecting our surroundings, it means being very selectly God's in any haphazard surroundings which He engineers for us. The characteristics we manifest in our immediate surroundings are indications of what we will be like in other surroundings.[7]

JUGGLING LIFE'S RESPONSIBILITIES

Have you committed your heart to God? Are you "very selectly" His? Have you surrendered your entire life to His planning and purposes—to His glory—so that He can use *you* to reach the lost?

EXTRA CREDIT ASSIGNMENT

Memorize this passage of Scripture by learning one verse at a time; then recite the passage to a minimum of five women.

> "Let love be without hypocrisy. Abhor what is evil. Cling to what is good. Be kindly affectionate to one another with brotherly love, in honor giving preference to one another; not lagging in diligence, fervent in spirit, serving the Lord; rejoicing in hope, patient in tribulation, continuing steadfastly in prayer; distributing to the needs of the saints, given to hospitality" (Romans 12:9–13).

STUDY GUIDE

1. Although 1 Peter 3:1–4 discusses a wife's relationship with her husband, how can these verses also apply to your testimony to a lost friend, coworker, or neighbor?
2. Read Proverbs 31:20 and list some ways you could apply this verse to your life.
3. According to Hebrews 13:1 and 2, what is *another* reason you should be quick to entertain—especially strangers?
4. Hospitality is hard work. What should our attitude be toward hospitality, according to 1 Peter 4:8 and 9? In what situations might you have to overlook the faults of others as you open your home to them?

Ministering to Lost People 277

5. List the good works of a godly widow in 1 Timothy 5:10.
6. Study James 2:15 and 16. How do these verses illustrate that our actions speak louder than our words?
7. Read 2 Corinthians 12:9. What are some of your reasons for *not* wanting to open up your home in hospitality? According to this verse, what should your response be?

GROUP PROJECT

Brainstorm some ways to incorporate missions in your homes *this month*. Choose a project, correspond with missionaries about needs they have, and list how you can partner with them. Be sure to include in your plan the youngest and oldest members of your families, as well as your husbands, if they are willing. Don't forget to pray!

EXTRA READING

✔ Child Evangelism Fellowship has excellent materials to help you teach missions to your children. Order a catalog at 1-800-748-7710 or cefonline.com.

✔ Greig, Doris W. *We Didn't Know They Were Angels: Discovering the Gift of Christian Hospitality* (Ventura, CA: GL Publications, Regal Books, 1987). Part 1 of this book is full of inspiring and practical ideas to motivate you to begin practicing hospitality and to help you know how to begin. Part 2 includes more than three hundred recipes and household hints to give you a start. This book is one of my favorites because the author makes hospitality sound easy!

✔ Johnstone, Patrick, and Jason Mandryk with Robyn Johnstone. *Operation World*. Rev. ed. Waynesboro, GA: Paternoster Lifestyle, 2001. An authoritative guide for systematically praying for the world. It is set up to help you pray daily for each country of the world, giving you information about the geography, people groups represented, political situations, and religions. It will also tell you how different Christians are working to penetrate the spiritual darkness in each country so that you can pray effectively. I could not find this book at most bookstores, but it is available at www.discerningreader.com.

✔ Kroll, Woodrow. *The Vanishing Ministry in the 21st Century: Calling a New Generation to Lifetime Service.* Rev. ed. Grand Rapids: Kregel Publications, 2002. I pray that you will read this book with an open mind to how God may be leading you and your family. The statistics about the church in America will shock you.

✔ Petersen, Jim. *Living Proof: Sharing the Gospel Naturally.* Colorado Springs: NavPress, 1989). As the author explains, "The life you live may be the part of the Gospel that speaks most convincingly to others." This book will give you practical advice on *how* to evangelize your friends, from your lifestyle to sharing what the Bible has to say.

✔ Schaeffer, Edith. *L'Abri.* Rev. ed. Wheaton, IL: Crossway Books, 1992. The inspiring, true-life account of a Swiss community that Schaeffer and her husband founded in order to give seekers a place to observe Christianity firsthand.

NOTES

1. Doris W. Greig, *We Didn't Know They Were Angels: Discovering the Gift of Christian Hospitality* (Ventura, CA: GL Publications, Regal Books, 1987), 60.

2. Greig, 22, 23.

3. Dewey M. Bertolini, *Back to the Heart of Youth Ministry* (Wheaton, IL: Scripture Press, Victor Books, 1989), 83

4. "Barna Addresses Four Top Ministry Issues of Church Leaders," (www.barna.org, September 25, 2000).

5. Woodroll Kroll, *The Vanishing Ministry in the 21st Century: Calling a New Generation to Lifetime Service, rev. ed.* (Grand Rapids: Kregel Publications, 2002), 109.

6. "Missions in the Home" (Cleveland: Baptist Mid-Missions, n.d.). Obtain information about missions projects from the Women's Department

of Baptist Mid-Missions at P.O. Box 308011, Cleveland, OH 44130-8011 or womensdept@bmm.org.

7. Oswald Chambers, *My Utmost for His Highest* (Dodd, Mead & Co., 1935; renewed 1963 Oswald Chambers Publications Association, Ltd. 1963), 187, 188.

CONCLUSION

God's Plan for Your Future

POINT TO PONDER

"Foolish fathers and mothers! Cruel families—who did not hand down true truth, but who handed down the opposite and led their children away from God. Look in your imaginations at the long lines waiting for their turn to run, grabbing the wrong flag, speeding in the wrong direction—in country after country and generation after generation" *(Edith Schaeffer).*[1]

By now you know my heart for families. You know I desire that *your* heart be turned toward *your* family. By now you know God has a heart for families too. We've learned a lot about what a Biblical woman looks like and how she can glorify God in her marriage. But if you're like me, you look around at families that are falling apart, and you wonder how God's ideal can ever be realized! It seems hopeless!

Well, don't despair. God has a plan! Remember the verse we read near the beginning of the book, "For I know the thoughts that I think toward you, says the LORD, thoughts of peace and not of evil, to give you a future and a hope" (Jer. 29:11)?

God has a great plan for His church, for families, and for you. First of all, God wants you to be in the center of His will. We can find everything God wills for us to know and do in His Word.

The only way we can be sure we are doing God's will is by surrendering every part of our lives to Him. Two of my favorite verses say,

> I beseech you therefore, brethren, by the mercies of God, that you present your bodies a living sacrifice, holy, acceptable to God, which is your reasonable service. And do not be conformed to this world, but be transformed by the renewing of your mind, *that you may prove what is that good and acceptable and perfect will of God* (Rom. 12:1, 2, emphasis added).

You see, as we sacrifice to God our own desires, our sinful nature, and walk clean in His sight ("holy, acceptable to God"), we can be sure we are doing God's will. As we renew our minds each day in His Word, our philosophy of life will be different from the world's and, therefore, our actions will be boldly different. We will *know* we are doing God's will because God Himself lives within and through us.

Obedience and good works are the heart of God's will. Knowing God's will isn't as nebulous as knowing where you'll live five years from now. It is as specific as walking in obedience to God's Word *today*. "And the world is passing away, and the lust of it; but he who does the will of God abides forever" (1 John 2:17).[2]

So let's review God's will for women in their marriages. God's plan starts for you right now. Throughout this book, you've read how a woman's character and her walk with God are most important. God wants women to "continue in faith, love, holiness, with self-control" (1 Tim. 2:15). God wants women to invest in their homes, in their children, and in their husbands—so that God's name will be lifted high.

Conclusion 283

> Admonish the young women to love their husbands, to love their children, to be discreet, chaste, homemakers, good, obedient to their own husbands, that the word of God may not be blasphemed (Titus 2:4, 5).

Could God's will be any clearer? Yet could it be any more radical in our society? If you follow God's plan, you may be ridiculed or looked down on. But God will honor those who honor Him.

God has a plan for the future as well. It involves the older women. If you're "older," don't think for a moment that God has no more use for you. That thought couldn't be further from the truth! You play an essential role in God's plan for passing on truth from your generation to the next. Without you, truth will quite simply not be continued! (Could this be what happened to America?)

God's plan for you, again, is that your character and relationship to Him be the first priority. As the younger women in the church look at the older women, they need to see those who are "reverent, not slanderers, temperate, faithful in all things" (1 Tim. 3:11). By the time you have reached your sixties, you should have a track record of godliness and good works that makes the younger women drool. Listen to what God expects of widows.

> Do not let a widow under sixty years old be taken into the number, and not unless she has been the wife of one man, well reported for good works: if she has brought up children, if she has lodged strangers, if she has washed the saints' feet, if she has relieved the afflicted, if she has diligently followed every good work" (1 Tim. 5:9, 10).

Most importantly, God wants the older women to be "teachers of good things" (Titus 2:3). This point is the key! If you are an older woman, please, please find a woman younger than yourself who wants to learn, and then invest time in her.

Younger women, if you don't have the pleasure of knowing an older, more experienced woman in your family or church, determine to become that woman yourself someday. If the past generation has dropped the ball, decide now to pick it up again when your turn comes.

May I also urge you to consider "mentoring" as a worthy career after your children are grown? Don't be too quick to jump back into the working world and thus rob yourself of valuable time that you could invest in others. You may gain more money for retirement, but you'll lose the eternal treasure that comes from serving God. Young women need older women who are *available* and *giving*.

If younger women would grow to become older women who follow God's plan, this world would certainly feel the impact! If the older women today would decide to follow God's plan of mentoring, all of us would reap the benefits!

What are the rewards for sticking with it and becoming the woman God has designed you to be? Let's return one final time to the beloved words of Proverbs 31:28–31.

> Her children rise up and call her blessed; her husband also, and he praises her: "Many daughters have done well, but you excel them all." Charm is deceitful and beauty is passing, but a woman who fears the LORD, she shall be praised. Give her of the fruit of her hands, and let her own works praise her in the gates.

NOTES

1. Edith Shaeffer, *What Is a Family?* (Grand Rapids: Baker Book House, A Raven's Ridge Book, 1975), 107.

2. See 1 Thessalonians 4:3 and 5:18, as well as 1 Peter 2:15.

If you would like to share with me what you've learned, write to me at

Anne Elliott
P.O. Box 918
Pinon, AZ 86510

Or visit me online, where you can learn more about all these topics through inspiring articles, links to informative Web sites, and support from other Christian women.

www.AnnesHomeyPlace.com.